Rebel Daughter

REBEL DAUGHTER

An Autobiography

DORIS ANDERSON

KEY PORTER BOOKS

Canadian Cataloguing in Publication Data

Anderson, Doris, 1921–
Rebel daughter : an autobiography

ISBN 1-55013-767-0

1. Anderson, Doris, 1921– .   2. Feminists – Canada – Biography.
3. Authors, Canadian (English) – 20th century – Biography.*
4. Women journalists – Canada – Biography.   I. Title.

HQ1455.A77A3   1996   305.42'092   C96-930921-X

The publisher gratefully acknowledges the assistance of
the Canada Council and the Ontario Arts Council.

Key Porter Books Limited
70 The Esplanade
Toronto, Ontario
Canada M5E 1R2

Electronic Formatting: Heidi Palfrey

Printed and bound in Canada

96 97 98 99 5 4 3 2 1

*To those indomitable women—my grandmother,
my mother and aunts; my mentors—male and female;
and my sisters everywhere.*

Contents

Acknowledgements

Other writers have approached me from time to time, with a proposal to do my biography. Perhaps they might have done a more objective job than I. But I believe it would be hard for anyone to write about my early childhood except me. Another reason that I always hesitated was pure conceit. I never felt my life was really "over"—nor do I yet. But as I approach seventy-five it surely must be close to the time to attempt the job!

In doing so, I half hoped that if I could see the whole of my life in one piece I might have more insight into why I took one path rather than another easier and more compelling one. Having finished, I am as mystified as ever. Perhaps the best reason for writing this book, in the end, is to remind younger women of "how it was."

The exercise has been rewarding. I count myself fortunate to have been born in this century, in this country, and with the opportunities I have had. As I look back, most of the journey has been buoyant, turbulent at times, and often filled with incredible joy.

I have many people to thank for helping me—Adrienne Clarkson and Anna Porter, who persisted in urging me to "tell my story"; my family, for details of our mutual past; friends who read and made suggestions about early drafts, including Sheila Kieran, Sylvia Fraser, Norma Scarborough, Deirdre O'Connell, Jean Wright, Julyan Reid, Keith Davey; my editor, Laurie Coulter, and copy editor, Alison Reid; as well as the computer department at the University of Prince Edward Island, who rescued a whole month's work on a mangled disc last summer; and last, but not least, my niece, Laurel McCubbin, who took the cover picture.

CHAPTER ONE

A Little World Run by Women

Like many women, I have never liked my name—or rather, my various names—and I've had quite a few. Only my married name was given to me with pride and love. It seemed to me I had been tagged from birth, for the convenience of society, with the names of mostly absent men.

Although I have been an ardent and outspoken supporter of the right of every woman to make her own decision about whether to carry a pregnancy to term, I have always known that had my own mother been given that option, I would not have been born. It's a piece of information that has never bothered me. From my earliest years, I saw too many women forced to have children they didn't want and couldn't properly care for. A demeaning and uncharitable lack of choice often blighted not only their own lives but the lives of their children as well.

I have been known for most of my professional life as Doris Anderson, but I was christened Hilda Doris Buck. Buck was the name of my mother's long-departed first husband. Girls in my mother's family were always given good solid first names favoured by the relatives: Elizabeth, Ann, Jane, Maggie, or Rebecca (my mother's name). But at my own birth, since I was illegitimate, it was not clear whether I was to become part of my mother's family at all. Hence Hilda and Doris.

Doris was a trendy name in the 1920s. I was called Hilda by my sentimental mother after an acquaintance's almost forgotten child who was "too good to live." By implication, I felt back then, I must have been "bad" indeed, by persisting in surviving—despite what must have been a clear wish by everyone concerned that I simply fade away like poor little Hilda.

My arrival on November 10, 1921, couldn't have been more untimely. Seven years before, my mother had been deserted by the infamous Alvin Buck. Before he left, he had persuaded my grandmother to take a mortgage on her only asset, a large boarding house in Calgary. He had assured her that he could double her money by investing the cash in a short-lived real estate boom. Having lost the funds, he slipped out of town with another woman, leaving his wife with their two children, Fred, aged four, and Reg, two. Just a month earlier they had lost a third little boy, who died in his sleep at just under a year. Alvin Buck, whose last name I bore for the first eight years of my life, neither sent money, nor ever attempted to see his sons again.

But his long shadow continued to fall over our lives. His picture always hung on Mama's bedroom wall. An arrogant-looking fellow with insolent, sleepy eyes, he wore a nicely cut suit and a derby hat perched on the back of a full head of dark curly hair. His hand rested authoritatively on a small table, and his legs were spread apart to show off his highly polished boots and a gold watch chain.

His picture was like an evil icon. He had been an overly strict, punishing father, from all accounts. He had certainly been an unfaithful husband, even before he took the train out of town. Buck continued to loom in our lives because, when I was a small child, my mother gave me the impression that he might return at any time. And I have no doubt that had he returned, he would have been received back. In those days women took all their status from their husbands. So necessary were men thought to be that even a thief, a tyrant, and a philanderer like Alvin Buck would have been allowed to return.

Mama was twenty-three when she became a single parent. Trained only for marriage, she had never worked outside the home except to help her mother in the boarding house. Deeply conscious of her own disgrace as a deserted wife, she took on the responsibility of her two small sons, her mother—a sixty-year-old widow—and the burden of paying off the mortgage Alvin Buck had incurred.

My mother's family had arrived in the West in the late 1880s. Her father, Joseph Laycock, seemed to have been a typical entrepreneurial man of his time. Born in 1850, the third son of a lowly barrel maker in England's Lake District, he left home early to make his fortune. A handsome man with light curly hair and a small moustache, he improved his prospects in 1872 by marrying Ann Leigh, the eldest daughter of a prominent farming family from the hamlet of Tockholes, near Blackburn in Lancastershire. Her family, which included Nightingales and Jepsons, had farmed in the area as far back as the church records go. Some of them were skilled masons and had constructed the church, houses, and stone fences in the surrounding countryside.

For a time Joseph Laycock prospered by selling real estate in Blackburn. In 1882 he told his wife he was off on a trip to Ireland in search of new opportunities. When next she heard from him, he had bought a tavern in Toronto on the corner of Sumach and King! (The tavern was always described as a "hotel" by the Leighs, who were teetotallers and considered the money Joseph made in his tavern "tainted.")

Ann had no choice but to pack up her small family—a twelve-year-old daughter, a ten-year-old son, and a baby girl—and come to Canada. She never saw England or her own relatives again. In the church records in Tockholes, after my grandmother's name, are the dismissive words "Gone to America"—not a line about whom she married or how many children she had. She might as well have sailed off the edge of the world.

Once established in Toronto, Joseph again prospered. The family lived in a house on King Street and kept servants. Two large oil paintings of Ann and Joseph were commissioned, together with several studio portraits of the children. Two more daughters were added to the family, one who died and my mother, Rebecca.

The new railway had just opened up the Canadian West, and the restless Joseph, like many Englishmen, saw an opportunity to make his dream of owning a large country property come true. In 1887 he once again set off, this time for Vancouver. The train broke down in Calgary, and during the stopover someone convinced him that the potential of the prairies was even greater than that of the West Coast.

Joseph's plan was to run a dairy farm that would supply the fast-growing little community. Although land in other areas was free, he bought a quarter section from the Canadian Pacific Railway on the north hill overlooking Calgary, in what is now Tuxedo Park. The next year he built an imposing eight-room two-storey house, along with a fifty-foot-long cow barn, a large horse barn, and several other buildings. He called his spread "the Grange."

In 1890, after arranging for prize cattle to be shipped from eastern Canada, as well as some purebred dogs and horses, Joseph moved his family out to their new home in Alberta. He farmed for only one year, though. Plagued by a weak heart from an earlier bout of rheumatic fever, Joseph died in 1891. He was only forty-two years old. The day before he died, my mother, born the year before, took her first steps across the floor towards him.

My grandmother, who was then thirty-nine, had had nine children. Of these, three were stillborn and two died of childhood diseases. She had four children to support—Maggie, eighteen; James, sixteen; Annie, seven; and Rebecca, twelve months.

After Joseph's death, Ann had nothing but bad luck. My grandfather had persuaded his brothers, William and Thomas, to come out from England and take up farms adjacent to his own, but they had large families and were pressed for money themselves. For two years after Joseph died, William farmed the Grange and Ann moved into town, where she had a large house built near the City Hall.

William found running two farms too difficult, so Ann was forced to move back to the Grange with her family. For three successive years she put in a crop with hired help, and for three successive years the crops were destroyed by hail and she had to buy feed for the cattle. The frigid Calgary weather took its toll on the prize cattle too; tough local cattle would have survived better in those early days. The money from selling milk and butter in Calgary wasn't enough to make the Grange profitable.

With his driving ambition, Joseph had insisted on good educations for his children and had been strict with them all, but he had been hardest on his only son. In the absence of his father's authoritarian presence, James, eighteen, became something of a playboy. My mother described wild chases in a buggy across the prairie, hunting down coyotes instead of fixing fences and doing other chores.

Mama was sent to the local one-room school. A shy, red-haired six-year-old, she didn't speak up loudly enough that first day, and the teacher strapped her. My grandmother refused to send her back, and from that time until they moved into Calgary, she was educated at home. In Calgary, she was sent to the convent, which my grandmother considered superior to the public schools, but my mother always felt her short, formal education was inferior to the schooling the other members of her family received.

In 1895, in the living room of the Grange, Mama's eldest sister, Maggie, married a flamboyant, red-haired cowboy called "Blue" Osborne. It was a love match. She was a tall, well-read, rather reserved young woman. Blue Osborne, on the other hand, was almost illiterate. Everyone said that had my grandfather been alive, he would never have approved of the marriage.

Blue Osborne hailed from Texas. He was barely twelve when his mother died, and he ran away from home to ride herd on the long cattle drives from Texas to the railway in the Midwest. He was dubbed "Blue" by his rough companions because of the colour of his shirt. His own name, Francis Marion, was considered too sissified for a cowboy.

For two years, Blue tried to run the Grange, but in 1898 he decided it was impossible to make it profitable. Joseph had been accustomed to small, neat English farms and hadn't realized farming in Canada required larger acreage. Finally Ann sold the cattle and equipment to Blue, and he took up a homestead at Rosebud, east of Calgary.

The story of that trek across the prairie in 1898 from the Grange to Rosebud, some hundred miles to the east, is a legend in my family. James and his fifteen-year-old sister, Annie, herded the cattle. My grandmother, with my mother beside her, drove one of two buckboard wagons loaded with supplies. Maggie drove the other wagon with her baby daughter, Eva, tucked under the seat.

At one point, they had to ford a fast-moving stream. Halfway across, my grandmother's horse got cramps. Blue rode out into the water and cut the animal loose. He managed to rescue my mother and grandmother but was unable to save the horse, which slipped under the water and drowned.

Ann stayed on the Grange one more year. Nobody would buy it at a time when there was plenty of free land to be had and very little money. In the end, the Grange was sold for taxes. My grandmother moved back into the Calgary house, put on a large addition, and began taking in boarders to support herself and her two youngest daughters. James joined the Great West Saddlery company and became a volunteer in Calgary's first fire brigade. In 1901 he married and set up a harness-and-saddlery business in Gleichen. Later he opened one of the West's first moving-picture theatres.

Blue Osborne ranched at Rosebud for several years, but deeply regretting his own lack of education, he was determined his own children would have more opportunities. To be near better schools, he sold the ranch and moved his family first to Calgary, and then to Medicine Hat, where he became a buyer and seller of cattle.

A strapping man, Blue considered himself indestructible. Mama remembered the last day he dropped in to see his Calgary relatives. He was running a fever, so my grandmother urged him to stay at the house and see a doctor. He replied that he had already been given a prescription for cough medicine, and he had a herd of cattle he was supposed to see. He flipped a coin to decide whether to go on the ride to assess the animals or back to the doctor. The coin came up in favour of the ride. He took two more swigs of the medicine and left. When he returned to Calgary, he was long past any doctor's help. He died two days later of pneumonia.

On the day of her husband's funeral, Maggie went into labour with their seventh child, a son. Blue's coffin was carried into the bedroom so that she could have a last look at him before he was buried. She was left with six children to raise; another baby son had died and her eldest daughter, Eva, was barely twelve. To support them, Maggie, like her mother, turned their home in Medicine Hat into a boarding house.

My mother's sister, Annie, considered the beauty of the family, married an Englishman in 1902 when she was eighteen. Although he seemed urbane, charming, and well off, he turned out to be a "remittance man." These were men who had brought dishonour on themselves back in England. They were sent to the colonies and given regular allowances, provided that they never returned. It wasn't long before Annie realized her new husband was an alcoholic with little desire to work. She separated from him soon after their daughter was born and supported herself and the baby for several years. After he died, Annie married another Englishman, who was able to provide a comfortable life for them.

Although all the women in my family had coped well with the changes in their lives, the lament that persisted throughout my childhood was "If only your grandfather had lived . . ." I was always given the impression that if Joseph Laycock had lived, everything would have been quite different. With his talent for making money, he would have succeeded in turning the Grange into a profitable proposition. Or he might have taken up another line of business in the growing town of Calgary and scaled down the Grange operation until property values went up twenty years later, when the land could have been sold for a good profit. If only he had lived, the doleful voices went on, he would have been a leading citizen of Calgary, an elder in the Pro-Cathedral Anglican Church we attended, a city councillor, and with his entrepreneurial gifts, one of those who had founded Calgary's celebrated Stampede.

And they might have been right. Even in my childhood, the Grange land had become a thriving suburb. I marvelled at the handsome people in their beautiful clothes and jewellery in the gold-embossed family album. An old hump-backed trunk filled with treasures was mute evidence of a much more affluent past—my grandmother's black silk evening bag with its silver handle, ostrich feathers that had once adorned a hat, a gold-handled silk umbrella, and the few remaining pieces of her jewellery.

As a teenager, I would pore over the hand-tooled family Bible with its gold clasps and its record of births, deaths, and marriages inscribed in my grandfather's fine hand. I would listen once again to my mother relate the tales of hardships and heartbreaks, and I would question why so much had depended on one man. "If all my grandmother needed was a man, why didn't she marry again?" I would ask. "She was a rich woman for those times. There must have been lots of men more than willing to take the Grange on."

"She was tired," Mama would say. "She'd been brought halfway around the world. She'd had nine children—and lost five of them. But probably the truth was she never thought she would find a man half as good as my father."

I was still puzzled by the remorse about the past. My grandmother, mother, and two aunts had raised their fourteen children well, educated them as best they could, and "kept their heads above water." In those days, when there was no form of social assistance, they paid their bills, coped with mortgages, called doctors when needed, and instilled in all of us standards of behaviour and work habits that have stood us in good stead throughout our lives.

As my grandmother grew older and arthritis prevented her from doing much of the housework, she turned to needlework, which was one of her great skills. She did all the mending, knitting, and quilt-making, as well as many of the sit-down jobs such as baking and preparing vegetables. It was said that one day when one of my brothers came home from school with wet mitts and couldn't find his spare pair, she knitted him a new pair in the time it took him to finish lunch!

✦ The First World War and the influenza epidemic of 1919 had been hard on my family. My mother's brother, James, and two little nephews had died, but although she had contracted the disease, Mama survived. The last calamity she needed was an extra, unwanted child. It was disgrace enough in those days to be a deserted wife, but bearing an illegitimate child was the ultimate humiliation for a woman.

Society at that time was not forgiving. Uncle William's wife had never forgiven one of her daughters who ran off with the hired man. Years later the daughter, living happily in Montana with her husband and four children, returned to Calgary to visit her brothers and sisters. She came face-to-face with her mother on Eighth Avenue. Her mother cut her dead.

My grandmother, who was nearly seventy, could not have been pleased when my mother told her she was pregnant. It was another blow to this family, once so full of optimism and pride.

I was born in Medicine Hat, where my mother's two sisters lived. She went there to avoid the curious eyes of her neighbours and relatives in the last months of her pregnancy. Her niece, Eva, who was now married, helped my grandmother in the boarding house while my mother was away. I was brought back to Calgary on the train and immediately put in a home for unwanted babies. Years later, my mother, who was given to dramatics, told me she almost put me out for adoption. I think I was supposed to be shocked, but being a rebellious teenager at the time, I remember almost wishing that she had.

I was a sickly baby. I am sure everyone, including my mother, half hoped I would die, but it's another thing to actually watch a baby die and do nothing. Like many a child in similar circumstances, I certainly didn't thrive in that home.

My mother's mistake, of course, was in continuing to visit me at all. I don't know what finally prompted her to keep me. Perhaps she could see that I was not being looked after well—and she would have been incensed at that. Perhaps my tenacity at clinging to life appealed to her. And so, after several months, she took me home. But even then it was a tentative acceptance. A bed was made from a bottom drawer—as though at any time I could be returned and the drawer put back in the bureau. Her story was that she was looking after a baby for money. This might have passed muster with casual acquaintances—she was always trying to make extra money—but I doubt that it worked with the relatives in her close-knit family.

I wasn't even a very successful baby. Ordinary milk didn't agree with me, and the doctor could suggest no alternative—milk was what babies drank in those days. A cousin, Will Laycock, a big jolly farmer, and a man I always liked, told Mama one of his children had had trouble with cow's milk but thrived on condensed milk. She tried that, and I began to flourish.

It was around this time that everyone decided they hated the name Hilda and began to call me Doris.

I must have seemed strange to my mother. Considered to be "a fine figure of a woman," she was tall, plump, and red-haired, like all the women in her family. I was thin, sickly, and even as a baby had long, dark hair. I couldn't have been a very attractive child because Mama, who was an avid photographer, took no pictures of me with her Box Brownie camera during the whole of my first year.

The earliest snapshot was taken around my first birthday. I am sitting on a sleigh. My brothers are dressed up for Sunday school in short belted jackets and knickers, boots, caps, and ties. I am all in white in a fake-fur coat, leggings, and mitts—all hand-me-downs from the daughter of an affluent friend of my mother's. Everyone else is smiling, but in the weak winter sun, even at that early age, I am looking at the world with a sceptical, almost resigned, expression.

I refused for years to face the fact that I probably carry some emotional scars from that abrupt separation from my mother right after I was born. I always believed she more than made up for it with affection later. However, although I was a lively, independent child, I was terrified of being abandoned. Mama could get instant obedience from me by threatening to put me in the bedroom by myself. She could control me with a single disapproving look. Later on, in all my closest relationships, partners always complained that I was too guarded.

My earliest memory is of the Calgary house. I recall emerging from my grandmother's bedroom closet, which had a pungent smell of out-of-season clothes. At two and a half, I had pulled on my grandmother's high boots and had tried to lace them up. As I staggered out into a large sunny room, I remember someone laughing and laughing on a kind of shiny dias across the room. I was told later that it was my grandmother, sitting up in her brass bed.

My next memory is standing in the snow beside a very deep hole. I looked up at my mother, who was weeping inconsolably. It must have been my grandmother's funeral. She died at seventy-two, when I was barely three.

That old house in its shabby neighbourhood—my first home—remains vividly in my mind even now. I was happy there. And to this day I never can pass an old, shabby house but that I mentally spruce it up with new paint and furniture. Today, one block north of the old City Hall stands Calgary's handsome public library, on the very same spot where our house once stood.

In my childhood, the boarding house and its neighbourhood were "going downhill," as my mother frequently lamented. We were the last of two original families on the street. All the rest were new Canadians— mostly Polish, Ukrainian, Jewish, and Chinese. Although Mama always insisted everyone was as good as everyone else and should be treated equally, I quickly realized this was, in fact, not the case. I was allowed to have the children of new Canadians over to play with me, but I wasn't allowed to go to their houses.

A livery barn stood across the road from our house, and a blacksmith shop was just down the street. Horses were far more common than cars at that time and were used to pull milk, bread, and ice wagons. In winter we children loved to sleigh ride down the slope of the livery stable's driveway. The owner, a fierce man in a black Stetson, would rush out, flourishing a long whip. Sleighs made the slope icy for the horses.

I remember those early years as being almost idyllic. My mother was enjoying an unusually independent period in her life. She had succeeded in supporting her family—her mother, her sons, and finally me, with no help from anyone. She enjoyed a close and happy relationship with her sisters, nieces, and other relatives. Aunt Maggie sent her daughters up to Calgary to take teacher's training and nursing. They boarded free with us in exchange for helping around the house. And Mama would occasionally send my brothers to Medicine Hat for short holidays and to work with her sisters in their gardens.

Deeply attached to her own mother, my mother turned to me after my grandmother's death, as the only other female in the house. She probably hoped to receive from me the same kind of help and support her own mother had always counted on from her daughters. I tagged along as she performed her chores around the house. One of my earliest expressions was "I can manage." At that time, she encouraged me to try to do things myself and she seemed to revel in my independent nature.

My mother's world was small and eminently sensible. Although she was greatly overworked and busy from morning to night, I felt well looked after. She could be sharp with me, because she had little time for dawdling and I was expected—as my brothers were—to do what I was told immediately. From an early age, we all learned to read her moods. We knew, for example, that she was short-tempered on Monday night after she had done the week's wash for our family and all the boarders. Sometimes, when she was really provoked, she could fly off the handle and administer a clap on the ear. Very occasionally, I got spanked with a hairbrush. Her physical punishments would not be approved of today, but I don't think it ever hurt us to learn to cope with another person's moods from a fairly early age.

Because I was almost constantly with her, my mother knew instantly when I was tired, or hurt, or when the world was too big and fearful for me, and she generally did something about it. Once, I decided I didn't want to go to Sunday school anymore. Nor did I want to see people, so when anyone came to the house, I would hide. Instead of scolding me, she accepted a four-year-old's temporary retreat from the world. She continued to talk about things I would miss—an outing in her niece's car or the Christmas party at the Sunday school. After about a week, I decided that the advantages of being part of the world outweighed the disadvantages. I went back to my usual activities and even recited a poem in front of the Sunday school at Christmas.

Children find beauty wherever they are. That old, shabby house seemed filled with sunshine to me. I remember in the late afternoon my wonder at a brilliant rainbow arcing across the worn linoleum from the glass in the china cabinet. The kitchen was the hub of the house, and my playroom. An oilcloth-covered table stood in the centre of the room. A canary chirped in its cage by the window. The table served as a playhouse, and a collection of stools—chairs with the backs broken off—became cars, streetcars, or airplanes.

I made up my own games—and although I had dolls and my busy mother had even made clothes for them, I rarely played house. Far more often the dolls and any pet cats were pressed into service as pupils in school, or as the audience while I was a concert pianist, or as passengers on a plane, that I, like Amelia Earhart, piloted.

Mama's treadle sewing machine sat before the window. At night I would go to sleep to its comforting sound as she made clothes for us. Almost everything I wore was run up on that machine, often from hand-me-down clothes from cousins or aunts. A worn-out shirt became rompers or a play dress for me, or patches for quilts. Purity Flour sacks were bleached and made into underwear, tea towels, and dish cloths. She also made all the sheets and pillowcases for the house. In her "spare time," she turned out dozens of black protector armbands men wore back then to keep their shirt sleeves clean. She made these for a men's store, which paid her a pittance, but it was extra money in those hard times.

An enormous iron stove burned gas at one end and wood and coal at the other. On it my mother cooked breakfast and dinner for our family, as well as eight or nine male boarders. But her pride and joy was a new Maytag electric washing machine, built like an armoured tank. It replaced an old wooden tub with a lever on the side that had to be pumped by hand. Mama used the "new" machine until she died—some forty years later. On either side of the kitchen were two big wooden racks, which were raised and lowered by pulleys and used for drying clothes. In winter everything was hung outside to dry and then brought in, stiff as boards, to finish drying in the kitchen.

Old newspapers were kept and used for lining drawers and shelves, making kites, paper hats, or copies of dress patterns. Magazines were kept for school projects. All string and paper bags were saved. Worn-out sheets and pillowcases were torn up for bandages. Even Christmas wrapping paper was ironed and recycled. Bottles and jars were used for jams and pickles that were put down every fall. In fact, so little was thrown out that only one large bag of garbage was collected each week from the whole household.

We raised vegetables in the back yard, which was large for a city lot. In one corner was a chicken coop where a rooster and several hens kept us supplied with eggs. Every spring newborn chicks were kept in a box in the kitchen with a gallon jug of heated water to keep them warm, until they were old enough to fend for themselves outside. From time to time they were killed for dinner, and I would sit at the table weeping over one of my pets being devoured so callously.

My mother was active in the Pro-Cathedral Anglican Church, as convenor of the Ladies Aid. Most of our social life revolved around the church or within Mama's large circle of relatives. Both my brothers were in the Boy Scouts, and one of them sang in the church choir.

From the time I was three, I was the Brownie mascot. The Brown Owl,

Mrs. Scrace, probably thought it would be good for her Brownie pack to have the experience of looking after a younger child. Perhaps she was also thinking it would be pleasant for my mother to have me out from under her feet for an hour or two every week. I loved the Brownies—the meetings in the parish hall, the songs and games, the church parades on special Sundays. Just by listening to the older girls, I knew so much lore by the time I was seven and became an actual Brownie that I immediately broke out in an armful of badges.

My half brothers were ten and eleven years older than I. Before rushing off to do their chores after school, they always had time to make a fuss over me, and they teased me mercilessly. Fred and Reg both had paper routes to earn extra money. As well, they helped my mother—running to the store for groceries, shovelling the walk in winter, digging the garden and watering it in summer. They helped with the meals by peeling potatoes, setting the table, and doing dishes, and they could press their own pants and even do elementary cooking. They also performed chores such as whitewashing the chicken house.

But they were not saints, and they were not diligent scholars. They frequently got into fights with each other and with other boys at school. Both had been given the strap—a not uncommon occurrence in those days, but one that greatly displeased Mama. They even played hookey, which brought the truant officer to the house from time to time. Always anxious about raising boys alone, my mother spent a great deal of time worrying about them.

As soon as I was able, I too had chores to perform. I had to keep my drawer in the bottom of the bureau tidy. I swept down the stairs with a brush and dustpan, and later dusted the whatnot—a table with fancy lower shelves and legs. I dried spoons, graduating in time to forks, knives and, finally, dishes.

We were all given allowances in return for our chores. I kept mine in an iron bank shaped like an elephant. My mother opened a bank account for me as soon as I could print my name, and I would be trotted down from time to time to put any little savings or windfalls in the bank. The rule was never, never to take out the money. It was there "for a rainy day." When I broke a meat platter, Mama thought I had been careless and decided to teach me a lesson by making me pay for it. It took me the best part of the winter to pay for my negligence out of my allowance. Dipping into my bank account never crossed my frugal little mind.

It's strange today to think back on that matriarchal world. My mother ran everything herself, and sensibly, in my opinion. She certainly took no nonsense from the boarders. If they came home drunk, used coarse language or—heaven forbid—tried to sneak a woman into the house, they were immediately given their walking papers.

I was surrounded by men, but we lived in an entirely separate world from the boarders. They were upstairs; we were downstairs. They ate in the dining room; we ate in the kitchen. Like a good concierge, Mama always knew who was in or out, who was reliable, who was likely to try to steal away without paying his rent, and who had too many girlfriends for his own good.

I observed the boarders curiously from afar, often from the front window as they came and went. I noticed how different the upstairs smelled—musty and smoky from their cigarettes and cigars and their sweaty clothes and socks. They seemed to own very few things. Their clothes hung limply in the closets—usually one good suit with one pair of black shoes suitable for a wedding—or a funeral. I marvelled at how different their talk was from that of women. They boasted a lot, made bets, challenged one another. And sometimes they whispered like bad schoolboys and then laughed uproariously.

The Price brothers, who worked at Imperial Oil, were particularly memorable—or at least their clothes were. My mother had to use cleaning fluid to try to remove the stains from them. One Monday morning, the tub burst into flames, and she had to call the fire department. At four, I remember holding the door open for the firemen. Mama's arm and face were burned, and a fair amount of damage was done to the kitchen. The worst disaster for her was the death of the canary.

With a houseful of men, my mother truly never let me out of her sight. She had no illusions about what lonely men might do to little girls—or boys. Without making me fearful, she made it clear that I was never to go upstairs and into any boarder's room without her, and she went into their rooms herself only to make their beds, change linen, wash their floors, and dust their dressers. When I went upstairs to the one bathroom in the house, I had to report to her first, and then report again when I got back.

Some of the boarders lived at the house for years, and they were allowed to josh with me. Occasionally they would offer me kisses or a "chin whisker," which meant rubbing their stubbly faces against mine. Mama always discouraged that kind of contact. I was never allowed to take money or candy from the boarders or any other stranger.

That was my world. A happy place, as I remember it. Cosy and too restricted even then, but wonderfully safe because my mother was completely in charge. She ran everything and it seemed to me at that time so long ago that she was all-seeing, all-knowing, and infallible.

CHAPTER TWO

The Real World of Men

I didn't find out who my father was until I was almost five. I wasn't even curious about him, since the absence of fathers in my family had been the rule, not the exception. My missing parent was first brought to my attention by two little girls who lived in "the block," a brick building housing an employment agency and some apartments that looked out on our back yard. Their father was a barber, and they wanted to know what mine did for a living. I said I didn't know. This piqued their curiosity. Where was my father? In a brilliant flash of inventiveness, I told them he had been killed in the war—a romantic idea that was clearly impossible if they had been able to count—but it seemed to satisfy them at the time.

My mother had begun to trust me to run small errands, and one day I was sent to the nearby market for a pound of butter. The friendly dairy man asked, "Where's your daddy?" I tried the war story on him. He laughed derisively, and that night after saying my prayers and kissing my mother good-night, I asked, "Everyone has a daddy but me. Who's my daddy?"

She must have been waiting for that question for a long time. Even at an early age, I realized that my mother had a penchant for making grand opera out of what seemed to me quite ordinary events. And with such a hard, work-a-day life, she could hardly be blamed. But this was no ordinary moment for either of us. Her eyes filled with tears. She took me in her arms, her voice breaking as she said, "Your father is Mr. McCubbin."

I knew something dramatic was expected of me, but instead of registering pleasure or even surprise, I was confused and disappointed. She must have known that—I wasn't clever at hiding my feelings—because she clung to me even harder, and then, still wiping her eyes, she kissed me again and put me in bed.

The truth was that I was not pleased by this revelation. I don't know what I had expected—a fairy prince, perhaps. But I was already well acquainted with Mr. McCubbin, and I had already decided that I didn't like him. He had only recently become a frequent visitor at our house; I don't remember much about him before that time. I owned an ivory dresser set that had been a gift from him. I barely remembered a purebred collie pup called Bowser that he had given me. The dog had to be tied up to keep him from knocking me over when I went out to play.

Thomas McCubbin was different from most of the other men in my life. He was better dressed than the boarders and the men hanging around the employment agency who sometimes peed into our garden. Photos of him at that time show a handsome, athletic-looking man. His colouring was unusual—pitch-black hair, strong, dark features, and light blue eyes. When he came to call, he was always nattily dressed in a suit, tie, and hat. Unlike my male relatives, he often brought my mother chocolates or flowers. After I had gone to bed, he would play cribbage with Mama, and she would make cocoa for them. He seemed to be able to drop in during the afternoon while most other men were at work. At other times, he would disappear for months.

His relationship to my mother puzzled me. Although she was generally pleasant and polite on the telephone, her voice at certain times would become cold and indifferent and she would say things such as "Well, I may be home, and then again, I may not." She would then hang up the receiver with a bang and come away looking flushed and angry. I always knew she had been talking to Mr. McCubbin.

My father came from a large farming family in Wigtownshire, Scotland, where the name McCubbin is as common as Smith. A great raconteur, he said his family had originally been McKibbons. "Some of them went to Ireland and got kicked out for sheep stealing. When they arrived back in Scotland, they couldn't spell their name, and so they became McCubbin," he would relate with relish. One of my Scottish aunts claimed to have traced the family back to the Stuarts, but my father said you could prove anything if you paid enough for it. Another, perhaps more authentic, theory was that the McCubbins originally came from the Isle of Man in the Irish Sea, but none of his family believed this. Not being a Scot was worse than being a sheep stealer.

He was bright in school, and his mother had wanted him to become a minister in the Presbyterian Church. But when he was fourteen, the teacher thrashed him for something he was convinced he hadn't done, and cracking the switch over his knee, my father walked out of the school forever. Afterwards, he was apprenticed at several jobs but couldn't settle down at anything. Finally his parents decided to send him to the colonies. "I was bound for Australia," he would say, "but the boat sank at the dock, so they put me on the next boat to Canada."

Although he admired his gentle father, and deeply loved his feisty little mother, as the third son, my father probably felt he never received his full share of attention in a family of nine. I think he always wanted to make it big and return home triumphantly. He was just eighteen and sporting a large black moustache when he arrived at his uncle's farm in Saskatchewan in 1909. That first Christmas, he spent most of what he earned buying his mother a beautiful gold watch with "Maple Creek Saskatchewan" engraved on its face. Years later, his family sent me the watch and his stiff little note: "Dear Mother, This is a little present for Christmas. I hope it pleases you and that you get it all right. Tam."

The following year, he persuaded his older brother, Peter, to come to Canada. They homesteaded in a log cabin in Saskatchewan on adjoining quarter sections. He used to tell us how they made porridge, which was so inedible that they tossed it out in the snow. It froze and they used it as a doorstop for the rest of the winter. After one year, Pete went back to Scotland to become a railroad engineer. My father, impatient with farming, and hearing rumours of a boom in Calgary, moved on. It was the same boom that had tempted my grandmother to take out a mortgage on her house and give Alvin Buck the money to invest.

Mama first noticed my father when he passed the house wearing a big fur hat, which she thought hilarious—and typical of "green" immigrants from the British Isles. Two or three days later, he was at the front door, inquiring about a room, and he became one of the boarders. Although my mother was a married, though deserted, woman, they fell in love. A year later, when the First World War broke out, my father immediately joined up. His reason for enlisting wasn't patriotism, he was always quick to tell us: it was the adventure that intrigued him. He was actually afraid that the war would be over before he got there.

He always held it against my mother that she refused to go down to the station to see him off when his troop train left Calgary. As a married woman, she thought it would have been scandalous to do that. Still, they wrote to each other. None of the letters has survived, but I have beautiful postcards from France with such sentiments as "Forget-me-not" embroidered on lawn and discreetly addressed "Dear Friend" and signed "Your friend, Mac." I also have a gold locket that he carried with him all through the war. In it is a curl of my mother's red hair.

My father spent four ghastly years in the trenches amid that terrible carnage. He was gassed and wounded, and although he was given promotions twice, he lost them for bad conduct. When the war ended, he returned to Canada bitter, disillusioned, and even more of a rebel. "He had a chip on his shoulder," Mama always said. He wanted to make up for lost time and be a big success, but he wanted to take shortcuts to become one.

Still recovering from the recent flu epidemic, my mother looked like a wraith when Father first saw her after he returned to Calgary. However, their romance continued, although two less well suited people could hardly be imagined.

My mother was extremely conventional. She wanted a normal, safe life, and above all a "good, steady man" who would offer her, after her disastrous first marriage, security and respectability. She was deeply religious and tolerant of other people, races, and religions. Generally uncritical, she would rarely say anything nasty about anyone, although people who knew her well could tell by the warmth in her voice—or the lack of it—exactly what she thought. She hated arguments and conflict. Politics mattered little to her. She usually voted Conservative, and mostly for people who belonged, as she did, to the original old Calgary families.

My father was the complete opposite. A born rebel, he was anti-establishment, anti-royalist and, having had too much Presbyterian religion as a boy ("You weren't even allowed to whistle on Sunday!"), a confirmed atheist. He was intolerant of foreigners and considered politicians and members of the clergy little more than charlatans. He distrusted lawyers, bankers, and even doctors. He would go out of his way to pick an argument with anyone. Fascinated by what was happening in Russia, he claimed to be a Communist. Although I have no evidence that he ever actually joined the party, he certainly always voted for it. And far from being a teetotaller, he enjoyed drinking far too much.

The one thing they had in common was a strong physical attraction, which resulted in her becoming pregnant with me. In later years, she told me the reason they couldn't marry before I was born was that she couldn't get a legal divorce. After she died, I discovered this was not true. After seven years, and an attempt to find a missing husband, a woman could obtain a divorce—with difficulty—at that time in Canada. And to prove it, there among her papers was a legal divorce granted to her, in time to marry my father one month before I was born.

I will never know why that marriage did not take place. I am sure the one thing my mother would have wanted was marriage. Why my father, as a single man, and one who claimed to love her, didn't do what was expected of him is one of the mysteries surrounding their passionate and peculiar attraction for each other.

To give him credit, Father always seemed an unusually honourable man, in spite of all his bluster against the establishment and convention. I would have expected him to immediately do the right thing. But with his rebellious nature, he might have felt he was being trapped into a conventional life, having to support a woman with an aging mother and two half-grown sons before he had really put the war behind him and launched himself in a career. Like many women of that time, my mother was always eager to be agreeable. There was a point, however, when her obdurate, red-haired Leigh temper took over, and she could be as stubborn and unforgiving as a stone. I can imagine that if my tactless father ever suggested that he felt trapped, she might have told him to go to blazes. That might have happened between them. It's the only explanation I have.

I do know that he met the train when she came back from Medicine Hat after my birth. They had probably agreed that I would be put out for adoption. Knowing my mother as I do, I'm sure she could not have held a baby in her arms and willingly have given it up. On that long train ride, perhaps she thought the sight of me would change everything between them. Knowing my macho father, I am also sure that had I been a boy, he probably would have insisted on marrying her on the spot. As it was, I must not have impressed him, and he took us, as had originally been planned, to the home where I spent the first few months of my life.

In retrospect, that was to prove one of the worst of many bad decisions my father made. Having to support a family might have provided him with some stability and the desire to stick with a particular line of work. In Calgary in the 1920s, many opportunities were opening up; instead, he frittered away those potentially productive years.

Veterans were being offered training by the government, and he took a mechanics course and opened a garage in Carbon. He soon gave it up when the little community failed to grow fast enough. He then heard of a gold find in Panama, and he and a friend flew there, only to find that the rumour had been false. For much of the twenties, he took jobs that offered fast money, such as working on a harvesting crew. Some winters he drove a car to Florida, where he would stay for several months and drive another car back. A born gambler who always believed his luck would turn, he played poker, bet on horses, and could never resist a lottery ticket—or the stock market. After my birth, I think my mother probably was not only bitter but also convinced, with some justification, that marriage to my father would be a disaster. For those few short years in my early childhood, she became the independent woman I knew and loved so much.

When I was four, Thomas McCubbin began to drift back into our lives on a regular basis. I found him interfering and demanding. I thought he had no more right to assume any authority over me than any of the boarders. He once bawled me out for running onto the street after a ball, although I was allowed to do that by my mother if I checked carefully that no cars were coming.

With time on his hands, he began to take an interest in my education and bought me jigsaw and metal puzzles. He would try to help me colour books, but I soon realized he couldn't tell green from blue. He would insist in his peremptory manner that he was right, which was unsettling to me. Adults were supposed to be infallible, especially in such obvious matters. I was fascinated by the tattoos on his arms—the result, I learned later, of a drunken leave during the war. Ashamed of them, he brushed my inquiries away.

He also bought me a Tinker Toy set—sticks and wheels that fitted together to make various carts, houses, and windmills—an unusual gift for a girl. The day he arrived with it, he insisted that all the pieces be laid out in the correct categories before we could begin to build anything. By the time that was done, I was bored. The children from next door wanted me to go out to play, and I left him in the middle of the floor surrounded by the pieces. He was exasperated. My mother was amused.

He was full of radical theories. One of them was that a child, forced to swim, would just naturally be able to do it, like a dog. One summer day, he threw me into the deep end of a swimming pool to test this theory. I sank to the bottom, gasping and screaming with fright, and he had to dive in to rescue me. My mother was furious and enrolled me in swimming classes at the Y. I managed to get over my fright and learned to swim quite adequately, in spite of my traumatic introduction to water.

An early fitness freak, my father worked out at the YMCA every day. He greatly admired the Edmonton Grads, an all-woman basketball team making headlines around the world. After Gertrude Ederle became the first woman to swim the English Channel in 1926, he decided to turn me into a super athlete and started me on a regimen of exercises. Every afternoon he would turn up about three o'clock. I would be required to stand on my head and perform cartwheels. He would also work out himself by walking all over the dining-room floor and out into the kitchen on his hands. Then, holding on to my legs, he would lift me over his shoulders. He also chinned himself on a beam over a bedroom door. To add to the weight, he would wrap his legs around me and lift me too. This put my face right up against his crotch, which I didn't like. After two weeks my mother stopped it, saying it was stretching me out too much and making me too muscular.

Looking back on those days, I think it must have been an uncomfortable time for my father. One day when I had been sent to the store, I bumped into him. He tried to give me a quarter, and I told him politely, "I am not allowed to take money from strangers."

But far worse for me than his growing presence in my life was his influence on my mother. Her attitude towards me began to change. I remember the day she took me aside and told me, "You're getting too bold." I knew what "bold" meant. It was a term used to describe little girls who were too spirited, girls who drew attention to themselves or showed off.

"People say you're getting a little too forward," she added.

"What people?" I asked. Then I remembered a birthday party I had recently attended for the daughter of my mother's girlhood friend Aunt Ethel. It had taken place in Elbow Park, all the way across the city in a much nicer neighbourhood. I knew none of the other girls, who were all a bit older. I think I behaved reasonably well, until we played Musical Chairs. It was my introduction to the game and I loved it. I managed to stay in until only three of us were left. The next time the music stopped, I wasn't in front of an empty chair, but I scrambled to grab a seat anyway, knocking another chair down in my eagerness. After a moment of shocked silence, Aunt Ethel said, with a tight little smile, that she thought we should play Fishes. Even at four, I knew I had made a social gaffe. Little girls were not supposed to compete too hard.

The incident no doubt had been related to Mama in a kindly way, but I soon realized the main pressure for change was coming from my father. In spite of his efforts to turn me into an athletic wonder, he also seemed to want, in his mysterious macho mind, a little doll for a daughter. He objected to a studio picture that had been taken of me at the time. In his opinion, I looked "too bold." He used to pull at the tiny hairs on my arms and say, "Hairy as an ape!" I knew this was not a compliment, and it had more edge to it than the gentle teasing I put up with from my brothers and the other men in the house.

My mother began a serious campaign to turn me not only into a little lady—exceptionally tidy, clean, and smarmily good—but also into a winsome and flirtatious young woman. These latter traits she certainly had never encouraged before, and to this day I am not comfortable with them in other women. Another more subtle message was, Don't lead any parades and don't be too bright—exactly the reverse of what she had seemed to like about me up to that time. Resenting the change, I naturally felt confused and vaguely unhappy.

For all these reasons, when I learned that the difficult and interfering Mr. McCubbin was my father, it was small wonder that I was not pleased. About the same time, I received two other unpleasant revelations—this time about my beloved older brothers.

Some money was missing from my elephant bank, and Mama, who knew to a cent where almost every penny in that household went, tracked the villain down. It was Reg. He said he had "just borrowed" it. I'm sure he intended to pay it back, but it shook my faith in him all the same.

Shortly after that, on a Saturday afternoon, I was left alone with Fred as my baby-sitter. He took me into the back bedroom, undressed me, and began to molest me. He certainly didn't hurt me and we were soon interrupted by Mr. McCubbin, who arrived unexpectedly and called out. When Fred hastily dressed me, I realized what we had been doing was wrong.

That night while I was being bathed, I related the incident to my mother. I will never forget the look of total shock on her face. She immediately summoned Fred. By the dressing-down she gave him, I realized he had committed a far more heinous crime than anything he had ever done before. I felt sorry for him and vaguely guilty, although Mama made it clear to me what had happened was not my fault.

I was becoming much more aware of the world outside our small neighbourhood. Through the church, I already knew that certain families were "better" than others. In her important position as convenor of the Ladies Aid, my mother organized the church suppers and teas, went to meetings, and even kept the books. At church functions she sweated away in the kitchen with her little band of women, and only came out wiping her hands on her apron to be thanked by the minister. Other women—the bishop's wife, the doctor's wife—officiated at the tea urn in silk-crepe dresses, elaborate hats, and ropes of pearls. They clearly patronized my mother, although they seemed to do no real work at all.

When I started at Central School (later James Short School), these class distinctions were driven home even more clearly. I had always lived in a multicultural neighbourhood. At school I discovered, as a white Anglo-Saxon Protestant, that I was in the privileged class compared with most of the children in my neighborhood.

I realized this one day when the boy in front of me accidentally hit my pencil with his elbow and it fell to the floor. In that austere schoolroom reeking of floor cleaner, we six-year-olds sat at desks screwed to the floor and wrote with large green pencils. If your pencil fell on the floor, even once, you were given a stubby black pencil. I'm sure if I had been one of the Ukrainian, Polish, Jewish, Chinese, or black children that day, I would have spent the rest of the year with a black pencil. My green pencil was returned to me.

Some little girls arrived in Grade 1 already equipped with a social Geiger counter about who was "in" and who was "out." They quickly formed cliques. I learned that it was better to be in the clique than not. Mary Fell was "out." A pretty child, and bright enough, she came to school inadequately clothed even on the coldest days. No mitts. Often only a thin cotton dress under a coat with missing buttons. Her sweet, resigned demeanour spelled "victim" as much as if it were stamped across her fore-head. The clique of little girls who ran Grade 1 ignored her and made fun of her. I knew deep in my heart that without my mother, I might have been a Mary Fell. I didn't have the courage back then to befriend her, but I have resented the kind of categorizing that ostracized her and have disliked the people who carry it out ever since.

It was clear to me from the beginning of school that men rated higher than women. All our teachers were women; the principal and vice-principal were men. The most puzzling lesson, which hadn't made an impression on me before, was that boys rated higher than girls. Up to that point, my experience with boys was that they weren't much different from girls. I played as often with the boys next door as with the girls from the block. The thing you had to watch about boys was that some of them were tough. They hit each other—and girls too, if you got in their way. Two boys had knocked me down and stolen 15 cents when I was on my way to the market one day. My mother didn't try to pursue the culprits. Typically and practically, she told me to take a safer route, be more watchful, and be prepared to run fast.

In school, boys seemed rather backward. They were slower to catch on to routines, much less nimble in dancing and other activities, and generally not as quick in learning their schoolwork as girls. Nonetheless, boys, particularly WASP boys, received special treatment from the teacher. In addition to more praise and attention, they were appointed to do special tasks such as helping the teacher marshal the class for fire drill. The fact that they received these unearned distinctions simply because of their sex seemed unfair to me even then, at the age of six.

In those archaic days, every child was graded scholastically on a report card and seated in the classroom according to ability. When I think of it today, it was a preposterous way to label children at such an early age, and wildly discriminatory, when you consider their diverse backgrounds and language skills. Some could barely speak English. Others couldn't see the blackboard clearly. Some came to school hungry. Others had serious psychological problems.

Because we were graded like eggs, two rows of Grade 1 children— almost a third of the class—were labelled inferior month after month and virtually ignored by the teacher. The other children called them "the dummies." One of them was a Chinese girl called Mary Sing who drew beautifully but didn't understand English.

In spite of my mother's campaign to turn me into a perfect little lady, I still managed to lead at least one more parade. Queen Victoria's birthday was celebrated on May 24 with a march past, the whole school saluting the old Canadian flag. Because I consistently stood first in Grade 1, I was chosen to lead my class that day.

We paraded to "Colonel Bogie's March" thumped out on the school piano. As we passed the flag, I shouted, "Eyes right!" and smartly saluted. Then, when I estimated that Grade 1 was past, I yelled, "Eyes front!" But nobody had told me when to stop, and I kept on marching stalwartly across the playground. It wasn't until a vice-principal ran after us to tell me we could be dismissed that we stopped.

When I rejoined my mother, a woman from the church was sitting beside her. I heard her say condescendingly, "Never mind, boys really should always have to do those jobs. They always seem able to do them much better than girls." Mama just looked uncomfortable, and I felt dashed.

By the late 1920s, my brothers had left school after Grade 8, had jobs, and were paying my mother room and board. Compared with what was to come later, those days were good, cheerful times, full of change and excitement. My mother got her long hair bobbed, and we all tried miniature golf—a new craze. My brothers taught me the Charleston. They dated girls in short dresses and cloches who, in Mama's opinion, wore too much make-up. Reg bought an old Model T and turned it into a "fliver," with slogans painted all over its sides. He frequently took me for rides. Fred came home drunk one night, and I can still hear my mother carrying on about having "nourished a viper in my bosom!"

At eighteen, Fred secretly married. Mama claimed that the girl, who was pregnant, was a trollop and that her son had been selected as the fall guy. The marriage ended in six months, after the baby was born. The girl returned to her family, and later she and Fred were divorced. Fred, who had large brown eyes like Alvin Buck, seemed to have a penchant for falling in love. His next liaison was with an older married woman, recently separated from her husband. One morning the husband appeared at the door with a gun, demanding to know where my romantic older brother was. Luckily he wasn't home.

During this period, my father's "job" was playing the stock market. Just before it crashed in the fall of 1929, he was supposed to have been worth quite a bit of money. He bought me a coat and hat—the first clothing I had ever owned that was not a hand-me-down or home-made. Even my cautious mother took a little gamble on the market and, to my father's disgust, cashed her stock in when she had made a modest profit. She and I took a short trip to Vancouver and the Okanagan Valley, where we visited some cousins.

Mama must have felt more secure financially at this time. Because my father was flush, she was probably getting some financial help from him. She stopped supplying board and only rented out rooms. We acquired a wind-up portable gramophone and traded in my grandmother's old player piano for an upright.

The stock-market crash made no impression on me, but it was to change my life profoundly. On the day before my eighth birthday, I had found a dead bird. I took it home, intending to bury it. As I rushed in the door to ask my mother for a box, both my parents were there, and obviously in a celebratory mood. I was lifted up by my father, as they told me proudly that they had just been married at the City Hall.

I think that, once again, I was expected to be jubilant. I was told it was a special present for my birthday. I would have preferred almost anything else.

Once ensconced, my father became even more demanding and dictatorial. One of his first edicts was that I had to eat porridge every morning. I hated it and refused to eat it the first day. I went to school without any breakfast. When I came home at noon, there it was—covered with a leathery skin. I refused to eat it again. By dinnertime I was so hungry that I ate it, gagging, and then cried through the rest of the meal. What made the whole exercise even more traumatic was that my sensible mother, to whom I had always been able to turn for help, sat through the whole performance, looking sad and sympathetic but saying not a word.

On another occasion, my father tried to teach me long division before I had fully grasped subtraction. I was afraid of being late for Sunday school, but he refused to let me go until I had mastered the concept. I burst into tears and he finally gave up, muttering that I was just being stubborn, rather than realizing that no one can learn under such pressure.

I think my mother truly believed that her husband, now the head of the family, had to be deferred to. I also think that in her typical fashion she was trying to please him and "get along."

On his side, my father had had very little experience with either children or a close relationship. He must have known we all resented him. In his better moods, he adopted a rather droll approach, which amuses me now, but puzzled and exasperated me then. He would say, "When I was a little girl, I always washed under my bangs," when he chided me for washing only the centre of my face. Or, "When I was a little girl, I kept my handkerchief spotless," when I had used mine to mop up ink at school.

Puzzled, I finally asked my mother, "Was he once a little girl?"

Most of the time, my brothers and I tried to avoid him. But we all had to gather at meals. This family ritual, which had always been a pleasure, became a nightmare. My father seemed to know how to communicate with other people only by arguing or haranguing them.

If it wasn't some remark of mine, it was something my brothers said that started his tirades. He constantly criticized us. Reg cut the bread too thick. Why did I separate my vegetables before eating them? We learned to sit as silently as possible, trying not to give him any opportunity for another diatribe. He soon alienated most of my mother's many relatives by picking arguments with them too. At his first Christmas as part of the family, he got roaring drunk, picked a fight with Aunt Maggie's eighteen-year-old son, Joe, and threw him out of the house.

One morning in late March 1930, I awoke to find I had been moved into the back bedroom in the night. My father was already up. Fred put his head around the door to tell me the news: I had a baby brother.

Except when she had me, my mother gave birth to her babies at home, attended by our family doctor. Her niece, Eva, moved in at those times and looked after us and the house. I remember going into the front room that morning, and Mama wanting me to come and kiss her. I had eyes only for the tiny bundle in her arms, with his scrunched-up eyes, long dark hair, and incredibly delicate hands and ears.

My father called his son Thomas John after himself and his favourite uncle back in Scotland, but he was always called Johnny. Immensely proud of having a son, my father kept bringing his old army friends to see Tarzan of the Apes, as he insisted on calling the baby. No one had to tell me that this event and this child were far more significant to my father than I could ever have been.

I didn't care. I had already realized any real affection between my father and myself was unlikely, although I continued to try to please him by striving at sports, without much success. Johnny, with whom I felt an immediate affinity, was far more important to me. Having been raised almost as an only child, I felt I had gained a wonderful live doll. In that tense, crowded, unhappy house, my little brother was a miracle—big, bright, active, curious, and oblivious to all the misery around him.

As soon as he could sit up, I involved Johnny in all my play, as well as including him in an imaginary world full of adventures for both of us. Realizing the importance of males, I always made him king, but a foolish king. I, of course, was the wise knight who always rescued him from his reckless and foolhardy adventures. I had learned early the handmaiden roles assigned to females.

Eighteen months later, on a hot August day, another son was born. My father called him Jim, after his younger brother who had come out to Canada a few years earlier. Once again, I fell in love instantly with this tiny perfect creature.

By this time Johnny was a strong, lively two-year-old. What seemed so miraculous about my brothers, and still fascinates me about babies, is how full of life, optimism, and boundless curiosity they are. I made a resolution back then that no matter what else I did, I wanted children of my own.

What also intrigued me about my brothers was the fact that although they were boys, they seemed, at that early age, very similar to me. They cried in sympathy when the cat got hurt. They were just as fearful of violence as I was—and just as caring. At age four, Johnny took Jim for a walk. They had to pass a large dog. John was afraid of dogs. Jim was not. But John put himself between his baby brother and the dog as they passed it.

Because little boys seemed as sensitive and caring as little girls, I began to wonder what happened to them. Why, by the time boys reached school, did they so often turn into boisterous hellions who pushed you, knocked you down, took your money, and relished fighting, hurting one another, and bullying younger children?

Even that wasn't much of a mystery. I couldn't help noticing how differently my brothers were treated than I had been. John once pulled the crocheted runner on the dining-room table and brought the big green jardiniere with my mother's prized ivy crashing to the floor. And Jim pulled a dresser scarf, sending the robin's-egg blue china set that had been painted by Aunt Maggie to the floor. Because my brothers were babies, these misdemeanours went unpunished. Mama was certainly vexed, mostly at herself—or me—for not keeping a closer eye on her lively little sons. Their father, on the other hand, positively celebrated all the mayhem. They were being "real boys." Unlike me, they were encouraged to get dirty, collect worms in their pockets, dig holes in the back yard, and even fight with each other.

Most of the time my father left the discipline and decisions about us entirely up to Mama. Occasionally he waded in, with disastrous results. One morning when John was barely two, too young to understand what was wanted of him, my father became so exasperated that he took off his leather belt and started whacking his son to "show him who's boss around here." Crying with terror, the baby crawled under the table, desperately trying to get away from him. Mama finally stopped this brutal scene but not quickly enough, in my opinion.

In other ways she continued to be a very good mother. When he was three, John started Sunday school. He was shy and balked at sitting on the children's seats in the class. My mother sat with him over to one side. After two or three weeks, he agreed to take his place, but she still had to be beside him. My father, and many another mother at that time, would have given him a shake and told him to "act like a little man." That she still had so much patience—as she had had when I was that age—has always been proof in my mind that she was a fine mother for small children.

She bowed to the prevailing social customs of the day as my brothers grew older. When Jim began school, the neighbourhood bully used to lie in wait for him. He would grab Jim by the collar of his mackintosh, jerk him back and forth, and throw him face down in the snow. By this time, I was a teenager. Enraged as I watched this from the house, I offered to rush out and box the bully's ears. My mother would have none of it. "He's got to learn to look out for himself," she said grimly.

And he did. He learned to go to school by another route, or always with other little boys or his brother. When he was ten, he could fight well enough to take the bully on, beat him, and knock him down—to the satisfaction of the whole neighbourhood.

I was learning other lessons as well. I was beginning to realize that it wasn't just that boys had more fun and freedom, but they also had many more opportunities in the world than I would have. I resolved that even if those doors were closed to me, my adored younger brothers had to be helped in every way possible. As soon as they could talk, I tried to teach them words and how to count. Later I drilled them in reading, spelling, and arithmetic—long before they were capable of even understanding such things. Both my parents thought I was being ridiculous.

CHAPTER THREE

Life in the Dirty Thirties

During what came to be known as the Dirty Thirties, Canada was still an outpost of the British Empire, where people talked wistfully about the old country. Calgary was about the same size as present-day Lethbridge, Alberta, or Cornwall, Ontario. In spite of all the newcomers from Europe, it was a remarkably WASP city, and dramatically different from the confident, booming western metropolis of today.

Our minister at the Pro-Cathedral Church had a plummy English accent. The choir was entirely male. (Later, when women were added in the war years because of a lack of men, they were banished to an out-of-sight gallery.) Policemen wore tall London-bobby hats. Our Brownie and Girl Guide manuals were filled with mysterious lore about blacking stoves and making coffee by letting it boil up in a saucepan three times before it settled—in a country where everyone owned a coffee pot.

Eighth Avenue, our main street, had stores straight out of an English village. Bloomfields sold "sweets" in tall glass containers. A rotund little milliner made hats to go with the navy, brown, or black crepe dresses with beaded surplice fronts our mothers wore. In the market, a man with a Cockney accent sold fresh West Coast fish in a stall called This Is the Plaice.

Militarism and patriotism were everywhere. Statues commemorating the Great-War dead stood in all the parks. In our church several stained-glass windows had been donated by families whose sons had been killed overseas. The imperialist exploits of the British Empire filled our readers and history books. Later on at Girl Guide camp, we were wakened every morning by a bugle call, as if we were army recruits. After breakfast we rolled up our beds, tidied our tents, and stood at attention under the blazing July sun in our navy uniforms, felt hats, and long black stockings while being inspected by the captain and her lieutenant.

Most women wore corsets, but no make-up except powder. They bobbed their hair, rinsed it in vinegar to get rid of the soap, and curled it with heated tongs or by winding it around leather or metal curlers. At twelve, girls were given a corselette—a one-piece garment with thin metal stays. (I took mine—a Christmas present—up to the bathroom, cut out the stays, and threw them behind the bathtub, where my mother discovered them and raised a great ruckus.)

The thirties were also a time of great social unrest. Every city had a soup kitchen. Unemployed men were gathered up and shipped off to relief camps in the bush. Calgary had its own "Red Square" in a vacant lot across from our house. Every weekend, and more frequently during the summer, political meetings were held there. Men would stand on boxes and harangue the crowd while a few policemen watched. I slipped away to listen to them as often as I could—these ragged men in caps, with anger in their eyes and voices. The most radical proposal was to blow up the City Hall, which thankfully came to nothing.

As the Depression deepened, Fred and Reg lost their jobs, and the tension in the house increased. Soon the battles between them and my father became so rancorous that they left home to ride the rails. Along with other desperate men, they would wait outside towns, then climb surreptitiously onto trains in the hope that they could find work somewhere else. Sometimes my mother wouldn't hear from her sons for months at a time.

Part of the reason for my father's vile temper was the position in which he now found himself. Aged forty and a proud man, he had only a few possessions and his small army pension of $13 a month to his name. All the money he was supposed to have made in the stock market had vanished. Having wasted his time during the twenties trying to "get rich quick," he had few marketable skills. Occasionally he was hired to take tickets at the hockey rink. He helped my mother as much as he could by taking over the garden and all the chores around the house, but it was not enough. To ease his misery, he invariably got drunk when he received his pension cheque and we soon learned that he was a nasty, quarrelsome drunk.

Mama didn't have to tell me she was deeply unhappy. As her closest female relative, I became her confidante at the age of eight. Beside herself with worry, she would weep, cling to me, and exclaim, "I'm so miserable I want to commit suicide!" Looking back on those scenes, I know now that she would never have done such a thing. Out of her own despair and neediness, she was looking for a dramatic reaction from me—which she certainly got. Those scenes had a shocking effect on me.

Almost hysterical at the thought of losing my mother and being left to cope with a truculent father, two small brothers, and all the work of the house, I would beg her not to leave me. I resolved that if she committed suicide, I would take my own life as well. I planned to drink the bottle of iodine marked Poison, which was kept on the top shelf in the kitchen. It's the only time in my life I have ever even considered such an act, but that's how desperate I felt.

In fact, I would never have been left to cope with the whole burden of the house and my father. I was a child myself. If anything had happened to my mother, the women in the family would have rallied around, as they always had, to look after us children. And Father, in spite of all his blustering independence, would have handed the job over to them. By putting me through those scenes, Mama robbed me, in a way, of my childhood.

I have often wondered why my mother didn't tell Thomas McCubbin to pack his bags and leave—or behave better. The house was hers. She was supporting the family. Years later, when I had sons of my own, I also wondered how she could have allowed Fred and Reg to roam the country risking their lives. Perhaps the prospect of being responsible for all three small children by herself at the age of forty daunted her.

At this time I was experiencing my own small hell. I had been taking piano lessons in a class of ten children at 25 cents a lesson at the school. In the spring of 1930, my teacher decided two of us were good enough to take the Toronto Conservatory examination. Not feeling nearly as confident about piano as I was about school, I was terrified that I would fail.

What made taking the test even more difficult was that my father couldn't abide the sound of my practising. "Why can't you play something with a tune?" he would thunder at the third or fourth repetition. Being able to practise only when he was out of the house added to my distress, for he was home most of the time. I longed to go to my mother and beg her to excuse me from taking the exam, but for the first time in my life I realized I couldn't bother her with my worries. She was far too troubled herself. Instead, I used to get up as soon as it was light and practise by moving my fingers over the keys without actually depressing them.

On the day of the exam, my teacher told me to print a list of all the pieces I would be playing on a paper to be given to the examiner, and to be sure to add at the end of the list, "All memorized." I did this, but not being quite sure how to spell "memorize," I asked my mother. Busy and harassed as she always was in those days, and never terribly strong in spelling, she told me to look it up in the dictionary.

My teacher met me at the Palliser Hotel, where the exam was to take place. Ernest MacMillan, the august head of the conservatory, was the examiner. To my annoyance, he chuckled all through my performance. When I was finished, my teacher asked to see my list. Instead of "All memorized" I had printed "All memorialized," which, after he had listened throughout the day to earnest amateurs thumping out scales and other musical clichés, must have amused him. When the results were published in the newspaper, far from failing, I had achieved First Class Honours. And I had learned a hard lesson: I could stand on my own in a crisis, and solve some of my own problems without my mother's help.

I became much more critical of my little world. The old house that had sheltered me so happily in earlier days I began to see as shabby and unfashionable. It was cold in winter because we had no central heating—only natural-gas radiators—and terribly overcrowded with one bathroom for fourteen people. Even the roomers had changed for the worse. Many were living on pensions or bits of money they had saved. They were defeated, sad men, living lonely, empty lives. Their rooms smelled. They received hardly any mail and had little to say to anyone. It was like living in a house full of surly zombies.

I took refuge in my avaricious appetite for books. Every Saturday I would walk across the city to the central library, where I took out four books at a time—the limit allowed. They would all be read by Sunday night, but I was not allowed to go back until the following Saturday. Returning the books was torture. A dragon lady would go through each page and give us a terrible dressing-down if she found a single mark. It's a wonder my generation learned to read at all!

I then devoured everything I could find in the house—my older brother's *Boys' Own Annuals* with their gory stories of conquests of the natives in the colonies and the mysterious world of British public schools. Before my mother could throw them out, I salvaged comics from the roomers and trashy magazines like *Liberty* and the *Chicago Examiner*, as well as *True Stories*, which featured young women who were always seduced, got pregnant, and in return for their "night of folly" paid and paid and paid.

My parents, far from encouraging me to read, were always insisting that I "Go outside and get some fresh air! You'll ruin your eyes with your head stuck in a book all day!" The thermometer on the front porch often hovered well below -15°F in the winter. When she finally accepted my addiction to reading, my mother attempted to divert my attention to the Elsie Dinsmore books about a dreary little saint who refused to play the piano on Sunday, and the *Girls' Own Annual*, full of stories about namby-pamby British schoolgirls called Bunty and Cuddles, whose most daring exploits were midnight feasts in one anothers' rooms. About this time I decided to write stories myself, and the next Christmas I received a small printing press. I did manage to print out a page or two, but the process was far too tedious to complete a short story.

One benefit my father brought into our lives was his younger brother, Jim. After emigrating from Scotland, he had started house painting, which later grew into a successful decorating business. A truly generous man, he bought me my first watch and pair of skates—the only pair of skates I owned as a child that were not second-hand. My father banked up snow in the back yard and with water from the hose produced a rink, on which I learned to skate. I didn't find it much fun skating around by myself, and few other kids in the neighbourhood owned skates.

In the fall, when I entered Grade 3, my parents said it was time to change my name. I was to tell the teacher that my mother had remarried and I was now to be called Doris McCubbin. Though my old name had nothing to do with me legally, I resented the change and felt I had somehow lost a piece of my old, secure identity.

Soon after that, the principal decided our Grade 3 class was too large, and twelve of us were moved in with a class of Grade 2s. No explanation was given to us or our parents—we were just abruptly moved. I later realized it was not a demotion, simply a matter of numbers, but I was deeply unhappy about it.

Then, for the first time since starting school, I stood second. I remember feeling so humiliated that I immediately burst into terrible sobs. Because I couldn't stop, the teacher, obviously annoyed and puzzled, asked me to leave the room.

I said nothing at home about this embarrassing incident. I thought Mama would dismiss my feelings as a silly reaction to a minor setback. My performance in school was quite unimportant compared with all her other worries. Even when I produced my report card, she signed it with only a passing comment on my second-place standing.

On that occasion the school came to my rescue. They phoned and asked my mother to come in for an interview. Whatever they said made an impression. For the first time in months, she sat down and actually tried to understand what was bothering me.

What was bothering me, of course, was the situation at home. I felt caught in the crossfire between my parents. With my older brothers gone, my father took all his frustration and anger out on me. He criticized the way I cut my boiled egg (too close to the top, the way my mother did it), my looks (not pretty enough), my habits (never tidy and clean enough). He insisted on a discussion at every meal, and it always ended in an argument. This was a game I could never win. Usually it went on until he reduced me to tears and I had to leave the table.

I couldn't tell my mother, because she was part of it. She could have stopped it. From time to time, my father would push her too far and her temper would suddenly flare. Then she would treat him with a coldness I couldn't have believed possible. Sometimes the silent war continued for weeks, the atmosphere in the house becoming more and more oppressive as the days went by. This treatment had an amazing effect on him: he would do anything to get back in her good books. I gradually began to despise these mysterious and exasperating male/female games.

While he bullied me, she would sit silently with the demeanour of a sympathetic martyr, signalling with her looks and pained expression her own distress. Only rarely did she intervene—and then mildly—in this daily verbal battering. Understandably, I soon began to hate my father, and perhaps, in retrospect, that's what she wanted. I was always destined to be her ally, not his.

Because I was miserable at home, I took refuge in books and in school. There I felt in control of things and successful. However, standing second had threatened even that secure corner of my world. The school's solution was not one I believe my mother agreed with, because she never wanted me to be pushed and she herself was actually afraid of too much success. However, since the school recommended it, she bowed to their decision.

Suddenly one morning, the principal, a dour, worried-looking man, appeared at my classroom door. Once again I was abruptly told to pack up my books and accompany him upstairs to a mixed class of Grade 3s and 4s. I was put into Grade 4. The move seemed to achieve its purpose. I felt challenged by more demanding work, and by the end of the first month I stood fourth. My mother muttered about pushing me too hard, but she was wrong, as she usually was when it came to her goals for me.

That fall I was given an unbelievable present—a bicycle. To this day I don't know how my parents managed to buy it because money was very tight. My mother must have realized some of the pressure I was under. The bicycle was a second-hand Raleigh—a good English make—but so ancient that it had wooden wheels, and the tread on the front tire had been completely worn off. I didn't care—it allowed me to explore the city, and later I rode it back and forth to high school.

Buying a licence every year and keeping the bike repaired kept me broke. Eventually I blew the old tires by overinflating them at the local filling station. Father took two metal wheels off a bike that had belonged to Reg, but the gears didn't quite fit, which meant the brakes were unreliable. I tore off the entire toe of a shoe trying to stop before the brakes were repaired. In time, tired of my father's complaints when he had to fix my bike, I learned to take it apart, clean it, repair it, and put it back together myself. I kept it going and in good shape until I left home.

By 1931 our financial situation was much worse. The rent Mama received for all the work she did was still pitifully small, and sometimes she couldn't rent all the rooms, although she charged only $2 a room a week, or 25 cents a night. Many desperate men couldn't even afford that, and my mother would often feed young men who came to the door asking for a handout. Sometimes she would give them a room for the night, and encourage them to take a bath, hoping someone else was doing the same for her own sons, wherever they were.

My parents struggled just to keep their heads above water. Still burdened by the mortgage, Mama was terrified she would lose her only security—the house she had inherited from my grandmother. The thought of a major illness in the family horrified both of them. Compared with many other people, we at least had a place to live and a few possessions. As working poor, we all felt as if we were under a long, endless siege.

About this time, our teacher told us to buy a bottle of India ink for art class. My mother did not even have an extra 10 cents for such a project. I found an old bottle of dried-up ink in a desk and tried to make India ink myself at home. When this failed, I told the teacher I had forgotten to buy the ink—an unlikely story for a pupil as diligent as I was. The boy across the aisle must have recognized my plight and lent me his bottle. I am still grateful to him, but then I burned with shame.

Because my father was a veteran, we were given the occasional food package by the Canadian Legion, including a turkey at Christmas. Once I received a pretty school dress—plaid with piqué collar and cuffs. I hated it. Although there were many children in our school on what was then called relief, the stigma of having to wear a dress that everyone knew was a hand-out from the Canadian Legion galled me and my parents.

Money was so tight that we walked everywhere, no matter how cold it was. In summer, to break the tedium, my mother would pile my brothers and a box of sandwiches in the baby buggy and we would walk across the city to Riley Park, which had a swimming and wading pool. On Sunday my father would take us to St. George's Island while my mother went to church. We would watch the progress made on the dinosaur models, visit the animals in the zoo, and play on the slides, swings, and teeter-totters. Each time he would grill me on the habits of the animals, which I think turned me off nature study forever.

Although you could get into a double feature on Saturday for 10 cents, I was allowed to spend my allowance on films only once a month. My mother said movies "affected" me too much. She was right. I could repeat almost every line of the dialogue, as I played them over and over in my head for days. I have been a devoted movie fan ever since.

From a cousin who was a radio ham, we acquired a small crystal radio with two sets of earphones. Four of us could listen at one time, sitting in close pairs and sharing a headpiece. We found our two local stations by fiddling with the little wire tuner in different areas of the crystal. My father took over the radio and listened to hockey games, country music, and the news—the latter a daily cause for tirades at the latest actions of R. B. Bennett's Conservative government in Ottawa.

To save money on haircuts, my father bought clippers and scissors and cut everyone's hair—badly. Mama's and my hair was cut far too short, while my brothers looked like refugees from a prison camp. Old newspapers were soaked in water, wrung out, and burned in the kitchen stove to help reduce the heating bill. And one year when tomatoes were 25 cents for a big basket, my parents bought a dollar's worth and made Tomato Marmalade. It was a disaster, but we had to eat the cursed mush all winter.

Clothing was made too big so that you would grow into it. Shoes were a great expense, and since I had narrow feet, mine were more costly. I was frequently scolded for not polishing them, or wearing the soles out too quickly. My father used to resole our shoes with rubber patches and cement he bought at Woolworth's, but in damp weather the rubber would come away from the shoes and slap the pavement like flippers as we walked.

Everything was repaired or made at home. Father became quite ingenious at keeping my grandmother's old mantel clock ticking away. When yo-yos came in, instead of the store-bought one I wanted, I received a homemade one. When my brother needed pads to play hockey, my father made them out of old tires. My parents even tried making their own soap.

Because there was no public-health insurance, people used all kinds of home remedies. Mustard plasters, goose grease, and a camphor bag around the neck were common ways to try to ward off colds. My father's cure for a boil was to put a bottle filled with steam from the kettle on it and then pour cold water on the bottle to form a vacuum and extract the boil. Usually a lot of skin came away too. In fact, most of his remedies were worse than the original affliction.

An early supporter of socialized medicine, Father believed that doctors should be paid to keep people healthy, not to cure them after they became sick. Dr. Follett, who had been our family physician for two generations, made house calls, but he was rarely summoned, and only when we were seriously ill. He never sent a bill, but my proud mother would call him up and demand one.

On the whole we were a healthy lot, partly because my father was a health-food addict long before it became fashionable. The garden kept us supplied with vegetables until Christmas. When eggs were plentiful in summer, they were put down in crocks for winter and served only on Sundays. We ate brown bread. Cheese and other processed foods were banned. Mama made lots of soups, stews, and casseroles with a little meat supplemented with beans, split peas, and macaroni. Pot roasts and stewing beef were staples, as was fish, because it was cheap. If my brothers and I cleaned our plates, we could have second helpings, but usually we were told to "fill up the corners with bread."

Instead of rich desserts, Mama served mostly fruit and puddings at the end of a meal. Her big treat was a one-egg cake with a boiled icing. We had very few sweets, and eating between meals was prohibited. Even cookies were rationed. Because buttermilk had all the goodness of milk without the fat, we drank huge quantities at 10 cents a gallon jug. I would lug these jugs home from the dairy with my brothers in tow—my parents' ruse, I realize now, to get us out of the house early Sunday morning so that they could make love.

I felt horribly deprived. During the thirties, Jersey milk was being widely advertised because of its high cream content. Good mothers baked rich desserts—angel-food cakes that used a dozen egg whites and golden cakes to use up all the egg yolks. I thought double chocolate cakes, as well as rich pastries and pies, were signs of a truly caring mother.

In one respect our diet was lethal. No bacon fat or gravy was ever thrown out. Any leftover fat was used for frying. Carrots, cauliflower, and cabbage all came to the table covered in white sauce. Later, when I would go home to visit, and Mama would cook a favourite dish for me, I was always surprised at how bland it seemed. Few spices and no garlic were ever used.

We all had great appetites, but no one was overweight because we ate sensibly and got lots of exercise. By the time I reached high school, I had to walk or bike two miles there and back, except in extremely cold weather when I took the streetcar. My younger brothers became track-and-field stars. I was less successful—usually the best I could manage was to be the slow member on the relay team.

Airplanes were still so rare that everyone ran outside if one flew overhead. Occasionally there were parachute jumps at the old Calgary airport, and a hat would be passed to compensate the daredevil flyers. Being quite fearless, I reasoned that jumping out of an airplane couldn't be that difficult—all you had to do was remember to pull the parachute string. I biked up to the airport and offered to do a jump just for the thrill of the plane ride. I was a skinny little kid of ten in a torn black dress and scraped knees. A big man in riding breeches and boots looked me over and laughed. "You wouldn't even land," he said. "You'd get blown away in the wind. And we can't waste a parachute."

I greatly admired a little girl about my age called Isabel, who came from a large impoverished family in the neighbourhood. She would scrounge records from somewhere and get into the skating rink free. My father used to praise her for being a hustler—which at that time had nothing to do with sex. I longed to be like her. There was nothing I wanted to do more than run free like a boy, without the heavy restrictions my mother imposed on me. But Mama said Isabel was "tough" and "running around like a wild thing without a mother." Years later, Isabel ended up in the Kingston women's prison on a drug charge, and I had to concede that, once again, my mother had been right.

It was not possible to live through the Great Depression and not become politically aware. Everyone around me talked constantly about politics. All kinds of wild suggestions for curing our economic ills were seriously discussed, including a technocracy—a North American form of dictatorship—and its opposite—socialism in the form of the new Co-operative Commonwealth Federation, the forerunner of today's New Democratic Party.

In 1935 the Social Credit Party of William Aberhart came to power in Alberta. Many of my mother's relatives voted for it, and even carried around the money issued by the provincial government. My father had great fun ridiculing Aberhart's "funny money" and his unsuccessful efforts to control the banks and muzzle the press.

As if that didn't get my argumentative parent into enough trouble, he was also an anti-royalist at a time when King George V and Queen Mary were almost deified in Canada. To our great embarrassment, my father would stomp out whenever "God Save the King" was struck up at any public event. On the other hand, he was a great promoter of his adopted country, as was my mother. Both my parents deeply resented the fact that they had to list Great Britain as their country of origin on the census form. They both proclaimed they were Canadian.

Between my timid, conservative mother and my radical, bombastic father, I was forced to think seriously about a great many issues. I discounted much of what my father said because he was a notorious and enthusiastic teller of tall tales. To give him credit, he constantly challenged us both mentally and physically with puzzles, riddles, and games. (At the time I felt all these exercises were designed to prove we were all idiots and the school was teaching us nothing.) In fact, with his collection of puzzles, his miscellany of weird bits of knowledge of geography, literature, science, and whatever else interested him, as well as his stubborn anti-establishment stance on almost everything, he was easily the most stimulating person around in my early life.

Today it is fashionable to think people like my mother deserve their lot in life. It's claimed that piling hardship on people already barely able to cope is good for them. It's supposed to inspire innovation and thrift. I can tell you, having lived through it firsthand, that such theories are the self-serving excuses made by the comfortable about the deprived.

I believe most people want, as my parents did, to take care of themselves. Women like my mother, especially if they have to go out to work, need child care. My parents scrimped and saved throughout their lives—in a way that deprived all of us—so that they would not be a burden on their children or the state in their old age. Poverty and adversity year after year make family members turn on one another. They rob good, hard-working people like my mother of hope and men like my father and older brothers of self-respect. And they blight the lives of children, leaving them with scars they will carry for the rest of their lives.

CHAPTER FOUR

To Be or Not to Be—a Woman?

As I approached my teens, I grew more and more apprehensive. I had watched feisty, active girls suddenly, on reaching adolescence, turn into giggling simpletons. I was determined I was not going to be one of them. At the age of eleven I felt I could hold my own with any boy. I could run faster, climb fences and trees better, was quicker in sizing up a situation and understanding what had to be done—and at least as clever scholastically as any boy I knew. All boys had going for them was size, muscle, and the fact that society seemed to value them much more highly than girls.

I came to a radical conclusion: instead of striving to catch a man, why not be a man? I began to fantasize about changing my sex. I dreamed of waking up and suddenly being a boy, with all the freedom boys had. I even imagined having a sex change—long before that became a medical possibility. I wanted boots, not Oxfords. I wanted plainer clothes instead of the frills my mother liked to deck me out in.

And I fervently wanted my father to be hit by a streetcar, particularly when we were waiting for dinner and he reeled in late, three sheets to the wind, and sat pontificating at the head of the table. At those times, I was sure my mother and I would get along just fine. I dreamed of growing up and looking after her forever. I would buy her that cosy house she craved in a better neighbourhood and everything else she had ever wanted.

My mother was not aware of my dreams. As I came closer to puberty, her efforts to turn me into a little lady increased. Disgusted, I went through another phase. I decided these dreary people could not possibly be my parents. The Duke of Windsor, later Edward VIII, who renounced his throne to marry Wallis Simpson, had bought a ranch in Alberta on a visit to Canada in 1919. The West was rife with rumours of romances he was supposed to have had during his brief prairie visit. I was sure he had to be my real father, and any day he would return and claim me. I collected every scrap of information on him I could—all of which I had to hide from my very real father, who would have been appalled by this adoration of the British royal family.

In the summer of 1933, my father began to work part-time as the door-man at the Canadian Legion. His main job was to prevent drunks from getting in and physically evicting any obstreperous customers who were causing trouble. His skill as an amateur wrestler and his generally pugnacious nature had finally paid off.

With a little more money coming in, Mama decided to take one of the excursions being offered by the CPR to Prince Rupert, where my brother Reg had finally found work. She took Jim, who was a toddler, with her. She was to be away a little more than a week, and because it was summer she left me in charge of the house, the roomers, and three-year-old John.

Besides making beds and cleaning the house, I cooked our meals— the most difficult job by far. I had helped my mother for years, but Father was fussy about his food. I did manage, although I didn't make the coffee strong enough and bought sausages he hated. A fairly good cook himself, he took the opportunity in my mother's absence to make a plum duff—a Scottish concoction a bit like a boiled Christmas pudding. It was filled with such good things as raisins, nuts, and currants. Unfortunately, he forgot to flour the cloth cooking bag and it turned into a soggy mess. We buried it in the back yard and he made me promise not to tell my mother. Of course, the minute she returned, she wanted to know why the supply of raisins and nuts was so depleted, and we had to confess.

While Mama was away, I realized that one of the boarders had taken a woman up to his room one night, no doubt thinking he could get away with it in my mother's absence. Asking my father to deal with this matter never even crossed my mind. With his bad temper, he would have thrown them out bodily. I did what my mother would have done. I waited and confronted the shame-faced man and the prostitute at the bottom of the stairs the next morning, and I told the man he would have to leave at once.

I was eleven years old.

That fall, the school wanted me to skip another grade, but my mother said I was already too young for my classmates. Although I was tall, I was quite unsophisticated. Most of the girls in my class were at least two years older. They wore high heels, as well as lipstick and nail polish—although make-up was forbidden in class—and they talked about quitting school and finding a job and a husband.

By the time I was twelve, it was no longer possible to ignore nature. Unless some extraordinary act of God took place, I was becoming a woman, no matter how much I wished to avoid it. I began to menstruate. When I went swimming, my budding bosom kept popping out over my swimsuit when I dived and I had to stay underwater, tucking myself back in before I could resurface.

After I entered high school at thirteen, I reluctantly made peace with my growing sexuality and began to take more interest in my clothes, grooming, and social life. My parents, of course, were thrilled. But Mother Nature and her hormones began to affect me in other strange ways. I would have fits of being incredibly exhilarated, and then of weeping. I started to develop secret crushes on both male and female teachers, Girl Guide leaders, obscure movie stars, and paper boys. These sudden emotional surges came and went with dizzying intensity.

Our vice-principal was short and balding. Behind his horn-rimmed glasses he constantly blinked, as though on perpetual alert for imminent disaster. Since he held all the power, why did he feel he had to stand so defiantly on guard as we marched into school, class after orderly class? I felt sorry for him. He probably represented order to me in a disorderly world. I imagined that he lived in one of the new suburbs, in a small, tidy house with a well cared for lawn, surrounded by a precisely clipped carrigana hedge. Inside, there would be matching chesterfield, dining-room, and bedroom suites, and broadloom on the floor. Respectability. I was in love with him all one spring.

It was about this time that I started to become critical of my mother. I not only hated her taste and the way the house was decorated—everything was old, worn, and crowded—but I was also growing impatient with her doom-and-gloom view of life. Unlike my father, who thought his luck would change at any moment, my mother lived—understandably, considering her history—with an expectation that the sky was about to fall. She cautioned me to keep my head down and not tempt fate, as if aiming too high would invite certain disaster. Far from showing her former pride in my accomplishments, she seemed slightly embarrassed by them.

I began to chafe against the kind of life she expected me to live, although her expectations were not more limited than those of most mothers of that time. I could take up one of three careers—secretary, nurse, or schoolteacher. Since I was bright and liked school, I was to be a teacher. "Get some training so that you will have something to fall back on in case of a rainy day." Or, heaven forbid, should an even worse calamity occur, she would add, "Or something to support yourself in case you're left hanging on the vine." Translation: if no one asked you to marry.

Mama always stressed that teaching was just a stopgap. My ultimate aim in life was to be marriage. "Marry a good steady man who will be a good provider" was a precept she herself had certainly not followed in either of her marriages. Along with this piece of perceived female wisdom was another cautionary bit of advice: "Don't expect too much."

Without putting it in so many words, she implied that I was average in appearance. Because there were lots of prettier girls, it would not be prudent of me to be too ambitious in the matrimonial sweepstakes. "Men will appreciate your type later on in life," she was fond of saying. This, of course, was no consolation at all for a teenager who wanted to wake up the day after tomorrow and be beautiful.

Even visiting relatives felt free to comment on a young woman's appearance. "Better put a brick on her head," they would say. "She's growing too tall for the boys." Or, "Don't encourage her to be too smart. You catch more flies with sugar than salt!"

A second-class boy was all I was led to believe I could expect. A dull but nice man would be quite sufficient, or even an ugly man who underneath his rough exterior might have a heart of gold—and a good job. As for that all-important job, almost anything with a steady paycheque seemed to fill the bill—a floor walker in Eaton's, a postman or milkman, perhaps.

My father, having long since given up on my swimming the English Channel in record time, or making the Edmonton Grads team, had no ambitions for me at all. Years later he told me with candour and surprise, "You were so attractive I just assumed that some guy would come along, knock you up, and you'd get married."

His comment astounded me. He couldn't possibly have had the slightest inkling of what was going on in my mind when I was an adolescent. He certainly had given me no impression that he thought me attractive. He had constantly pointed out that my nose was too pug, my skin was blemished, and my manner wasn't winsome enough to please any man.

Little did my father know, but I had already decided not to marry young, if at all, and never to put myself in the position of being wholly dependent on a man. My strongest motivation at that time, in fact, was to make sure I didn't get trapped into a marriage with someone like him.

Years later, I asked my mother why her hopes for me were so limited. She replied, "Actually, you were quite attractive. I just didn't want you to get a swelled head."

As I was growing up, I knew of very few examples of what I would call happy marriages. Most of my friends lived in homes that duplicated— except for the roomers—my own. The women ran the house and raised the children; the men made money, but rarely enough. Money, however, gave men the authority to rule the roost, and the household generally revolved around them. They decided what was to be listened to on the radio. They frequently made scenes about trivial matters. My father, for instance, once woke up the whole house when he came home one night and discovered that his slippers had been moved from their usual place. Men often got drunk and abusive. And in the infrequent event of a divorce, it was almost always the men who divorced the women. People quite candidly would say of an uppity woman that she needed "a good one across the face" to straighten her out.

A few of my friends who came from upper-middle-class homes had mothers who seemed freer in their relationships with their husbands. They kidded them, even made fun of them from time to time. But most women flattered their husbands and formed a kind of pact with the children. They knew how to "handle" Daddy, as if he were some kind of unpredictable troll who had to be endured. It was a bad bargain for everybody. Men were cut off from intimacy with their own children and an honest relationship with their wives. Women became little better than legal concubines and hypocrites. Girls particularly, if in competition with their mothers for their fathers' affection, were contemptuous of their mothers' lot in life. But they had nothing except unrealistic fairy tales with which to try to fashion anything better.

I turned to teachers as the only other role models around, and looking back, I think they were quite exceptional. Many of them were excellent scholars and could easily have been teaching in a university, but during the Depression there were few openings for men and almost no women teaching at universities.

Because none of my female teachers married—they were instantly dismissed if they did—or had children, they poured a lot of their own ambitions into their students. They dressed better than most of our mothers. They took long holidays in summer and even travelled abroad. They frequently had their own apartments and cars. A few of them, such as Betty Mitchell, who taught drama, were even glamorous. Naturally I fell in love with almost every one of them.

My mother and her female relatives and friends used to look down on them. "Poor old dried-up things," they would say. But I wondered why. Having a husband didn't, to my way of thinking, make up for all the advantages teachers had.

In Calgary, there was one other woman who seemed to hold down a job with any real authority. She worked at the Bank of Commerce, where I had my account. She sat at a desk, but she wasn't a typist. Men and women came to her and she signed pieces of paper. She had short hair like a man, and she was not glamorous, young, or beautiful. Nor was she married.

She reminded me of one of my teachers, Miss Boucher. As I turned away from my own mother, I began to long for a different kind of role model—a powerful woman who could look after me better and stand up to men like my father. Miss Boucher was stout with short iron grey hair and a gap between her two front teeth. While most teachers simpered and played up to the principal and vice-principal, who were always men, Miss Boucher did not seem at all intimidated by them. In her presence even the principal was nervous, tucking in his chin even more importantly, and talking more authoritatively in his effort to control her. Miss Boucher had the kind of independence I wanted, but I had trouble fitting her into the other half of the picture that was gradually forming in my mind.

I had been carried away by a woman singing at the grandstand at the Calgary Stampede. Her voice rising to the open sky thrilled me. She seemed both successful and feminine. Suddenly I saw it all—the big house, the adoring husband, the children. Surely a woman like that could have everything. A brilliant career and a family.

But there was another question gnawing away in the back of my mind. Of course the man would be nice to the woman because he loved her. Yet my father, in his way, loved my mother. Perhaps it would be different for my dream woman because she was so good, so beautiful, and so talented.

Did this mean I had to have all those qualities to make marriage work? Because I was neither good nor beautiful, was I headed for the same kind of unhappiness as my mother?

Try as I would, I couldn't fit Miss Boucher into romance or marriage at all. Although she dressed in plaid, pleated skirts and tweed jackets and wore no-nonsense shoes, in my imagination I would clothe her in white satin with long kid gloves and a corsage of roses. I tried to imagine her waltzing with some man in the ballroom of our local hotel, but the picture never worked. Were women like Miss Boucher, whom I admired, doomed never to be mothers because there was no man in their lives?

The movies offered other scenarios. Actresses such as Bette Davis, Katharine Hepburn, and Rosalind Russell frequently had roles as beautiful, young, and glamorous career women. They ran cosmetic or newspaper empires from offices big enough to engulf our whole house. Legions of flunkies scurried about at their beck and call. Of course there was always a devilishly handsome, slightly difficult man in the picture, and of course, after some plot complications, they fell in love. Movies were always vague about what happened then. The implication was that these women gave up their careers and turned into housewives like my mother. I thought the plots were ridiculous. Why not keep the job and the man? But that never happened. Women who chose careers over love always lost the man. The lesson was so inviolate that it could have been written on stone tablets.

Although I continued to get top grades, conditions at home made it hard to study. The only place to work was at the dining-room table, while my brothers played on the floor. The old crystal set had been replaced by a small mantel radio—a gift from my brother Fred, who was now a miner in British Columbia. My father took it over, playing hockey games or western music full blast. I used to study, two or three hours every night, with my fingers in my ears.

In Grade 9, I met an exceptional teacher, Catherine Barclay, who had a profound effect on my life. She had a mass of red hair and the ramrod posture of a Victorian aunt, which is what she often seemed like to me. Although she could be charming and witty, she could also turn a class of fourteen-year-olds into utter silence with a single glance when she was displeased.

She and her sister, Mary, had started the youth-hostel movement in Canada. She got me and other young people interested in hostelling, and we would go on hikes or work parties over the weekend, cleaning out a granary or building bunks, or pulling raw wool batts to make comforters.

In our English class, Miss Barclay made us write at least five hundred words every week, which she corrected in red ink down to the last delinquent comma. When I think of the hours she spent toiling over our hastily composed, bungled creations, I am still filled with awe. She made us get up in front of the class and give a speech at least once a month. To make sure we had something worthwhile to talk about, we were encouraged to research a topic in a file of clippings she had cut from her copies of the *Christian Science Monitor*. Public speaking was torture for me then, and there have been many days since when I've been grateful to her for making me conquer that particular terror in the relatively safe setting of Class 9B in East Calgary High School.

By the time most children graduated from high school, we could conjugate fifty-six irregular French verbs, but few of us could speak more than a few hundred words of the language. Miss Barclay persuaded me to join the French Club, where I watched French movies for the first time. Some of them were wonderfully risqué compared with the Hollywood product, although I'm not sure what our parents would have thought of them, had they known.

The most important thing Catherine Barclay did for me was to convince me that whatever else I did, I had to go to university. At the end of Grade 9, I tried for what seemed at the time my only chance, an IODE scholarship. It would have paid my tuition through university. I came second in the city. Discouraged and chafing at my home life, I longed to get out on my own. I decided to quit high school, take a commercial course, find a job as a secretary, and begin to run my own life.

My parents were surprised but didn't really object. High school was expensive and if I wanted to work, that was my business. But Mama had the good sense to phone the principal. He asked her to come in and told her that under no condition should I quit school. When Catherine Barclay heard of my plan, she was appalled. She persuaded me that no matter how impossible I found my home life, I should stick it out through high school, take teacher training, and then save my teaching salary to pay for university.

By Grade 10, I was faced with another unexpected complication. Boys now began to have crushes on me. Sadly, they were rarely the boys I admired. When the first blushing teenager asked me to accompany him to the Halloween Hop, I couldn't think of anything to say but yes. My poor quaking escort arrived at my door to pick me up and was grilled by my father, as though he were asking for my hand in marriage. During the intermission at the dance, he bought me an Orange Crush and a hot dog. I was impressed. "How long has this been going on?" I remember thinking. I found it wasn't much fun being propelled backwards in a straight line, in the sweaty grip of an awkward young man breathing heavily and concentrating on his feet. After depositing me at my door, he asked for a kiss. I automatically said no.

In Grade 10, I fell in love for the first time, with the boy across the aisle. Even now I think he was rather a superior boy, not at all what Mama had thought I would ever be able to attract or expect. Tall, with wavy, sandy hair and lovely light blue eyes, he was an exceptional student. I felt horribly awkward, badly dressed, and my skin had begun to break out. I took refuge in my ability to wisecrack, and we carried on a brisk repartee all through the year.

Once he offered to be my partner in a school debate. He made the sensible suggestion that he come over to my house some night to discuss our strategy. There was nothing I would have liked better than to spend a night sitting close to him discussing anything in the world. But the thought of his having to meet my father in that cramped house was impossible. He lived in a nice bungalow in a good neighbourhood. I told him I thought we could talk about our strategy after school, which we did. He eventually started dating the girl who sat behind me in class, to my mortification.

Mama had always taken pride in never lying to her children. When I asked as a small child whether there was a Santa Claus, she'd simply said, "No, but some people want their children to believe in Santa Claus so don't tell them." Even at four, living in a crowded house with no fireplace, I didn't have to be very clever to realize a fat man in a red suit would have trouble sliding down our skinny chimney to shower us with toys.

When I asked my mother about sex, I was given the impression—common at that time among my friends—that boys were ravening beasts, and even sharing a streetcar seat with one of them was dangerous. But I knew my mother enjoyed sex. Every Sunday morning she would appear flushed and happy, and I knew she and my father—that terrible man she merely endured most of the time—had been rolling around in bed. She would catch my eye and immediately go on the defensive. "What are you standing around for?" she'd demand sharply. "Why aren't the breakfast dishes cleared away?" Or "What are your brothers up to? I can't leave you alone for two minutes but that you go off into that dream world of yours!" She knew she wasn't fooling me.

I didn't find boys exactly ravening—more often than not, they were nervous, fumbling, and inept. But I was astonished at how easily I could be aroused, even by someone I really didn't care for much. To protect myself, I dated boys I thought would be safe and studious and just as anxious as I was not to "get into trouble."

My father, on the other hand, assumed every boy was up to no good at all. One Easter a girlfriend and I decided to go hostelling. My friend's father insisted that we take a boy along for protection. Father vetoed such an idea, and the hike was cancelled.

Mama had given me a book called *What Every Young Girl Should Know*. It was hilarious. The experts were starchy-looking women with pince-nez or sober-looking clergymen from the nineteenth century. The book went on at length about birds and bees, with little real information. I again tackled my mother on the subject of sex, and she proved to be a much more reliable source.

I didn't have to ask her what most of the four-letter words meant. In our neighbourhood, I couldn't remember when I hadn't known. My mother coyly answered my questions about birth, babies, how often people "did it," and so on, but for the most part straightforwardly. I think she enjoyed our discussion.

Later on, the conversations became a game between us. She would say to me, "Never kiss a man until you're engaged."

"If I wait that long, I'll never get engaged," I would retort. "Besides, how will I know if I like him if I don't at least do a little petting?"

She would pretend to be shocked. Then I would declare that I planned to become a prostitute for a few years after high school, and use my savings to put myself through university. Horrified, she would point out all the dangers of disease and that I would be ruined for any "decent man" and "never be able to show my face in Calgary again" before she realized I was goading her.

We had other discussions that were not so amicable. She had always sewn my clothes, and although I bore no resemblance at all to Shirley Temple, she decked me out in frills and bows, and vainly tried to curl my straight dark brown hair. When I was fourteen, the rows became so frequent that she told me, "I am washing my hands of you! You can have your clothes allowance and you can dress yourself!" The allowance was sufficient only if my clothes continued to be sewn at home. I was a fair seamstress, but not nearly as expert as she was.

That Christmas, I was invited to three different parties. I needed something more festive than the "good" dresses I wore to Sunday school. I took my entire clothes allowance downtown to buy material and my first pair of pumps. Once in the store, I got carried away by a beautiful silk rust velvet in a pattern that would have looked smashing on Joan Crawford or some other sexy vamp in a New York penthouse.

To my dismay, I had no money left for the black pumps. I think that if I had been my mother, I would have advanced a loan, but my uncompromising parent let me live with my mistake. I was forced to wear my old school brogues to all three parties with a dress that was far too sophisticated for any fourteen-year-old to carry off.

In the spring of the year I was fifteen, my father was finally taken on full-time as doorman at the Canadian Legion. At just about the same time, the grocery store around the corner from our house decided to expand. They made us an offer for the house and the lot. My father thought the offer was too low, but my mother deemed it fair and sold it for $2,000.

For more than twenty years, Mama had been paying interest on the mortgage. It was held by a tiny woman called Mrs. Venables, who would come once a year to collect the money, carrying a big black pigskin bag with gold clasps. My mother was always nervous before this encounter. We would be sent outside while she and Mrs. Venables discussed their business over tea served with our best china.

My father always said my mother would have been further ahead had she let the house go years before, but a debt was a debt, and she paid it no matter how hard up we were. The sale of the old house and lot allowed her to pay off the mortgage and buy a modest brick bungalow on the north hill in a much better neighbourhood.

Thrilled at the possibility of our finally becoming respectable, and even living like other people, I urged Mama to splurge on a rug for the living room and a matching chesterfield suite. We still had only one bathroom, and my brothers had to share a room, but for the first time in my life I had a room of my own, with its own closet, dresser, and a desk I made out of orange crates.

Although the "new" house had central heating with a gas furnace, the thermostat was still set quite low. Even in the depths of a Calgary winter, the bill never went over $10 a month. I studied in sweaters and heavy socks, but I didn't care. I finally had some privacy.

I was my mother's weekly cleaning woman. Every Saturday morning, I would clean the house from top to bottom—taking rugs out to be beaten, since we didn't own a vacuum, as well as doing all the dusting, polishing, and floor washing. The pay was 50 cents a week. If I worked hard, I could be through by one o'clock. If I dawdled, it took me until half past two or three. I also baby-sat twice a week for neighbours, which brought in extra money.

I don't think that experience hurt me at all. Like my brothers, who also had to cook, wash dishes, press their own pants, and generally look after themselves, I learned to do most household tasks quickly and efficiently, which has proved to be a lifelong asset.

Those last years of high school were relatively happy. I had a close circle of friends, I wrote and edited for the school paper, I was on the debating team, and I even had a minor part in the annual school play.

That Christmas Eve, I ran into my algebra teacher on the street. She stopped me, wished me a Merry Christmas, and asked me whether I planned to go to university. I said no, I was going to teachers' college. "If you want to go to university," she said, "I will lend you the money, and you can pay me back after you are through." I was not only astonished by this offer but also embarrassed. I thanked her and didn't even mention it to my parents. The idea of borrowing such a large sum of money from a relative stranger seemed inappropriate to me, as I was sure it would have to them.

About the same time, my father finally came to the conclusion that I might be learning something useful in school. He had given me another one of his puzzles. "How high," he asked me, "would a paper be if it was one-sixteenth of an inch thick and could be folded 150 times?" I'm sure he had laboriously figured it out by multiplication. I went upstairs, used logarithm tables, and came down with the answer in five minutes. He was not only astonished but quite put out.

I, in turn, began to appreciate his sense of humour a little more. One day Mama and I came back from a shopping expedition. Father was playing solitaire at the kitchen table. He had an empty bottle of Scotch beside him. He nodded up at the budgie's cage, which hung in the window.

"I thought the budgie looked a little peaked," he said. "So I decided to give him a wee drop of Scotch. Then I decided to have a drink myself. Then I gave the budgie another drink. And I had another drink. And between the two of us we finished the bottle."

At the end of high school, I had a party at my house. All my friends, boys and girls, were there. Parties in those days were almost always chaperoned. No liquor was ever served, although some of the boys in a faster crowd in our school carried flasks. If you weren't home by half past eleven, your parents would start phoning to find out where you were. Few boys had permission to drive their parents' cars—if their parents had one.

Because we were a fairly serious bunch, we sat around over a supper of sandwiches, cakes, and cookies and talked about our future. A few of the boys were going to university. One was to work for a bank; others hoped to line up jobs and take night courses. Most of the girls planned to be teachers or secretaries.

It was 1939 and we talked about the imminent possibility of war. As children of men who had served in the First World War, we knew about the horrors of battle. That night all the boys around the table declared that if war broke out, they would not join up.

That fall, as I was about to enrol in teachers' college, the Second World War did break out. A year later, all the boys who had been at my party were in one of the services—most of them chose the air force. Only half of them came back. I remember where I was and how I felt when I heard the news of each of their deaths.

Although I think the Second World War was "just," I abhor all war. I remember the faces of those young, reluctant heroes who had just been through the Great Depression, as I had, and the lives that they never got to live, and I weep.

CHAPTER FIVE

Running My Own Show

In June 1940 I graduated from teachers' college. With the prospect of soon earning a regular salary, I cleaned out my entire bank account of $25—the accumulation of all my savings since the age of five. I blew the entire sum on a second-hand portable typewriter.

Catherine Barclay, my former teacher, wanted me to attend a two-week French course at the Banff School of Fine Arts that summer, but I needed a small financial supplement to do it. As a graduation gift, Mama offered me one of three choices: a typing course—which is what I wanted; a studio portrait of myself—which is what she wanted; or the money to go to Banff.

I opted for the typing course. Because my mother wanted the portrait, she also paid for that. Then Catherine Barclay virtually shamed her into paying for the Banff course, and I ended up with all three. It was the first time in my memory that Mama had been "soft" with one of her children, no doubt a sign of the better times we were experiencing.

In reply to my applications, I received an offer to begin teaching in September at a one-room school about a hundred miles north of Calgary and fifteen miles west of Red Deer. The salary was $750 a year. My mother was shocked. "You will be earning more than your father," she said with some indignation.

At Banff, I camped in a tent with two other students to save money. Rather than sit around all weekend, I decided to hike around Mount Rundle to Canmore and stay overnight at the youth hostel. The next day, I took the much less travelled trail back, around the other side of the mountain.

I wasn't disturbed by the sound of moose and deer crashing through the bush, or even the sight of a couple of little black bears. But I was startled to look up suddenly and see the dirtiest man I had ever encountered, advancing along the path towards me. There hadn't been another soul for miles. I must have looked perturbed, because a grin split his blackened face and he muttered something about there being more like him coming along the trail. And there were—about thirty men covered in soot. They were fire fighters.

Until that moment, it had never occurred to me that what I was doing—hiking some forty miles in the wilderness around a mountain all by myself—might be dangerous.

In addition to French, I took drama at Banff. Having read my way through all the plays of the previous twenty years, in our local library, I was stage-struck. Back in Calgary, I wanted to return to Banff and the drama classes so badly that I wrote my first free-lance article about my experience there and sent it to the *Calgary Herald*. I was elated when I was called by the editor, Richard Needham, to come in to see him. A short, dark-haired man, who looked up rather shyly over his glasses, he later became an editorial writer and a widely read columnist for the *Globe and Mail*.

I immediately asked him how much I was going to be paid. "That's a very mercenary question," he said, somewhat disapprovingly. The modest sum of $5 and my by-line in print was gratifying, but the money was not enough to take me back to Banff. It was my first hint that writing was never going to be a wildly lucrative profession.

With the war, jobs were opening up. Although I had taken a two-week typing course, my first summer job was working at the meat counter in Eaton's. The very first day I was given a demonstration of how to clean a chicken. All the men stood around while one of them began a suggestive monologue: "First we lay her on her back. Then we spread her legs . . ." While they sniggered, I stood, face red, trying not to show any feelings whatever. There was absolutely nothing any woman at that time could do about such offensive remarks—except quit, or do what I did—pretend not to understand.

Within a week, I was offered a job at the newly established sugar-rationing board at twice the pay. I took it immediately and gave Eaton's my notice. I telephoned my mother to tell her the good news. Typically, she was greatly distressed. "Do you think you're doing the right thing?" she wailed. The idea of quitting a big firm like Eaton's seemed foolhardy to her.

My new job was checking and verifying applications for ration cards for sugar, tea, and coffee. I was fired after the first week for no particular reason. I think the man running the office decided to show he was the boss. He picked on me and another woman, probably because we both talked a lot—although that wasn't forbidden. Not willing to give up my much-needed job, I managed to talk myself back into the manager's good graces by being suitably contrite. It was a useful lesson. The knowledge that this unimpressive man had the power to cut me off was sobering.

In preparation for taking up my position as a teacher, I blew my clothes allowance and bought a new Harris tweed coat—the second store-bought coat I had ever possessed. My mother donated a trunk. Even packed with all of my worldly possessions, it was still half-empty. I filled it with newspaper to keep the clothes in place.

I left home by bus for my new school on the Sunday of the September holiday weekend. Just the day before, my mother had reminded me to put on my rubbers because it had started to rain. That evening I would begin my new life in a rural community as its leading citizen. I was just eighteen years old.

My training consisted of a single year of instruction in Calgary's normal school, where I had received something of a stamp of approval: at our graduation I gave the valedictory address and won a medal for athletics—the latter a mystery to me to this day. It must have been awarded on the basis of my written test not my physical performance. My father, as usual, was not impressed.

In preparation for teaching, we had been crammed full of John Dewey's theories of education, which had just been taken up by Alberta's department of education. Dewey, an American philosopher and educator, believed schools should be a preparation for living in a democracy. Children would learn by doing rather than being talked at. Desks were no longer to be screwed to the floor. Teaching methods that would involve "the whole child" were to replace the old-fashioned teach-memorize-test style.

As a product of the old system, I did not have to be convinced that it had failed deplorably to meet the needs of many children—like the two rows of "dummies" in my Grade 1 class. However, applying Dewey's ideas to one-room rural schools with thirty-five to forty pupils in Grades 1 to 9, and with teachers as green as the prairie grass, was a brave but rather unrealistic strategy.

To start the revolution, we had been equipped with a few rudimentary teaching aids. One was a recipe for papier mâché from salt, flour, and old newspapers. The second was a wooden frame filled with a purple jelly-like pad on which we pressed master copies and then pulled off reprints for each pupil. Both of these aids proved to be quite useful. The third, however, consisted of several bulky brown wrapping-paper maps with punched-out dots outlining the continents. By banging chalk-laden brushes against the holes, we could reproduce maps on blackboards. I discarded these almost immediately as too cumbersome.

It was dusk when I reached my destination. Word of my arrival had brought out a small crowd to inspect the new teacher. The father of two of my pupils stepped forward and took me to the farm where I would be boarding. One of the poorer farms in the area, it had been chosen because the farmer and his wife needed the money.

Besides a bed and dresser, my room included a washbasin and pitcher—with hot water supplied morning and evening—and a chamber pot in the cupboard underneath. The privy was a two-holer with an Eaton's catalogue for toilet paper. I read and prepared lessons at the kitchen table by the surprisingly bright light of a lamp fuelled by naphtha gas.

My landlord had not met me himself because his car was thought to be too dilapidated. It certainly was, even for those times. One side was held on with bailing wire, and mice nested in the holes in the seat. Mr. Kelso also had an unnerving habit of turning off the engine at the top of long hills and coasting down to save on gas.

I visited the school the next day. It was a standard, one-room structure, with a divided cloakroom for boys and girls, windows down one side, blackboards on the front and side wall, and a teacher's desk with a bell, strap, Bible, and register. There was a good basement equipped with a coal furnace and a large room where children played on cold days.

The next morning, quaking in my shoes, I met my pupils. Some were as tall as I was and only two or three years younger. We sized up one another. Drawing on my own school experience, I was convinced that teachers who tried to be too friendly and popular at the beginning of the year often lost control of the class and the respect of their students. I decided to adopt a fairly stern demeanour. I put them to work as soon as I had sorted them out. The first pupil to talk or misbehave was dealt with severely, to let the others know I would put up with no nonsense.

From that time on, I had little trouble with the pupils. The mice were another matter. It was impossible to get rid of them, even though we constantly set traps. With children bringing lunches to school and the winter coming on, the mice naturally moved indoors. After school, when I was alone, they got bolder. I would keep a little cache of stones to throw at them. Sometimes there were so many of them, I would sit on my chair on top of the desk to keep away from them.

I found I actually loved teaching and threw myself into my job with great energy and enthusiasm. In fact, there was very little else to do. I would arrive at the school about eight-thirty every morning, and stay until the light was gone. I always took home a big bundle of exercise books to mark and lessons to prepare for the following day.

What was so rewarding about teaching back then, compared with today, was the relative lack of sophistication of the children. Almost all families had radios, but few homes had many books. There was no television. My students eagerly welcomed anything I could give them that stimulated their curiosity. Following Catherine Barclay's example, I got them interested in current affairs by putting up pictures of people in the news on the bulletin board, and asking them to bring news items to school. We constructed a Mayan village of papier mâché with much less success. The project took up far too much time for what they learned.

I believe now, after that experience and watching my own children, that bright students will learn no matter what you do with them. Others with less aptitude for book learning may be extremely clever at drawing or music or doing things with their hands but need extra help in standard school subjects. No amount of trying to make learning fun replaces repetition and testing. Not recognizing that fact early enough, I'm afraid some of my pupils slid back in the basics that year.

My landlord, a wheat farmer on a single quarter section of land, with three horses, a cow, and a few chickens, ran a marginal operation even then. Each farmer cut his own grain and stacked it in upright stooks to dry. A threshing crew would move from farm to farm, harvesting it. One of the first questions Mrs. Kelso asked me when I moved in was whether I would help serve dinner to the threshing crew of eight or ten men. Eager to please, I agreed. Having the local teacher as a waitress, I discovered as I moved between the tables, was an extra attraction for the men—and a bonus for Mr. Kelso.

Although my landlady was not considered a notorious gossip, I soon knew all about the district—what couples "had to get married," ancient romances that had gone on for years and then soured, feuds that were still in progress, the relative monetary worth and farming ability of every man, and the managing and baking skill of every woman in the area.

Once harvesting was over and the winter set in, dances were held at the school. Mrs. Kelso's father ran the general store in Blackfalds, the nearest town. He was a ski enthusiast, and persuaded me to try it. I bought a second-hand pair of slats that buckled onto my overshoes and skied to school and back all that winter. My thick woollen ski slacks served a double purpose: on cold nights, as I listened to the wind whistling around the house and the coyotes howling, I wore the pants to bed to keep warm.

Every Christmas the teacher was responsible for putting on a concert and people for miles around attended. At the end of the performance, Santa would appear and hand out presents. My concert was a big flop. I reasoned that if children were going to spend so much time time memorizing and rehearsing plays, poetry, and songs, the material should be of some literary value. Afterwards I was told kindly that country people preferred something a little bawdy. The year before, one of the older girls had stuffed a pillow down her front and performed a monologue, with lots of double meanings, about the joys of being pregnant. She had brought the house down.

My landlady attended church in Blackfalds every Sunday night. She made it clear that she thought it unsuitable for me to stay at home with her husband, a dour Scot old enough to be my father, who, I am sure, had as little interest in me as I had in him. However, to keep my reputation unsullied, I went to church. I didn't mind at first. I was curious, and still am, about any sincerely held belief.

I was no longer a churchgoer. At eleven, I had been pressed to take communion and formally join the Pro-Cathedral, but I had begun to be quite critical of the church and disillusioned by the hypocrisy of some of its leading members. My older brothers, who had been confirmed, later left the church. Believing they had been too young to make the decision to join, in my case, Mama left the choice up to me—and I quit going to Sunday school.

By this time Mama had become interested in Christian Science and alternated between their service and the Pro-Cathedral on Sundays. For a while, I attended the much smaller Christian Science Sunday school. My father mocked the whole premise of Christian Science healing as no more worthy of respect than teacup reading. When we got sick, Mama would read passages from Mary Baker Eddy, but if that didn't seem to work, she called the doctor.

In my last years of high school, a friend and I had visited several different churches from spiritualist to Catholic. I have never been a member of a formal church since. Today I am a humanist. I believe the universe is so complex and so beyond our understanding that I can readily believe a superior intellect might have fashioned it. Although each formal religion claims to be the true faith, and millions of people have been slaughtered because of religion, I believe no one church has a monopoly on the truth.

My attendance at church in Blackfalds had another purpose besides saving my soul and my reputation. Young men in rural areas took bets on who would date the teacher. Mrs. Kelso's nephew, an aspiring minister in the Pentecostal Church, was one of them. I certainly couldn't see myself as a minister's wife, and I soon made sure I was invited to other homes in the area on Sunday night. A number of my friends from teachers' college did fall in love, marry, and settle down for life in whatever area their first year of teaching had taken them.

Although I liked that first school, I wanted to be closer to Calgary so I could go home more often than just at Christmas and Easter. In my second year of teaching, I taught at Macpherson Coulee School in the Airdrie district, about twenty miles north of Calgary.

My new school was almost too much of a challenge. The previous year, two teachers had found the students so hard to handle that they had left without completing the year. But the boarding arrangements helped make up for the problems at the school. I stayed at the Howard Wright farm, one of the largest and most prosperous in the area. My room in the handsome, well-furnished house was the most luxurious I was to enjoy for many a year. Mr. and Mrs. Wright were stimulating, generous people who seemed to be a truly well-suited couple. I spent hours talking about life and love with Augusta Wright, and I kept in touch with them for years.

I had lots of company in addition to the Wrights—the farm manager and his family, two hired men, a maid, and often a young man getting some practical experience before attending agricultural college. With so many young people around, there were lots of high jinks. The hired man put a dead mouse in my overshoe. In the exuberance of spring we chased one another around the property in wild water fights. We attended local dances, where I learned to appear to take a swig from a bottle—my strategy was to stick my tongue in the neck. Although I wanted to be a good sport, I didn't intend to give anyone the satisfaction of getting the teacher drunk.

Macpherson Coulee School was a different matter. Among my problems were twins who had epileptic seizures simultaneously. All four children in another family were said to be slow learners. They came to school with jam cans full of slabs of bread and cold boiled cabbage, and spoke a peculiar lingo only they could understand. The youngest was a girl in Grade 1. Unlike her brothers, she seemed quite bright. She bossed them around, showing some spunk and ingenuity. The mother obviously needed counselling, and the boys needed special classes, while the little girl needed more confidence. I did what I could to give her that, but with no available social services, and the whole district convinced that the family were hopeless pariahs, it was hard to change anything.

Another family made their way to school in a little cart with a pony. The two older boys were high-spirited and mischievous but settled down to be good students after the first week or two. Their younger brother, on the other hand, was considered delicate. Whenever his class took reading, he claimed to be sick and left the room. I tried individual help, and finally, in desperation, told him he had to stay in his seat no matter how sick he felt. He blubbered all through the class, but thankfully didn't throw up. His older brothers were incensed at this harsh treatment, and I knew they would report it to their father, one of the school trustees.

The next day the father came to the school, prepared to take me to task. I explained that I believed his son had to get over his phobia about reading and he wasn't going to do it in the cloakroom. He reluctantly gave me the benefit of the doubt, and after a few more scenes, the boy did begin to read. It might have turned out differently—but I was right that time.

My biggest problem—literally—was a Grade 9 pupil who was older and certainly a lot bigger than I. His mother had been the local teacher forty years before, and she was determined that her son finish school, although he showed little interest in or aptitude for it. He rarely shaved and regarded me with an insolent, sleepy stare to let me know that whatever was going on in his head, it was not lessons. Fortunately, although he was surly and difficult, he never really defied me. At that age, I would have had no idea what to do if he had.

To add to our difficulties that fall, some tramps broke into the school and started a fire that burned the building to the ground. Another abandoned and much older school was hauled in to replace it, and we made do with that for the rest of the year.

By the summer of 1943, I had saved $800, which I thought would be enough to repay my parents their $100 for my teachers' college tuition and put myself through two years of university. How had I done it? In the country, there had been little to spend money on. Every summer I worked when I wasn't taking courses, and I saved money by making most of my own clothes in my spare time.

My only indulgence was photography and developing pictures. Uncle Jim was a good amateur photographer, and my father had bought a small Kodak from him. Mama's snaps taken on her old Box Brownie always turned out better, and in disgust, he had given me the camera. After reading up on photography, I bought some equipment and began developing my own film. I used the same camera with great success for years.

Most of my family and even my friends were mystified by my determination to go to university. Friends who had not married were looking forward to getting a job on the Calgary school board, buying a fur coat, and perhaps even a car. Uncle Jim's wife, Alice, thought she had the answer to why I didn't want to do the same. "I know why you want to go to university," she said triumphantly. "You will meet a better class of man there!"

Tuition for one year was $120. To make my money go as far as possible, I planned to take my first year at Mount Royal, a junior college in Calgary. I would be able to live at home and pay my mother board, as well as earn extra money working in the Safeway meat department on Saturdays.

Home was a more congenial place. Everything still revolved around my father, but Mama had her own circle of friends in the neighbourhood. She was the convenor of a little group of eight women who knitted "soakers"— a kind of outer baby diaper—as well as sweaters, caps, and bootees for refugee children, and scarfs and mitts for the troops. The knitting group became the focus of my mother's social life. She and her friends talked on the telephone almost every day. After the war ended, they continued meeting at one anothers' homes for the rest of their lives.

One of my most pleasant memories from that year was the half-hour walk to class in the early morning. No matter how cold it is, the sun always shines in Alberta. As I would come over the hill to take the path down to the Centre Street Bridge, the sun would illuminate the Rockies in all their snowy splendour on the western horizon—this was a wonderful, bracing way to begin the day.

The classes themselves were dreary, the instructors uninspiring. To make up for what I was certain was inferior schooling, I worked extremely hard, and not only passed with distinction in all my subjects but also won two bursaries—one in English and one in history. At the end of the final term, I gave the valedictory address.

With the war continuing, many teachers left the profession either to join up or take better-paying jobs. I found a summer job at a school in the foothills. Its teacher had joined the army in the winter and no replacement had been found that spring. A friend of mine, who was also attending university, took over a neighbouring school. One weekend I hiked over to visit her, and she introduced me to one of her Grade 9 pupils, a strapping farm boy. To my way of thinking, she was much too friendly with him. "If he ever gets fresh with you," she warned me, "scratch his face. He hates having his face marked." I remember being quite astonished at this method of handling a Grade 9 pupil.

A few weeks later, I went over again for a visit. The same young man turned up after dinner and offered to walk me partway home. After a few miles, he suddenly grabbed me, tried to kiss me, and when I pushed him away, he ripped open my blouse, sending the buttons flying in all directions. He then tried to throw me to the ground. There was no question that he was going to try to rape me. Although I was a strong young woman, I realized I was no match for him.

I then remembered my friend's advice. I raked my fingers down the side of his face, and while he stood cursing me, I took to my heels. I'm sure he could have caught me, but scratching his face seemed to have cooled his ardour, and I managed to get away.

I never told anyone. I felt ashamed somehow at being put in such a position by a pupil. I also wasn't sure whether the community would support me or decide that I had encouraged him in some way. He even had the gall to turn up, looking as cocky as ever—though his face still bore evidence of my attack—at our school picnic a day or two later.

But that wasn't the end of my trouble with men that summer. My friend had a brother in the navy who turned up late one afternoon at the one-room teacherage where I was living. He was on his way to see his sister, but wanted to come in for a drink of water. Because he was burdened with a large dufflebag, I tried getting him a ride with neighbours, with no luck. I then fed him dinner and told him under no circumstances could he stay. He agreed, and set off for his sister's.

About four in the morning, he was back at the door, begging to be let in. Apparently, he had decided he was too tired to walk, had returned to the teacherage, slung a hammock between two trees, and gone to sleep. Now he said he was freezing to death. Against my better judgement, I allowed him to curl up on the couch. At seven I woke him and told him he'd have to leave or my reputation in the area would be ruined—if it wasn't already.

Just as he was leaving, a neighbour's truck went by. I also noticed that this stupid fellow had taken down the hammock. Knowing the story that he had spent the night in the teacherage would soon be all over the neighbourhood, I gave up, fed him breakfast, and sent him on his way. Although nothing had happened between us, for the rest of my stay in that area I was a scarlet woman!

All the time I had been teaching, the five o'clock train to Edmonton with its urgent, mournful whistle had been like a daily promise of a more sophisticated future. But after my first month at the University of Alberta I was so disappointed—after all my work and saving—that I almost quit. I don't know what I had hoped for—some great, sophisticated hub of learning, I suppose. To my dismay, my fellow students, who were three years younger than I, seemed like high-school students—which, of course, they were.

Since I had won the first-year bursary in history, I decided to try for an honours degree, which would take an extra year. I reasoned that I could probably get some scholarship money to help, and went to see the head of the department about it. An impressive older man, he took great pleasure in telling me that he had never given a woman a first in all his years of teaching. Realizing I was wasting my time, I opted for a standard Bachelor of Arts degree.

In retrospect, I understand that he did me a favour. I might have been tempted to go through for a Ph.D. and embark on an academic career. With the war ending, it had become even more difficult for women to get appointments to university posts, and many women who had taught during the war were let go. It wasn't until thirty years later, when women in academia started agitating for better working conditions, that they began to be treated with anything like equality, and there are great inequities even today.

With a university career unavailable to me, I decided to work hard but play a lot more than I had originally planned. In spite of my initial disappointment, and the fact that it was wartime and far fewer men were around, I had a ball at university. I got involved in the debating society, played interfaculty basketball, joined the drama club and wrote for the *Gateway*, the university paper. Although many of my best friends were in fraternities, I not only could not afford to join one but didn't approve of them.

Today, when I go back to visit the campus, I can hardly find the small college I attended in the complex of buildings that now make up the University of Alberta. In 1943, its enrolment was small, so it was possible to know people in every faculty. Some of my happiest hours were spent sitting in the old Tuck Shop across from the campus, where we bought coffee and doughnuts and argued interminably about the future of the world. We believed the Allies would win. If they didn't, we were sure civilization was doomed. As children of the Depression, most of us talked about helping the poor, eliminating hunger, and making universities free for bright students.

Because the residences were occupied by the air force, I found a tiny room in the basement of a large house close to the campus, where I could make meals on a hot plate shared by other students. Our landlady was a curious woman who kept lecturing us on the evils of "leading men on" unless we planned to have sex. I don't know what she expected us to do. The Pill hadn't been invented. Yet this apostle of free love, like all our landladies, would never allow us to have men in our rooms. There was a lot of necking at the door, and in the back seats of cars, but the frigid Alberta weather cooled off even the most ardent lovers.

Although I was still a virgin, some of my friends had "gone all the way." One couple had sex in the boy's frat house every day at noon. When the girl's parents found out, she was abruptly pulled out of school and sent to another university. It was a scandal at the time—mostly because of the very public way the parents dealt with the matter. The couple later married, and it all seems quite silly to me today.

During the war, it didn't seem appropriate to engage in the usual university high jinks. There were no inter-university football games. We all did military drilling or other war work; coeds, for example, served in the Edmonton army canteen. In the era of the big bands—Glenn Miller, Artie Shaw, Benny Goodman, and the Dorsey Brothers—we waltzed, fox-trotted, and jitter-bugged to "In the Mood," "Sentimental Journey," and "Deep Purple." In the spring I attended balls on three successive nights with three different men. I had one evening dress, which was white. It got badly soiled in the rain in the middle of my social whirl. Having no time to take it to the cleaners, I just rinsed out the hem and went merrily on.

In my final year I only had enough money to pay my tuition and a few months' board. I had to find other work to get me through the rest of the year. The dean of women, Mary Winspear, took me aside and offered a loan through a university fund, but I hated the idea of being in debt, and, in any case, I had other plans.

I applied to the *Edmonton Journal* for the job of stringer on university affairs. The managing editor seemed impressed but sent me over to see the editor of the society page. She asked, "Who is your father?" I replied that he was Mr. McCubbin. "But who is he?" she continued impatiently. "What are his connections?"

Although I had to admit he didn't have any, I got the job. I was so incensed at her snobbish attitude that I walked over to the *Bulletin,* an older but smaller paper, and applied for a job there. I was hired by John Oliver, the editor, without any folderol about my pedigree. I immediately phoned the *Journal* and told them to keep their job.

Being a stringer meant I covered all university news. Because I was paid 5 cents an inch, the more diligent I was in scaring up news, the more money I made. On the whole, I did quite well. I even reported on football games— which I knew almost nothing about—with coaching from a helpful boyfriend.

To make sure I had enough money, I also applied for a job working part-time in the university library. The librarian clearly did not want me, probably because she considered me far too talkative and gregarious. Because my grades were good and the dean of women supported my application, she was forced to take me on.

One of my duties was to open the library every morning. To get there on time, as well as have something to eat, I would swallow a vitamin pill and a raw egg in a glass of water and then race for the arts building to arrive at a quarter to eight. By the end of the year, my reluctant boss had apparently changed her mind about me. She urged me repeatedly to take a librarian's course. Sorting books and magazines, however, wasn't what I had in mind. Writing them seemed much more fun.

That year I became features editor of the *Gateway*. The editor, Don Cormie, was a law student who later headed a trust company where thousands of Albertans lost their life savings. Another budding lawyer, Roger Belzil, was advertising manager. He seemed totally disinterested in our various campaigns and crusades, concentrating only on selling ads and earning his commission. Being highly idealistic, I once told him in disgust that I expected him to become one of those crooked lawyers who ended up in jail. Imagine my surprise years later when he was appointed to the Supreme Court of Alberta!

In 1945 one of my friends, Libby McCullough, and I appeared in a one-act play, *The Ten Pound Note* by J. M. Barrie, and I won an award as best actress. We were asked to put the play on for the troops over at the canteen, but Barrie was not what the troops were looking for, and it was a total flop. At one point, I had to open up a typewriter. The lid completely hid me from the audience. It seemed like the crowning catastrophe in a terrible evening, and I collapsed with laughter behind the lid, leaving poor Libby standing helplessly in the middle of the stage until I recovered.

A much more successful and popular affair that spring was Cabaret Night, staged by Joe Shoctor, who later founded Edmonton's Citadel Theatre. A highly sophisticated affair with the latest Broadway songs, it was a harbinger of the great era of post-war musicals and Shoctor's brilliant future career. I regret to say at the time I was a confirmed cultural snob. I didn't even attend.

I made some friends at university whom I have kept for life—Libby McCullough Jensen and Mar Walker and her husband, Wilf. I also counted two outstanding professors among my friends—Mary Winspear and F. M. Salter.

Mary Winspear, in addition to being dean of women, also taught a course in the modern novel, which I found engrossing. Although she was an excellent teacher, at the end of the war she was let go; men were returning from overseas and all the teaching jobs were reserved for them. She later founded a school in Montreal. I kept in touch with her for many years.

My most memorable professor was F. M. Salter, who taught one of the few courses in Canada at that time in creative writing. Several distinguished writers, including W. O. Mitchell and Rudy Wiebe, studied with him.

 ᴖ I remember the first day of his class well. More than a hundred students crowded into the classroom, all of them keen on becoming writers. Salter came in—a small dark-haired man with a little black moustache and huge limpid brown eyes behind large glasses. He glared at the roomful of students and proceeded to tell us he was the toughest teacher around. If we took his class, we were going to have to produce three thousand words a week—or we were out. Then he left.

At the next class, the ranks were considerably thinned; only about thirty students showed up. He was even more intimidating. He told us he would not put up with mangled syntax, bad spelling, or sloppy construction. We were supposed to have mastered all those basic skills in high school. Then he marched out again.

When he returned the next time, seven of us were left. I don't think he could have got rid of us no matter what he said. From then on he couldn't have been more solicitous. He fussed over our embryonic prose like a mother hen and tried to get us published in the *Atlantic Monthly*. Years later, Salter would look me up and be very disappointed that I had done nothing more with my writing than editing a women's magazine.

The other memorable course I took was modern European history from Dr. G. M. Smith, an impressive lecturer and the man who had discouraged me from taking an honours degree. We were only a month into the course when he was moved to Ottawa on an assignment related to the war. Five of us in the class decided to continue without a professor. We each agreed to prepare a lecture every fifth class—a formidable undertaking. Another professor in the department supervised us and set the exam. We worked hard: it was a matter of pride not to let the others down. In the end, we all received first-class honours.

Although many young men were in the forces, they still outnumbered women at university, and once again, I fell in love. Everything about the future seemed wonderfully clear to the young man I was interested in—

but not to me. He saw himself taking a Ph.D. and then having a brilliant career. Like all university men, he took it for granted that some woman, perhaps myself, would be happy to give up her own ambitions and look after all the mundane details of his life—such as making sure there was toilet paper in the bathroom, getting the kids to dental appointments, sending his clothes to the cleaners, and managing his social life.

I suppose I should have been delighted at even the possibility of snagging one of these potentially "prize" husbands. They were highly sought after and certainly superior to anything my mother had anticipated for me. However, my own goals were becoming clearer. I wanted to marry and have children, but I knew that after all my hard work, I also wanted a career. Whenever I hinted at such an idea, the young man looked at me as though I had suddenly grown two heads.

Mama and Aunt Annie attended my graduation. I was the first member of the family to have gone through university. My thrifty mother bought me a second-hand gold watch to replace the nickel one from Uncle Jim. It looked second-hand, and while my friends were showing off spanking-new graduation presents, I hid mine, I am ashamed to admit. My graduation went by in a lovely blur of corsages from various balls preserved in tea cups, parties, letters and cards of congratulation, and fervent goodbyes.

University had given me three great years. My most important discovery was that I was not the misfit I had believed myself to be back in high school. I had also been privileged to study under at least two exceptional professors, Salter and Winspear. Even more important, a university degree in 1945 gave me a big advantage in the job market—which is, alas, no longer true.

Once again, people tried to both influence and help me. Salter offered me a job as assistant to an American professor who was researching Alberta's pioneers. He thought the pioneers' tall tales of the Canadian West would be a rich source of material for writing. I am sure it would have been, but I was impatient to see more of the world.

John Oliver at the *Bulletin* also offered me a job as a reporter. I had already realized, however, that women reporters were confined mostly to the society page, writing items about teas, weddings, and women's clubs. I was convinced that there had to be a better job somewhere in journalism.

I was also offered another option—marriage, to an engineer I had been dating. Even if most of my friends were pairing off and heading for matrimony as routinely as lemmings going down to the sea, I wasn't ready for marriage. I promised my engineer that I would consider it, but I needed more time. As he was going off to an overseas job, we decided we would continue to keep in touch by writing to each other. This arrangement gave me the advantage, when I chose to use it, of telling my mother and her friends, and men I wasn't interested in, that I had a serious commitment elsewhere.

At the end of graduation, I had enough money left to buy a one-way train ticket to Toronto, the centre of Canadian journalism. I planned to work there for a few years, gain experience, and then move on to what seemed to me at the time the epitome of sophistication—New York City.

At the urging of Mary Winspear, I had paid one week's board and room in advance at the Women's Christian Temperance Union on Gerrard Street, off Yonge Street in Toronto. I calculated that if I ate frugally on the train I would have about $11 by the time I arrived at Union Station, and I was positive that I would be able to find some kind of a job within a week.

I didn't have a worry in the world. When I look back today on my confidence—and naïvety—it blows my mind.

CHAPTER SIX

"Why Isn't a Nice Girl Like You Married?"

Toronto in the summer of 1945 was hot, humid, and crowded with far more people than it could comfortably accommodate. Far from the cosmopolitan metropolis I had anticipated, it seemed provincial, smug, and dull. As the hub of industrial Canada, it drew people like me from all over the country. For years I regarded the city much as a mail-order bride would a dour, uptight husband. We were in a marriage of convenience with no love lost on either side.

Shortly after I arrived, Toronto's relentlessly WASP, politically Conservative, and stuffy nature was revealed. A huge Orangemen's Parade led by the mayor completely blocked downtown traffic. The parade and the Canadian National Exhibition in the fall—a tame and highly commercial affair compared with Calgary's rowdy, whoop-de-doo stampede—comprised the summer's entertainment. There was one important break that year. In August the war in the Far East ended, and I, along with thousands of other people, poured out into Yonge Street to celebrate.

Even the infamously dull Toronto Sundays were worse than I had expected. There was nowhere to go for people like me, except churches, the Art Gallery, and the Royal Ontario Museum. Even Eaton's windows had drawn curtains, following the edict of its founder, Timothy, who believed the piety of the populace should not be contaminated by commercialism on the Sabbath. If you didn't attend church followed by a gargantuan family dinner with roast beef, mashed potatoes, veg, and pie, God help you.

I was no connoisseur of restaurants, but even slightly unusual eating places were rare. The most popular, which was located on Bloor Street, had the unappetizing name of the Diet Kitchen. The tawdry old Royal Alexandra was the only theatre—and most of the time it was either dark or running third-rate road shows.

Coming as I did from a prairie province, I had highly romantic ideas about the possibilities of life beside a huge lake. I dreamed of slipping down for a cool dip at noon or after work. Unfortunately, with all its floating debris, Lake Ontario had little allure, even for a prairie gopher like me. The ferry to Centre Island provided transportation to sandy beaches, and a little less garbage, but to my disgust the city had fewer public swimming pools than Calgary, a city one-quarter its size.

In my father's opinion, Toronto had one enormous asset—Maple Leaf Gardens. "Toronto—the home of a nation's sport," he kept repeating reverently, like a mantra, before I left the West. He had been quite excited at the thought of a daughter of his being able to watch players like Rocket Richard and Teeder Kennedy skirmishing on the ice on a Saturday night. Once again I disappointed him. It was fifteen years before I actually attended a hockey game.

My conviction that I would easily find a job proved to be sound. Within a week, I was hired by the *Star Weekly* as a copyeditor. Despite no training at all except my stints on the *Bulletin* and student publications, I plunged into writing headlines and blurbs as well as cutting and editing copy. Among the syndicated articles I dealt with were ones written by the "Red Dean"—the Archbishop of Canterbury—who composed rapturous accounts of life in the U.S.S.R. These were soon dropped in the aftermath of the war, when the U.S.S.R., no longer our "gallant ally," became "the Red Menace."

An introductory letter from F. M. Salter put me in touch with one of his former students, and through her contacts I moved into a rooming house on Spadina Road that was full of media people. One of my first purchases that summer was a little radio. I revelled in listening to whatever I pleased, instead of the country and western music interspersed with news and sports that I had endured for so many years at home.

In September I applied for and got what promised to be a much more stimulating job—in addition to a $10 raise—as the "leg woman" for Claire Wallace.

At that time, there were local daytime radio shows for the woman in the home. Female hosts cheerily dispensed a mix of news tidbits, spiced with recipes, lightly larded with household hints, and packaged with frequent plugs from sponsors. There were also two national shows. One, sponsored by Tamblyn's drugstore chain, was hosted by Kate Aitken, who also wrote cookbooks and organized shows for women at the exhibition.

The other was hosted by Claire Wallace and sponsored by Robin Hood Flour. These two women hotly competed for national audiences and were probably the best-known and highest-paid media women in the country.

Claire Wallace, who came from a family of journalists, had established her name as a "stunt writer" at the *Toronto Star*. In her own highly personal style, she took on offbeat assignments, then reported on the experience to her stay-at-home audience. She would answer an ad for a maid, then "tell all" to her readers. Or, at a time when people still believed that allowing a woman to go down a mine brought bad luck, Claire would wangle her way into one and relate what kind of reception she got. Her most frequently used punctuation was the exclamation mark.

A striking woman—tall, blond, radiating charm and confidence—Claire was my first encounter with a media celebrity. She never entered a public place—not even the corner store—without turning on a great expectant smile at the possibility of being recognized.

My job was to research and write her scripts. Realizing all the skills I would have to master almost overnight, I thought it was a wonderful opportunity for a novice. I would have to become instantly familiar with Toronto and all its personalities, as well as scramble successfully for my share of stories in the media scrums. Undeterred, I plunged in as I had at the *Star Weekly*, but my new job almost sent me back to the West forever.

Claire needed at least five items a day. The stories had to be a mix—for example, a three-minute distillation of an interview with a nuclear physicist, a heart-warming item about a dancing dog, a curious, little-known fact about a common household item like baking soda, a bit of hot celebrity gossip, and, to end the show, some little item that Claire could cleverly personalize.

Soon after I was hired, the Metropolitan Opera came to town and played to sell-out houses at Maple Leaf Gardens. I interviewed the stars, Lily Pons and Nino Martini, and I blush today at how uninformed I—the culture snob—was about opera, and what inconsequential questions I must have asked.

Martini showed me a gold cross nestled among the hairs on his chest. He gave me a complimentary ticket to *La Traviata* and asked me to meet him for dinner after the show. I was entranced by the performance but got cold feet when it came to the dinner. Something about the way he had bared his chest warned me that more than just dinner was planned. I slunk away instead of meeting him backstage.

My interview with Benny Goodman wasn't much better. He was staying in a rather sleazy hotel room across from City Hall. He was brusque and impatient, and when I persisted with my questions, he began to take off his pants. I fled.

One of Claire's stunts was to fly over Niagara Falls in a small plane. I supplied all the factual details about the falls, which she breathlessly related to her listeners—and I got my long-wished-for airplane ride. A few weeks later, we went to Ottawa for the state visit of Britain's prime minister, Clement Atlee. It was my first glimpse of our nation's capital and of Mackenzie King, our prime minister. I was struck by how short both men were and how much older and less distinguished they seemed in the flesh than they appeared in the newsreels in movie theatres.

In those first few months I found most of the Toronto press women competitive but friendly. Alexandrine Gibb, one of the few women sportswriters in Canada, had introduced herself to me at the *Star Weekly*. A large, expansive woman, she was said to have knocked down a fellow reporter in a scrum when he tore her fur coat. I was awe-struck meeting Lotta Dempsey, whose by-line I had noted for years in my mother's *Chatelaine* magazines. Breezy, outgoing, friendly, and humorously self-deprecating, she welcomed me as a fellow Albertan.

June Callwood, a reporter for the *Globe and Mail*, looked as she does today—beautiful. Although she was about my age, the fact that she was married and had a baby made her seem infinitely more mature. Lillian Foster, the fashion editor of the Toronto *Telegram*, was a grumpy but well-loved character who dressed more like a bag lady than a fashion doyenne. She bluntly dismissed me when I was introduced as Claire Wallace's new researcher. "Claire has a new researcher every two or three weeks," she sniffed.

Lillian's gloomy prediction was not only accurate, but also solved the mystery of why I was hired. Dozens of young women had worked for Claire—and left. Although she drove herself hard, she drove her staff, consisting of me and a long-time, adoring secretary, even harder. Her moods were mercurial: she could easily waste an hour relating her exploits of the night before, modelling a new outfit, or reading her fan mail out loud to us. Five minutes later, she would be ripping to shreds a script I had toiled over for the entire previous night. It then had to be completely revised and ready for her broadcast at two o'clock.

Eager to succeed, I would pore over scripts she liked, trying to discern why one had pleased her, and why another with the same mix was not worth using for garbage wrap. I could find little logic or consistency in her criticisms. Even more worrisome, she would actually alter facts in my stories if she didn't feel they were startling enough. I resented her assumption that it wasn't important to give her female audience accurate information.

In fact, Claire was ahead of her time. Entertainment was far more important than dispensing knowledge on her show. And it was even more vital to constantly polish and enhance her image as a media star. I think she would have been right at home on today's confessional, let-everything-hang-out TV shows.

I had no life of my own at all while I worked for her. I was expected to be at her beck and call at every hour of the day or night and even on weekends. This was not really a big problem—I knew few people and I certainly didn't mind working long hours. I did, however, need some respite from her hyperactive, controlling presence. Even when I was invited away for a Thanksgiving weekend, she insisted that I check in with her regularly by phone.

If Claire had been willing to offer me guidance, I think we might have spent a mutually productive few years together. However, she not only demanded all my time, she was also personally critical, and not very constructively. In retrospect, I realize she built up her own ego by tearing down everyone else around her, especially her rival, Kate Aitken, who always seemed calmer, more balanced, and able, therefore, to accomplish much more.

Claire criticized my appearance. I was required to buy expensive outfits from a shop she patronized. As she was twice my age, I felt her clothes were more suitable for my mother than for me. She mimicked my western drawl—a way of speaking I have never lost. She dismissed my hard-earned education as being inferior to her own because I had graduated from "one of those western universities" and she had attended, as she never ceased to inform me, a private girls' school.

Working such long hours, I caught several colds that fall. When she learned that I had never had my tonsils removed, she demanded that I have them out on my next holiday—my three days off at Christmas. I didn't mind—I was homesick anyway, and the prospect of being looked after in a hospital for a day seemed almost attractive.

Looking back, I realize I was raw, bumptious, and lacking in sophistication. I certainly could have used some polishing and shaping. But although I had eagerly taken direction from both men and women all my life, this was different. Claire Wallace was a Queen Bee—one of several I was to meet—a woman who had "made it," no doubt with a great deal of difficulty and effort. She was prepared to be neither kind nor helpful to other members of her sex. Other women fell into two categories—slavish handmaidens, willing to flatter her, run her errands, and do the dirty humdrum work while she took all the credit and praise—or arch enemies.

Twice that fall I became so discouraged under the constant barrage of criticism that I quit. She must have found me useful, though, because each time she not only urged me to stay but raised my salary too. She would turn on all her considerable charm and that was my Achilles heel: I had always associated charm in a woman with breeding, not guile. Claire would change before my eyes into a facsimile of all those lovely women in the movies and the ads—the beautiful creatures we had been taught to model ourselves after and idealize.

She would be contrite. We had both been working too hard. We needed to take time out and get to know each other better. I must come to dinner on Sunday. I must meet her son, Wally, and her second husband, Jim. We must talk more. She would give me some little thing—usually, I realize now, something she didn't want. Even as she talked, I suspected that I was being conned again, but each time I kept hoping she meant what she said and that this monster boss would really transform herself into the utterly charming woman before me.

There were two other reasons I stayed. One was greed. I was earning $75 a week, a miraculous salary for someone as inexperienced as I was at the time. The other was that I was trapped by my own background. Deep down, I harboured the naïve and foolish notion that if something hurt enough, it had to be good for me.

Of course nothing changed. After six months I was so unhappy that all I could think of doing was quitting, heading back out West, and completely giving up on my hopes of a career in journalism. In March, I finally handed in my resignation and nothing she did or said could persuade me to stay.

I decided to give myself two weeks to deliberate about my future. I tried to write short stories during that troubled time, but was far too drained and emotionally upset to produce anything at all. In the end, I wisely determined to put the experience behind me and give myself another chance.

I sat down and wrote applications to more than twenty prospective employers, including the city's major publishing houses, advertising agencies, and news outlets. I toiled over those letters, and they must have been quite persuasive because I received replies to every application and ten interviews. When I think of how difficult it is for young people today, outfitted as they are with polished CVs and superior qualifications, to even get a reply to the applications they send out, I know there is something sadly amiss.

Not every letter was encouraging. One from Dent Publishing went something like this: "Thank you for offering your considerable talents and skills to our firm. But I am afraid our small, somewhat quiet and modest little publishing house could not possibly accommodate someone as vigorous and dynamic as you present yourself to be."

Disappointingly, it turned out that most of the jobs I was offered were for glorified secretaries. In the post-war period, when all the good jobs were reserved for returning servicemen, women, who had enjoyed filling in for men during the war, were given a clear message: handmaiden jobs only. I could work in a small advertising firm with the remote possibility of someday writing copy, but my main task was to answer the phone and do the secretarial work. I could work in a publishing firm and perform the same phone-and-letter-answering tasks, with the chance that in my spare time I would be allowed to read manuscripts.

I finally settled for a job in the advertising department at Eaton's, and a salary of $25 a week, because there were no secretarial strings attached. I was one of a pool of young women who wrote the store's ads for the two dailies—the *Star* and the now-defunct *Telegram*. Six departments, including notions, ladies' shoes, and lingerie, were my responsibility. In the next three years, a fairly large turnover in copywriters allowed me to work my way up to writing fashion-department copy, and even going out on fashion shoots.

Besides the pool of women writers, there were a few men who wrote copy for the men's departments, furniture, hardware, and radios. There was also a contingent of artists and an office staff of four. All the bosses were men. Four young men took our copy down to the departments for approval. Unlike most of the women, few men had a university degree. They all knew they were on trial, and if they made good, they could end up as department managers, or in the executive suite. One of them, a fresh-faced choirboy from St. Catharines, Ted Gittings, eventually became advertising manager of *Chatelaine* magazine and later, president of COMAC publications.

Such heady possibilities were, of course, inconceivable for the female copywriters. Even if we stayed at Eaton's for the rest of our lives, the most we might achieve was to become the writer of the back-page fashion copy for the *Globe and Mail* when the incumbent writer, Aileen Adams, retired.

The office manager had been the former riding master for the store's president, John David Eaton, and his siblings. He had no qualifications whatever for running an office that I knew of, and no concept that writing might involve thinking before you touched fingers to typewriter. We called him "Cyclops." When he patrolled the office, about once every hour, we knew we had to type furiously. If you were caught sitting, or God forbid, thinking, you were considered a slacker.

Everyone at Eaton's had to clock in. In our department we signed a time sheet four times a day. If we were late arriving in the morning or over-stayed lunch hour, it was recorded in Cyclops's black book. As it was entirely up to him whether an employee got paid for sick days, keeping on his good side was important. We always tried to look busy by rushing out of the office with a big sheaf of papers, as though on terribly momentous business with the departments.

Those fundamentals established, since we were all young and high-spirited, we generally had a good time. If we worked hard, we could have most of what we had to do finished by noon. I kept myself busy the rest of the time writing short stories, typing a novel for a friend, and shopping for bargains using my employee's 10 per cent discount.

One week all the women copywriters went on an orange-and-consommé diet. The office reeked of citrus fruit. The men complained, but nobody ever suggested we desist. As long as we behaved like silly young women exclaiming over bargains and fad diets, we were indulged.

All I had to know about copywriting I learned in the first week. If anything, we tried far too hard to be original in those mundane ads. The real lessons to be learned at Eaton's were how to get along with a wide variety of mostly male bosses.

Every department was run like a little fiefdom. The managers had absolute veto over ad copy and artwork. It was our job, as copywriters and women, to keep all those quirky egos happy. The head of the millinery department would often just slash through my heading and blurb with a black pencil and send it back. Later that day, looking over my revised copy, he would compliment me on a "vastly improved" effort. Usually I had given him almost identical copy, knowing his mood "improved vastly" by the afternoon.

I found that writing ads and trying to con people into spending money on things they probably couldn't afford was not a job I could take much pride in. I also thought all the fashion hoopla was ridiculous. Every spring Paris would proclaim hemlines were going up or down, sleeves were puffed or plain. The Canadian fashion industry would knock off some outfits from the New York shows. Stores like Eaton's would respond with uninspired themes such as "It's a Green Spring!" and people like me would write the copy.

Eaton's had been founded some seventy years before by Timothy Eaton, on some truly far-sighted principles: cash sales, not credit, and Goods Satisfactory or Money Refunded. Highly successful, with coast-to-coast stores, and a huge mail-order business, Eaton's was a Canadian institution.

Most of the people who worked there stayed for life. During the Depression, the store did try to shield its employees from mass firings, but by the time I worked there, I could not understand why the people around me were so loyal and passive or why almost all of them voted for the Conservative provincial government of George Drew. They reminded me of my mother, with her allegiance to the old Calgary families, and her belief that the way to success was to stay with one firm for life.

Every week, Eaton's house organ, *Flash*—a misnomer if there ever was one—would carry pictures of retirees. Some poor soul who had toiled in the factory or the bedding department for forty or fifty years was leaving, and all he would have to show for his labour was a going-away gift of something like a birdbath! There was no pension plan and no sick leave, except on the whim of managers like Cyclops. Salaries were arbitrarily set by the department heads. You could be fired with one week's notice. There was no unemployment insurance, no medicare, no maternity leave, no workers' compensation, and little protection against accidents on the job or choice about overtime. Sexual harassment was so common that it was rarely even talked about.

In 1946 a drive was started to unionize Eaton's. When we left the store after work on the first day of the campaign, union people handed us pamphlets. Most of the employees immediately threw them away as though John David Eaton, the founder's grandson, was personally watching them. I signed up right away. I had never seen a place where a union was needed more.

Soon afterwards, Eileen Suffrin, who was heading the drive, contacted me and I tried to persuade other people in my department to join, with little success. Most of the women felt they wouldn't be working there long—they expected to marry, and didn't want to get into any trouble. Older employees were probably afraid they would be fired, a possibility I have to admit I didn't care about one way or another.

The campaign to unionize Eaton's went on for more than a year. The firm reluctantly brought in a measly pension plan and sick leave. But after one of the biggest and most expensive union drives in the country at that time, the final vote was a failure.

Once I had my first year behind me, I began to find I could have a lot of fun in starchy, staid Toronto. I met men through friends at work, and I was off dancing at the Top Hat, Casa Loma, or the Royal York supper dance once or twice a month.

In my second summer in Toronto, I travelled by train to New York for a weekend, then hitchhiked all over the province and to Montreal with a friend from the copy department. Back then, two young women could hitchhike safely, although proper Torontonians frowned on the practice. In my opinion, it certainly beat staying cooped up in the steaming city every weekend. Fortunately, the family of one of my co-workers owned a cottage and a small sailboat on Beaver Lake. A gang of us would pile in his father's car and take off for a weekend. Being from the almost lakeless West, I have had a love affair with cottages ever since.

In the winter, I played badminton at the Strathgowan Badminton Club, and once again took up skiing, this time with proper skis and boots. Early Sunday morning we would take the Yonge streetcar to the end of the line, then a bus to Summit—a range of hills north of the city equipped with a rope tow, long line-ups, and packed slopes.

Growing up on a starvation diet of one movie a month, I wallowed in all the post-war movies from Italy and France, as well as the great pre-war

Russian and German films being shown at a film club I had joined. Often on Friday night, a fellow copywriter, Deirdre O'Connell, and I would have dinner at Mary John's, a small restaurant in what was then the Village on Gerrard between Bay and University. The meal was 50 cents, the movie 25 cents, and we felt we had had a grand evening.

One winter I enrolled in two night courses in psychology. At that time, we were all busy analyzing one another and trying to figure out how to undo the supposed damage of our various childhoods. I read everything by Karen Horney, as well as a good deal of Freud and Jung. I also continued my voracious reading of both fiction and non-fiction.

Through Leone Kennedy, a small, chain-smoking, wise-cracking news-woman who worked at Canadian Press, I met a lot of CPers. They were great drinkers. Whenever anyone arrived from an out-of-town bureau, there would be a room at the Royal York where everyone gathered, the men lugging along cases of beer. The more they drank, the better their tales—ripping off copy, meeting deadlines, covering up for one another when hung over. Gillis Purcell, the boss, took on the dimensions of Orson Welles in *Citizen Kane*. I was quite surprised years later when I actually met him and found him to be of medium height, gentle, literate, and witty.

At these and other parties, the air was so thick that you couldn't see across the room. Everyone smoked—it was considered sophisticated. I could never inhale and didn't like smoking much. Years later, when it became clear that smoking caused cancer, I had no trouble quitting cold turkey.

Although I was happy and fully occupied, my job was not very stimu-lating and had no future, so I constantly applied for other work. Nothing seemed much better than what I had. Then I was offered a job on *Maclean's* magazine in 1947.

Maclean's had always been Canada's biggest and most successful gener-al magazine. Under its editor, Arthur Irwin, it was changing from a stodgy pre-war journal (when Beverley Baxter's "Letter from London" was often its most sprightly item) into what was probably one of the best magazines in North America. Men who had chronicled the war—Ralph Allen, John Clare, Pierre Berton, and Gerry Anglin—had been hired. Articles began to appear on LSD and other new experimental drugs, along with tough, revealing profiles on celebrities like the CBC's "Not So Happy Gang" and astonishing political pieces like the one on Mackenzie King, who had run the country during the war with advice, through a medium, from his dead dog and dead mother.

There was one woman writer on staff—blond, vivacious Eva-Lis Wuorio, who wrote colourful profiles and, with her appealing Finnish accent and excellent social connections, was rumoured to have had romances with several men in high places.

No wonder the idea of working at *Maclean's* was almost beyond my wildest dreams. I was interviewed by Irwin himself, a shy man who scarcely raised his eyes from his desk blotter all through the interview. He was painfully honest with me. *Maclean's* needed a copyeditor and that was all. He made it clear that I would be sitting in a small windowless room editing copy forever, without any hope of ever getting a chance to write. If I had the slightest yearning beyond becoming the best goddamn copyeditor on the best goddamn magazine in Canada, I had better forget it.

Being equally honest, I turned the job down.

My short stint on the *Star Weekly* had convinced me that copyediting was highly necessary, but for myself just about the dullest job in a writer's world. Although I believed you could do almost anything if you had to, I didn't want to try to be a copyeditor—not even if I had to pass up the chance to say I had worked on *Maclean's*. I hated checking other people's work, and I wasn't a particularly good speller.

Everyone I knew thought I had made a terrible mistake, and perhaps I had, but almost fifty years later, I don't think so. During the fifties and sixties, many North American magazines employed women to do the research while men wrote the stories and got the by-lines. Although one or two women eventually did manage to become staff writers on *Maclean's*, other women became researchers for some pretty mediocre male writers. That might have been my fate.

A little later, I was one of about fifty women interviewed for a job as assistant to the editor on a new picture magazine that was being launched in Canada. I realized during the interview that the publisher seemed a lot more interested in my legs and my bosom than my qualifications. I didn't get the job. Years later, a friend who did confirmed my suspicions: "Of course I had to sleep with him, but I actually found him quite attractive." The magazine lasted less than two years.

I joined the CCF Party, and Morden Lazarus, its Ontario secretary, persuaded me to write for the *CCF News*. At the publication's office, I met a lanky, red-haired, extremely confident young man from the West, Pierre Berton, who was making a name for himself at *Maclean's*. Although he was about my age, he acted as though he was much older—and an expert on writing and editing, which, compared with me, he was. I learned from him and we've been friends ever since.

I found the meetings in the local riding dreary: the men did all the talking, the women took notes, and made the coffee. Disillusioned, I soon stopped attending.

In 1946 I had been kicked out of my rather elegant rooming house because I had almost started a fire. Fearful of leaving cleaning rags in the wastebasket, I burned them on the stone windowsill of my third-floor room. The fire lasted all of a minute, but the occupants of a passing car saw it and called the fire department. The landlady was so incensed that she demanded I leave.

Rooms were still scarce. No landlord ever painted anything, nor did they replace broken springs in beds, or even light bulbs. If you objected to peeling paint and grubby furniture, you redecorated yourself. I moved three times and found all the rules too restrictive. In one place, I wasn't allowed to use a second-hand sewing machine I had bought. In another, I was chastised for reading in the middle of the night and moving about my room—a nocturnal habit I have always had, and that I consider my own business.

My living arrangements took a turn for the better when my friend Libby McCullough, who had been sharing an apartment with three friends, left in 1948, and I replaced her. It was the fully furnished top floor of an old house in wealthy Forest Hill Village. The rent was $48 a month, which amounted to $12 a month each. Everything was old and kept breaking down, but it was a splendid pad for four young women.

We had elaborate charts about whose turn it was to make meals, clean, and shop, but of course there were always some slip-ups and arguments. Margarine had just been made legal. As a sop to the dairy industry, it had to be sold without color: it looked like lard, and the colouring—a hideous egg-yolk powder—had to be mixed in by popping a pigment capsule in its plastic bag and distributing the colour by kneading and squeezing. One of my room-mates refused to eat it, although it was a lot cheaper than butter. Another insisted that all potatoes be put through the ricer, as well as being mashed. We measured the coffee carefully, but never the water or how long the coffee perked. Beer was ordered by the case; each of us was supposed to put a check beside her name when she or a friend drank a bottle. We were always short half a dozen bottles when the case was empty.

Sometimes I would come home to find couples on every landing ardently saying good-night. Or sometimes I would walk out in the morning and find a total stranger asleep on the living-room sofa. We must have driven the woman doctor in the apartment below us mad with our noise and company: she was always banging a broom on her ceiling.

When I went back to Calgary for a visit that summer, I was struck by how "western" my home town looked. Cowboy hats were common on Eighth Avenue, and even the natives around the Queen's Hotel seemed exotic to my eastern eyes. My mother was impressed with my new clothes, but I could hear her on the telephone trying to explain away a more serious deficiency to her knitting group: "No, not yet. She's taking her time, I guess." At twenty-six, I think my parents would have been happy to see me married to any breathing male.

In Toronto I had made friendships that would become lifelong and met many current—and future—Canadian celebrities. The top theatrical event in Canada at the time was Andrew Allan's Sunday night "Stage Series" on radio. Alice Frick, a former student of F. M. Salter's was Andrew Allan's right-hand woman. She introduced me to her pale, rather languid boss, who was worshipped by everyone around him. I also met the "Stage" actors and writers—Tommy Tweed, John Drainie, Bernie Braden, and Fletcher Markle. Through a room-mate, I was introduced to Robert Weaver, who became one of the founders of the literary magazine *The Tamarack Review*, as well as the producer of the CBC's short-story series. For a year I did volunteer work on a small literary publication called *Reading*, the brainchild of Lister Sinclair, Fletcher Markle, and Alan Anderson, Alice Frick's husband. They and their friends wrote and edited. I and the other women volunteers worked on address labelling and mailing.

Emissaries from the West came to town occasionally. My aunt Maggie, who had remarried, had a pass provided by her railwayman husband. She arrived to visit a son, married and living in Toronto. I was summoned to Union Station for an audience.

Aunt Maggie had never been my favourite aunt, although I admired her. She was far too Victorian for me. Sixteen years older than my mother, she had raised six children entirely by herself. She had lived most of her life in Medicine Hat in a quaint old house built into the side of a hill. It looked like a cottage from the street, but stood three storeys high at the back and was lit by gaslights. Medicine Hat, as geologists said, was "a town sitting on hell"—a huge natural-gas field. When the town decided to replace gas with electricity, my aunt refused to have her gaslights changed. Visiting her was like stepping into a Gothic novel.

Now seventy-four, sitting in Union Station in the middle of June, she was wrapped in a fur coat, her tiny nose moist with perspiration, her prominent blue eyes cold with disapproval. Unlike my mother, she had been given a good education during the time the family lived in Toronto. Informed about what was being read and talked about, she quizzed me on my current interests, habits, and work. After I described my job, she sniffed and said reprovingly, "Why can't you do that kind of writing out West?"

It was a good question, and the message was clear: the family thought that I had had my fling. No great career had developed for me. It was now time to go back out West and settle down to teaching or marriage, as any dutiful and only daughter should.

Mama arrived the following summer. I had great fun showing her the sights—especially the corner of Sumach and King where her father's tavern had stood. We visited Niagara Falls and Casa Loma, and I even coaxed her into one of Toronto's new bars. (The previous February we had lined up for blocks in frigid weather to be able to say we had had a drink at the Silver Rail, Toronto's first cocktail bar.) I ordered my mother a Singapore Sling, which I thought she might not find much different from a soft drink. But teetotaller that she was, she shuddered with distaste at every sip and made me promise never to tell my younger brothers that she had been in a bar.

Looking back on those years, I realize I had a very good time. I might have gone on that way for a few more years, met someone, and married, as most of my friends were doing. My engineer friend had returned, and we decided we had both changed too much to consider marrying. Yet far from being immune to romance, I look back in bewilderment on how much time I spent in emotional turmoil over men I can barely remember today.

The pressure to marry was formidable. I was constantly being challenged by both men and women who implied that I was not married because I had not been asked. "What's a nice girl like you doing not married?" men would ask. Their wives condescended to me in much the same way my mother had looked down on my female teachers. They thought, charitably, that I was a sex-starved virgin.

In fact, I could no longer claim that dubious distinction. Curious about sex, and tired of wrestling matches in the back seats of cars and on narrow sofas, I had lost my virginity with a man I was very fond of but not in love with. Prudent soul that I was, I went to a doctor first and was fitted with a diaphragm. (To get it, I had to lie and pretend to be engaged.) From that time on, although I was discreet and certainly not promiscuous, I had sexual relations with anyone I felt genuinely attracted to, much as young women do today.

New suburbs were springing up on the outskirts of every Canadian city. Babies were being born in record numbers. Magazines and papers were filled with articles about families and the joys of parenthood. I wanted that, just as most of the young men I knew did. For them it was simply a case of becoming solvent enough to take on marriage with some young woman, who would then look after the domestic side of living, while they forged ahead in their careers. And who could fault them for that? My potential role in that scenario continued to bother me.

I felt out of step with my peers, even abnormal, for being so marriage-shy. I certainly hadn't found the splendid career I had been seeking. And as a single woman, I was depressed at how many married men propositioned me and were willing to cheat on their wives. I still stubbornly wanted both a career and marriage—but a more egalitarian marriage—even though the term had not yet been coined.

I continued to try to find a better job. I had some success in writing radio scripts for a local program, "Toronto Today." I also did some free-lance advertising and promotion. Try as I might, no more promising job materialized. With all the men flooding back into the work force, women were being squeezed out everywhere.

I had already been job hunting in New York. There were jobs, but not at salaries I could live on. I was interviewed by a senior editor at *Mademoiselle*, in her picture hat and Chanel suit, a vision of sophistication and success. As we talked, the unmistakable smell of soup wafted over an elegant screen in the corner. Finally the soup she had been heating for lunch boiled over with a hiss—and ended my illusions about the high life on a New York magazine.

In fact, young women from top universities in the U.S. were often subsidized by their families in order to get experience working for a magazine. For me, there was the added problem of getting a green card that would allow me to work in the U.S. at all.

I started reading, on a free-lance basis, the slush pile of unsolicited short-fiction stories that were sent to *Maclean's* every week. W. O. Mitchell, the author of the 1947 best-seller *Who Has Seen the Wind* had taken over as fiction editor. He knew of me through Salter. Mitchell, a wonderfully folksy, droll man, was trying to find better Canadian fiction than the formula stuff most magazines were publishing. Contrary to what he wanted, I had been trying to write formula fiction for the booming post-war U.S. market, but to date all I had to show for my efforts was a pile of rejection slips.

Frustrated in my efforts to find a better job, I regarded writing formula fiction as a good alternative. The plots were banal and basically the same. A young couple—they always had to be young—met in some "cute" way. Dog leashes got entwined. Identical-looking luggage was retrieved by the wrong owners. A favourite cliché was an initial introduction when they instantly hated each other. Then came some complication that forced them together under trying circumstances. True love blossomed. Clinch.

To finance my career as a fiction writer I needed a nest egg, and once again I had some money—$700—a fortune in those days. I had accumulated it in the same way I'd saved to put myself through university, by scrimping. I lived either in a tiny room or with other people. I always paid cash, abhorred debt, and still made many of my own clothes. Almost everyone I knew had a fur coat, but that, like a car, seemed extravagant to me. I wore cloth coats, which always seemed more fashionable than fur, and took taxis on the few occasions when I couldn't use public transportation.

With my little hoard, I planned to take another gamble on my future. In the spring of 1949, the Dominion Drama Festival was held in Toronto, and Deirdre O'Connell and I had bought tickets. Already a connoisseur of furniture and antiques, as well as being a lively conversationalist, Deirdre was a fashion plate compared with me. She had just departed from Eaton's and landed an excellent job promoting Walt Disney's commercial spin-offs, such as Mickey Mouse hats and T-shirts, in Canada.

She claims I had a different plan of action every night of the festival. The first night, I was going to go back to university and earn a Ph.D. The second, I was convinced that I should settle for a secretary-reader's job in a book-publishing firm and hope to become an editor. My next plan was to take another crack at New York. In a more practical mood, the following evening I decided to stick to advertising, buy a house, and, if I didn't marry, eventually try to adopt children—almost an impossibility in those days. Actually, that plan had little appeal. I hated advertising and I wanted my own children.

On the last night, I told her I was going to take all my money, quit Eaton's, and give myself a year to make it as a fiction writer. I intended to go to Europe to do it. As a good loyal friend, she was supportive, but I think she thought I was a bit mad.

In November 1949, a crowd of people saw me off at Union Station; I took the overnight train to Montreal, where I was to board the *Empress of Canada* and sail to England. In the week before my departure, three young men who had never given me any indication that we were anything more than casual friends suddenly decided they couldn't live without me. I didn't take any of this very seriously. One was gay. Another was "in love" with every second woman he saw, while the third really wanted to run off as I was doing but lacked the courage.

I've always advised young women who feel their lives are in the doldrums, at work or emotionally, to pull up stakes and strike out on their own, if they can. There is never a better time to do it, and it crystallizes a lot of things, including relationships with indecisive young men.

CHAPTER SEVEN

My Short, Unhappy Life of Sin

There is a snapshot taken of me in 1949 with my two younger brothers on the dock in Montreal. Eighteen and twenty at the time, they are tall, handsome young men, and I look unusually smart in a new coat, hat, and shoes. We make an attractive threesome, and what could be more natural than my brothers coming to Montreal to see me off to Europe?

The picture is deceptive: Jim and John were in Montreal quite by accident. They had driven from Alberta with two other young men to try out for the British Empire Games. I am clothed completely in going-away bargains from various departments at Eaton's. Even the collapsible umbrella I'm carrying is a farewell gift from my pals in the advertising department. Down in the hold of the ship is a set of unmatched luggage, as well as my old trunk, filled with all my worldly goods except my radio, record player, and second-hand sewing machine, which had been sold.

We look far more carefree and prosperous than we really were. Later that week, my brothers didn't even have the satisfaction of being chosen to compete in the games after their long drive. The snapshot, however, exemplifies something of the transformation that had taken place in Canada and in our family since the Depression. Few people would recognize this laughing, confident-looking threesome as the bedraggled little kids who had to walk across Calgary to the public pool at Riley Park because they couldn't afford a streetcar ticket.

During the war, Canada changed from an agricultural to a manufacturing country, and although we didn't know it then, we in the western world were about to enjoy an unprecedented period of prosperity.

My brothers and I were typical of our generation. We had grown up in poverty and hated it. We were determined to use whatever opportunities we were given to avoid that kind of privation. Although any child of the Great Depression was never sure that it couldn't happen again, we were modestly confident that with some luck, our lives would be a decided improvement on those of our parents—a hope my children and other young Canadians can no longer count on.

Travelling second class, I shared a cabin with three elderly British women who were returning to the Old Country after lengthy visits with daughters who had married Canadians during the war. They took to their beds as soon as we left the St. Lawrence and remained there for most of the trip. I don't think they were really seasick; they just enjoyed the luxury of staying in bed and having food brought to them by the stewards.

In fact, about half the passengers kept to their cabins on that choppy November crossing. Luckily, I turned out to be a good sailor and found lots of company among the rest of the passengers—some Canadian sailors en route to Britain, a gay couple from Vancouver, and a forthright former nurse from Rhodesia who, disgusted at life in B.C. with her retired brother, was heading back to Africa in spite of the troubles there. After diversions such as movies, crab races, or dancing, I would creep into my cabin sometime after midnight to the grumblings of my cabin-mates. "Every penny she has is on her back!" I heard one of them mutter.

Everything about the trip fascinated me, from the "coffee" served in the lounge the first day—it turned out to be half milk—to the strange Mulligatawny soup put before us at dinner. The strict hierarchy of the ship's staff and their obsequiousness particularly offended my more egalitarian North American sensibilities. Each day, as I took my chilly constitutional around the deck, I would hang over the rail, awed by the throbbing, confident sound of the ship's engines in that vast ocean. Sometimes the sea sloshed about as innocently as suds in a washing machine, and at other times it almost reached the deck in its cold, lashing rage.

As I became better acquainted with my cabin-mates, each related her story about the war. One, so British-looking that her face might have adorned a Toby jug, had had the side of her house blown away while she was taking a bath. Her sister had had to dig her own daughter out from under a pile of rubble after a raid. "'Ardly a scratch! Not 'er! It would take more than 'itler's buzz bombs to finish 'er off!" With their stalwart pride in simply having survived, they were typical of the Brits I was about to meet.

Not wanting to waste any opportunity to see something of England, I had decided to stay in Liverpool for a day before taking the train to London. I caught the flu just before we landed. That night, I had my first experience of life in Britain under coal rationing. I sat fully clothed and shivering in the cavernous dining room of the Adelphi Hotel, which was almost empty except for a few customers and four morose-looking waiters in tail coats. Unable to eat a thing, I returned to my room, where the chill seemed even worse. Though I piled my coat and sweaters on the bed, I spent a night of misery, either shaking and frigid or throwing up in the bathroom.

This inauspicious introduction to England did not improve the next day. In spite of aching joints and chills, I went out, determined to explore the city. It was a grim sight. Black with soot, its bombed-out buildings stood as dark testaments to the devastation of the war. I, an overdressed, pampered product of North American central heating, marvelled at the little British schoolboys with their bare knees, short open jackets, and long woollen scarves—their only concession to the cold.

That afternoon, the rain drizzled down the window of my train compartment as more of the war-scarred Midlands slid by. I left my trunk at Euston station and took a cab to the Montana hotel, a converted mansion in Kensington that had been recommended by a friend. I spent the next three days in a lumpy bed, sick to death with the flu. When I finally emerged, still weak and shivery, I ventured into the Underground and was thrilled to hear familiar names as they were sonorously announced at the stops: "Hyde Park Corner . . . Green Park . . . Piccadilly Circus. Watch the doors, please."

I got out at Leicester Square and wandered down to Trafalgar Square and Westminster Abbey. I fell in love with London, even in its shabby, scarred post-war state, that rainy November afternoon, and the love affair continues to this day. It still seems to me to be one of the most civilized and engaging cities in the world.

Once I had recovered, I found a room—little more than a clothes cupboard with a bed—on Nevern Road near the Earl's Court tube station. A gas heater kept the room cosy, and I could do simple cooking on an attached gas ring. For 13 shillings, I rented a radio for the entire winter and enjoyed the catholic and idiosyncratic programming of the BBC with its smorgasbord of offerings—from the habits of the nuthatch to Benjamin Britten's new opera, *Peter Grimes*. I caught up on Canadian news and collected my mail at Canada House on Trafalgar Square. Most Canadians living in Britain registered there, and after the first visit, the old Scottish doorman welcomed you by name.

I bought cheap Covent Garden season tickets for both opera and ballet, and sat "in the gods," enthralled by such post-war plays as *The Lady's Not for Burning* with John Gielgud. I also took advantage of the excellent free lectures at the National Gallery and the Tate, and the Italian, French, German, and British movies had never been better.

I would start writing at eight in the morning, take a break at ten and at lunch, then work until about three or four. Every afternoon I took off to either explore London or attend a lecture. At night I usually dined at a pub—pub food was good and cheap—near whatever theatre I was attending that night.

Mama acted as my agent. I would send a story off to an American magazine with a return envelope addressed to her in Calgary. I had provided her with the addresses of the magazines she was to send my story to next— if it was rejected—as well as money for stamps and envelopes. She also bought and mailed me copies of the U.S. women's magazines I was trying to write for, because they weren't available in England.

Ever since I had left home, besides her weekly letter, my mother sent me a box about every two months. It usually contained home-made cookies and other treats such as bed socks, home-made hand lotion, snapshots, and clippings. She continued the practice while I was in England. My friends at Eaton's also sent me CARE packages of tinned meat, cheese, tea, and coffee.

Four years after the war had ended, certain foods were still rationed, including sugar, tea, coffee, eggs, and meat. While standing in a sugar-rationing line-up, I noticed two young women with Canadian passports. The taller one, looking studiously bored, had the longest cigarette holder I had ever seen. Her more sociable companion and I started talking. They were both from Winnipeg and had worked for the Canadian Press. Vera Boysyk was living with friends outside London, and Enid Nemy, the smoker, was working in Bermuda and on a holiday in London. We had all heard of one another through Canadian Press pals, and soon became close friends, attending plays and pooling rations to eat in one anothers' digs.

A friend back in Canada had written to an older man she knew in London and supplied him with my address. He looked me up and entertained me royally at several posh restaurants I could never have afforded myself. After a few dates, he took me to see a handsome apartment in

Chelsea. I was so naïve that it didn't dawn on me until later that this fifty-year-old man was proposing to set me up there. Because I seemed indifferent to the idea, he continued to take me out without expecting any particular favours. He seemed to enjoy being seen with young women.

Another friend sent me two pairs of nylon stockings, which were almost impossible to get in London. He listed himself as "Rev. Montgomery" on the packing slip, and the package went through customs without being opened. I needed money more than nylons, so I sold them on the black market one dark night on lower Regent Street. It took almost no time at all. A man in a leather jacket came up to me and asked, "Selling something, luv?"

I replied, "Two pairs of nylons."

"How much?"

"Five pounds," I blurted out.

"Fine, luv." He handed me the money and disappeared.

Any further ideas I had about making money on the black market disappeared when I realized he could just as easily have been an undercover detective.

At a theatre matinee one afternoon in the spring of 1950, I sat beside an elegant young man who introduced himself as Arthur Truscott, a student from Oxford. After the play, he asked me to come along to a sherry party. As he handed me into a cab afterwards, he invited me to Oxford for a weekend and hastily scribbled down his address.

Not wanting to undertake this expedition on my own, I invited Vera Boysyk. The night before we were to leave, she didn't get around to washing her hair and decided not to come! I took the train to Oxford the next morning and was met by Arthur and his friend Hugh, who, with his even features, wavy hair, and glasses, looked like a shorter, more intellectual version of Rex Harrison, the movie star. The three of us spent the day sight-seeing—lunch at the Welch Pony, punting on the river, touring the various colleges. After dinner, we went back to Hugh's place to drink beer and talk. Around midnight we suddenly realized I was going to be locked out of my hotel if I didn't get an "after-hours" key.

Hugh raced off and came back with a six-inch-long piece of iron that looked like the key to the Tower of London rather than to a hotel. As I left his room, his landlady peered disapprovingly around the door. The next day, he was told he had to leave for having a woman in his room after hours. I also received a frosty reception from the porter, who clearly thought I was a low-life American debauching the cream of England's youth.

⌐ Soon after my weekend at Oxford, a letter arrived telling me I had sold a short story to *Maclean's*. Almost in the next mail, I got a letter from Almeda Glassey, the fiction editor of *Chatelaine*, to say they had bought one of my stories as well. Flushed with my sudden streak of luck, I decided to go to Paris at the end of March.

Before I left, I had another trip to make. I received a rare letter from my father, pointing out that all his many relatives lived in Scotland and I had not, as yet, paid them a visit. Shortly after this letter arrived, a tall young Scot appeared at my rooming house—an emissary from Aunt Bessie, my father's youngest sister. He, too, wanted to know when I was going to visit my Scottish relatives.

In mid-March, I left for Scotland for a two-week visit with Aunt Bessie and her husband, Davie, a burly red-haired Scot, at their home in Newton Stewart in Wigtownshire. A Scot is immediately treated like a member of the clan, so I was entertained warmly everywhere.

Two of my father's brothers and one sister lived on prosperous farms. Uncle Peter, who looked uncannily like my father, was about to retire with a good pension from the railway. One of Aunt Annie's sons, Peter, a brilliant scholar, was now working for British Petroleum in England. Aunt Janet, married to a tailor, Bob Straiton, lived in the next village with their four children. Her eldest daughter, Mara, was a teacher about my age. In Glasgow, Aunt Agnes's husband had just retired as chief meat inspector for Scotland. All my father's brothers and sisters, I realized, were far better off than my own family.

Meeting my Scottish relations helped me to understand my father better. Many of them were as outspoken as he was—but about Scottish nationalism. They had signed the Covenant declaring their wish to separate from England, and they argued vehemently that Scotland would be much better off as a separate nation.

In 1745, after the defeat of Bonnie Prince Charlie, the English carried out a genocide of the rebel clans. They forbade Scots to speak Gaelic, wear the kilt, and play the bagpipes. Such vengeful stupidity only made the Scots cling more fiercely to their native ways. Never forgetting what their ancestors had endured, they passed on their resentment like a virus from generation to generation. Sadly, the same kind of savage attempts to stamp out the heritage of various groups goes on all over the world to this day.

I must have seemed a curious, overgrown, decadent North American species to the hardy McCubbins. I was at least a foot taller than any of my female relatives. I caught a cold soon after I arrived, and because there was no central heating, they moved an electric heater into every room to warm it before I was allowed to enter. I was further embarrassed by my inability to master the way the toilet chain had to be pulled when I used Aunt Bessie's bathroom.

My dear little aunt Bessie with her beautiful wide forehead, fine features, and blue eyes was puzzled about why I had stayed in London so long and why I was going to Paris. She wanted me to remain with her and Davie and get on with my writing. She fervently hoped I would choose Scotland as the next setting for one of my stories. Later I found out that she also had a passion for writing. After she died, Violet McIntosh, her niece, discovered that she had secretly been writing love stories for the popular Scottish press.

After returning to London, I was in the middle of packing for Paris when Hugh, Arthur Truscott's friend, phoned and asked me out for a night on the town. Grandly, he took me to dinner at the Trocadero, where Edmundo Ross's big band was performing. It turned out that he had borrowed the money for this handsome blow-out, but had underestimated the cost by several pounds. Luckily I never left home without extra money, and we managed to pay the bill. By that time the Underground had shut for the night, and without taxi fare, we had to walk across London in the cold. It was not an auspicious start to our relationship.

Two days later I took the train to Dover, then the ferry and another train to Paris. I arrived at sunset, and as my taxi whirled me through the city, I caught heart-stopping glimpses of the Eiffel Tower and the Champs Elysées. After checking in at my Left Bank hotel, I ventured out to dinner on the Boulevard St. Germain des Prés, ordering a fine meal and a half bottle of wine. When the waiter brought a full bottle instead, I was too embarrassed to admit my mistake, so I drank it all and happily weaved my way back to the hotel and bed.

It was spring in Paris, but a cold spring. In April all heat is turned off on a set date, no matter what the temperature. I moved into a smaller, cosier hotel room on Boulevard Raspail, where I soon became *la grande Canadienne*. I continued writing in the morning, going out for a coffee and croissant, working some more, then sight-seeing and gallery-going in the afternoon. I went on foot—Paris is a wonderful city to walk in—and I found the Métro more like an underground streetcar than a subway. At night I ate at one of the many small restaurants on the Left Bank, its menu written by hand in purple ink and its waiters resplendent in long white wrap-around aprons.

I never lacked company. Paris in 1950 was full of American students and veterans using their G.I. credits for study. And the Left Bank was a United Nations of people—Africans, Asians, refugees from the Spanish Civil War, artists of every nationality and colour, and people of every sexual orientation. To find someone to talk to, all you had to do was sit in a bar.

One of my contacts was a Canadian who was living in Paris and trying to write. I will call her Katie. Although she came from a well-known and wealthy English-speaking Montreal family, she and her siblings were fluently bilingual. With dark curly hair, big blue eyes, and a lively wit, she was both brilliant and beautiful—and, at twenty-four, a remittance woman. Her family had packed her off to Paris, provided her with enough money to support herself, and hoped she wouldn't come home until she had decided what she wanted to do with her life.

When I met Katie, she was living in what had been the maid's quarters in a large apartment on Avenue Mozart near the Eiffel Tower. Because rents were controlled, she was paying a ludicrous sum equivalent to $12 a month for a small flat with skylights, a kitchen, a bath, and two bedrooms. She asked me to move in with her, which I eagerly did.

My new friend also owned an ancient Austin coupe just made for beetling around the narrow streets of the Left Bank. She introduced me to poetry and play readings, musicals, and small undiscovered restaurants off the tourist track. The Austin regularly broke down, and each time about a dozen Frenchmen would quickly converge to try to solve the problem. It was a great way to meet men.

To say I had a good time is ridiculous—I had the time of my life. Our favourite bar was the Bar Verte, run by a sad-looking Frenchwoman and her bustling little teenage son. Any night of the week you could get into a discussion about anything you wanted with people from all over the world.

One night, a soulful Spaniard sang love songs to me. Another evening, I argued fiercely with a group of Americans that if the U.S.S.R. was a threat on the left, I worried—as long ago as 1950—about their country's growing drift to the right.

Another night, we were sitting with an American poet and a rather boring American Ph.D. student who hoped to be hired by the U.S. State Department. A well-dressed French couple joined our group and bought us drinks. Around midnight, when the proprietor and her son were closing up, the couple suggested we go back to their place for a brandy.

They drove away with the poet, who was quite drunk. Katie, the other American, and I followed in her car. The husband drove at a furious speed, zipping into tiny streets and passageways as though he wanted to lose us. Katie, who knew the Left Bank as well as any native, was challenged by his manoeuvring, and we arrived at the couple's handsome apartment building almost at the same time they did.

More drinks were poured. Mr. State Department got more and more boring, the poet more and more drunk. The couple were polite but seemed strangely watchful and sober for people intent only on having a good time. Suddenly I wanted out of there. There was no use talking to Katie, who never wanted to go home, but I managed to attract the attention of the would-be Washington expert, and told him I thought our nice couple had some sinister plan.

I'm sure he thought they were Russian spies looking for recruits, and worried about his future career, he sprang into action. Gathering everyone up quite officiously, he herded us all out, including the poet, who could barely stand. A few days later, I was told the couple were well known on the Left Bank: they habitually picked up young men or women, got them drunk, and took them to their apartment for sex.

I might have stayed in Paris all summer except for Katie. Far more sexually active than I, she kept disappearing with men she had just met. She admitted she generally regretted these escapades, and wanted me to stop her from getting into them. It was a hopeless and unpleasant role trying to be her keeper. Sometimes she would disappear for days at a time while I fretted, checked the papers for dead bodies in the Seine, and wondered whether I should be informing the police.

Then Hugh arrived. He had managed to sell a story to the prestigious

New Statesman and Nation, and with the money he had come to Paris. We spent about four days together, and before he left I promised to go back to England to attend the ball at Balliol College in June. In any event, Vera and I had talked about hitchhiking around the British Isles in July. As I was getting ready to leave Paris, Hugh wrote that Arthur Truscott had been killed in a car accident, which made it seem even more important to go to England.

I never saw Katie again after she took me to the train, although we wrote for the next year. I received an invitation to her wedding to a penniless Spaniard I had met, a man who had slapped her around a bit even before I left. Then I lost track of her. A mutual friend later told me she had had three children, eventually divorced, then married an aristocrat and moved to the south of France.

By the time I returned to England, I was flat broke. The cheque from *Maclean's* had arrived and been spent in Paris. I had counted on the one from *Chatelaine* to finance my stay in England, but it hadn't been made payable through a European bank, and I couldn't cash it. In desperation, I had endorsed it and forwarded it to my bank in Canada, with instructions to put it in my account and send the money in care of Barclay's Bank in London.

When I got back, as I had feared, the money still hadn't arrived. As a back-up, I had written to my mother, explaining my predicament. I needed immediate cash, which I would pay back. At Canada House, I was elated to find a letter from her—and astonished by her postal note for $5. "This is from the money you left with me for stamps. I hope it helps. But I'm sure you will figure something out. You always do."

I realized then that I had been taking care of myself for so long that she couldn't imagine my not coping. Indeed, I did cope. I dug out my badminton and tennis rackets and sold them, which gave me enough money for the train fare to Oxford. I expected to bunk with one of Hugh's friends for the night.

I needn't have worried. I never got to bed. My stay was like something from Evelyn Waugh's *Brideshead Revisited*. As guests of one of Hugh's wealthy friends, we enjoyed a lavish spread of food and drank nothing but champagne all night long. One entire wall of the friend's room at Oxford had been decorated with orchids. The next morning, after a champagne breakfast, Hugh saw me off on the train back to London.

At some point during the evening, he had asked me to marry him. I countered that seeing him only at gala events in London, Paris, and Oxford wasn't a good way to judge whether we were marriage material. After more talk, I airily suggested we set up trial housekeeping after I got back from my travels around the British Isles. I probably believed this would never happen.

Once I was back in London, the bank draft from Canada had finally arrived and I was again solvent. The next day, I donned jeans and a T-shirt and, with a haversack on my back, set off with Vera on our hitchhiking tour.

We explored the south first—Stonehenge, Salisbury, Torquay, Plymouth, and Land's End—staying at youth hostels or guest houses. We had no trouble getting rides. People, particularly truck drivers, were always willing to pick us up. Often they went out of their way to make sure we got to a hostel for the night.

Then we started up the middle of England—Bath, Warwick, and through the Lake District to Scotland. Having been to Land's End, Vera insisted we go all the way to the top of Scotland to John O'Groats. On the way back, we spent a weekend on the Isle of Skye where, in spite of teeming rain, I fell in love with its rocky, rugged splendour, and the shaggy Highland sheep standing against the grey-green hills like orange dust-mops. (They had been dipped in an orange pesticide to kill ticks.)

We sailed to Ireland and travelled to Connemara on the west coast—a beautiful but stony land where Cromwell had driven the Irish in the seventeenth century. People lived in tiny houses built of stones; each had a goat and some chickens in a small yard with a stone fence. Most of the women wore black and looked far older than they probably were. Little boys were often dressed as girls because it was thought the fairies, who liked boys, would carry them off.

Outside Dublin we had trouble getting a ride. With night coming, we took refuge in a haystack. I wouldn't recommend it. We were cold and uncomfortable, as well as being kept awake all night by other haystack residents—mice. At dawn we were out on the road, anxiously awaiting a lift. Along came a donkey cart. Although it was slow, we were grateful for any kind of transportation to the next village and a hot breakfast.

We arrived in London one sunny afternoon at the end of July and headed straight for Canada House to pick up our mail. In our haste, we almost barged straight into an entourage headed by Queen Mary, the Queen Mother, who had been paying an official visit. I realized how unkempt we were from the startled look on her face.

A friend of Vera's tipped off the BBC about our odyssey around the British Isles, and within a week we appeared on one of the network's most popular shows, "In Town Tonight." They wanted publicity pictures, and we posed outside the BBC in jeans, T-shirts, and haversacks, while the photographer took low-angle shots from the pavement and kept asking us to thrust out our bosoms a little more. One of the other guests that night was Jimmy Stewart, the movie actor, whose "aw shucks" manner was the same on and off the screen. Later on, I sold a series of stories on the trip to the Calgary *Albertan*.

In the meantime, Hugh had rented a large housekeeping room with a hot plate and a shared bath down the hall in the Notting Hill Gate area of London. He had even purchased a few pots and pans, and, thoughtfully, a rather worn-looking second-hand wedding ring. He had informed the landlady that his wife would be joining him.

Since this had been my suggestion, I gamely moved in with him, but far from settling down in an idyllic love nest, I went into a state of catatonic shock. I was a hopeless amateur at "living in sin." I told my friends a cock-eyed story about bunking in temporarily with a distant cousin of my mother's in Surrey. (There actually was a cousin, and I had visited her for one weekend soon after I'd arrived in London.) I avoided giving anyone her phone number or name, using the excuse that she was old and crotchety. (She was married, middle-aged, and quite charming.) I still collected my mail at Canada House.

Anytime I wanted to see someone, I had to phone from the corner phone booth. Whenever I met a friend, I had to remember to remove the wedding ring, which I kept misplacing—at least once a day.

In my disturbed state, my writing routine completely fell apart. I would sit in front of the typewriter for hours, staring at the blank page. The inane plots of women's magazine fiction seemed absurd compared with all the turmoil I was experiencing at the time.

There was one aspect of being a stay-at-home wife that I think I carried out reasonably well. I religiously shopped and cleaned and had a hot meal ready every night—as my mother had taught me to do. And my old Girl Guide lore about making coffee the English way came in handy. In turn, Hugh instructed me how the English kept milk fresh without a fridge (by putting it on the windowsill in cold water, with a towel wrapped around it).

Hugh seemed blissfully happy with our arrangement. He had graduated in history with first-class honours from Oxford. While he was deciding on a permanent career, he had a temporary summer job arranging accommodation for foreign students. We argued quite a bit about his career. In England, a great deal depended on contacts. Being Canadian, I simply couldn't understand why he didn't just blanket possible prospects with letters of application, as you would in Canada.

As for my own troubled situation, in my logical way I spent my days making lists of the pros and cons. On the pro side, I found I actually liked living with a man—the companionship, the sex, the cosiness of reading Sunday papers in bed and then going out for breakfast. On the con side— far outweighing all the pluses—were the implications of taking the next, and to my mind irrevocable, step into marriage—which still frightened me.

At the end of August, Hugh landed a promising job writing editorials for the Liverpool *Post*, and once again urged me to marry him. He wanted me to find some kind of job in Liverpool as a start, and once we were more established, we would buy a house and have a family. Logically and intellectually, there was nothing the matter with this plan, but I still could not come to terms with the idea that everything I did from then on—except as a wife and mother—would be peripheral and not taken seriously.

Much as I admired and loved Hugh, I realized he was a normal man of the times. Marriage would make him more settled in his ways and more dictatorial—like most husbands—my father, particularly. Everything in my life and the lives of our children would be subject to his wishes. I had already noticed little stubborn traits and a tendency to want his own way. I could easily cope with them as an equal partner, but these would become much more pronounced if we married.

I could imagine myself countering these aspects of his character by jollying him along, catering to his whims, keeping peace in the family. In other words, we would settle down into a conventional marriage. In my heart, like having the ability to write shlock fiction, I knew I had all the skills needed for this wifely role. The real question was, Did I want it? The whole process seemed to diminish not only me but Hugh too.

Almost every morning, I awoke from a recurring dream in which I was pushing one of those tall English prams up a dark narrow passageway in Liverpool. The place was deserted, as lifeless as a city after a plague.

Worse, there wasn't even a real baby in the pram. I would be filled with ominous doubts.

On the plus side, I told myself I could continue writing, as I juggled the various jobs of the wife of an ambitious young man—looking after babies, maintaining a household, and entertaining friends and associates. However, I had already realized, the appeal of writing shlock fiction had completely evaporated. Having proved that I could do it, I knew that way of earning a living had lost all of its attraction.

There was another strong factor almost propelling me into marriage. True to my upbringing, I felt that having lived "in sin," I could only set my life right by marrying. And so, just before he left for Liverpool, I told Hugh I would marry him. I insisted that I go back to Canada first, to "get my feet back on the ground." Even as I told him, and he accepted this plan, I knew I was stalling for time.

After seeing Hugh off on the train for Liverpool, I moved in with a friend for the weekend. Since it was raining, we did almost nothing but sit in front of the fire in her cosy living room. It was like being back in my mother's kitchen. I mostly listened as the talk flowed over me—about her cats, the afghan she was knitting, the state of her plants, her plans for a trip to Spain—soothing, easy women's talk that required little response from me. I was grateful that she seemed completely unaware of the turbulence inside me.

After a short stay with Aunt Bessie, I spent a last weekend with Hugh in Liverpool, where he saw me off on the boat to Canada. As the huge mooring ropes splashed into the water and the horns sounded, my eyes streamed with tears. I looked like a devoted young woman distraught at separating from her handsome lover on the dock.

I was crying, I know now, not because we were parting but because I felt sorry for him, and angry at myself. He seemed so trusting and worthy and sure that everything would work out. And I? I was still overwhelmed by all my old doubts.

CHAPTER EIGHT

Editor-in-Waiting

"What's it going to be, gals?" The waitress's hearty familiarity was a shock after a year of English decorum. I was back in Canada. At 6:00 a.m. on a cool fall day, Deirdre and I were having coffee while waiting for my luggage to be unloaded from the train. She told me Eaton's had a job for me in the copy department, if I wanted it. Almost broke, I took it, and after a few days staying with her, I found a housekeeping room on Poplar Plains Road.

To the casual observer, I might never have left at all. But I had eliminated one option overseas. I knew that, although I could write popular fiction and probably support myself, I no longer wanted to. Now I faced a different dilemma: I still yearned to do something more substantial as a journalist, but I was engaged to be married in England, where an interesting job for a woman in any of the writing professions seemed even less likely than in Canada.

Toronto had changed while I was away. By 1950 it was beginning to transform itself from the uptight, WASP-run provincial city I had left into a modest version of the great cosmopolitan metropolis it is today. Bursting with newcomers from Europe fleeing the past, the city was undergoing a building boom. People were moving back to Rosedale and the Annex, renovating former rooming houses for family living. Toronto's perimeters were being pushed out to encompass surrounding farmlands, themselves turned into look-alike suburbs to accommodate the burgeoning post-war populace. Even a few international restaurants had opened—beyond the Italian and Chinese varieties.

Hugh's job as an editorial writer, it turned out, was much more limited than he had hoped it would be. And, like me, he was not fond of Liverpool. Britain, like a war-ravaged soldier, was taking a long time to recover, while Canada was enjoying a post-war boom. We gradually came to the conclusion that he should come to Canada, as many other Brits were doing.

Buying sheets, towels, and blankets for the first time, I began to assemble a modest "hope chest." Cooking pots, which had earlier been cast-offs from friends moving up in the world or five-and-dime bargains, became carefully shopped for items with a possible long-term future.

In the spring of 1951, I met Hugh's train at Union Station and took him to the room I had arranged for him. Almost immediately, he landed a job working at Current Publications, a small publishing firm. His job on *Quill & Quire*, a magazine for the book trade, was one I would dearly have loved for myself. Although I was a bit put out at how easily he had landed such a prize, I was not surprised. Almost all trade publications at that time were edited by men.

We moved for the summer to Centre Island, where I rented a self-contained flat with its own kitchen and bathroom, opening onto a little garden. When I signed the lease, the yard was still covered in snow, but well into a very wet July, it was a muddy pond with ducks swimming around, quacking happily. Although Hugh rented a small cabin close by, he spent most of his time at my place. We were living together yet not living together, because common-law relationships were severely censured back then.

Hugh expected that we would be married as soon as possible. I, on the other hand, kept putting off setting a date until we were more established. In fact, being "established" was really of no consequence to me then, or now. What still bothered me was putting myself into such a dependent position with anyone—even a young man who gave me every reason in the world to believe he loved me.

Then, in the fall of 1951, when I was almost thirty years old, I got my first real break. Byrne Hope Sanders, the editor of *Chatelaine* magazine, was looking for a new advertising promotion person. I applied for the job and was hired.

Sanders, a fine motherly figure, was a trail blazer for her time. Born in South Africa but educated in Canada, she had worked on newspapers before being named the second woman editor of *Chatelaine* since its launch in 1928. Until the 1960s, Maclean Hunter had a rule that if two people on the staff married, one of them had to quit. It invariably meant that the woman left. When Byrne married her art director, it was he who quit and free-lanced from home, while she stayed on as editor, even after the birth of her two children.

She was one of a small number of Canadian women who had any kind of public profile—and a good job outside the traditional teaching, nursing, or secretarial work. By the time she interviewed me, she was a Canadian institution—*Chatelaine*'s editor for more than twenty years as well as a Commander of the British Empire for her stint away from the magazine, heading up the Wartime Prices and Trade Board.

The job I was hired to do turned out to be something of a non-job. The salesmen had a bad habit of phoning editorial people for tips on features, and even pressing editors to include certain products, to help them sell ads. With an office in editorial, I was to be the liaison between the advertising and editorial departments—a kind of spy for the ad men. I also arranged promotions. I would approach Eaton's, Simpson's, or the Dominion grocery stores to try to persuade them to support some upcoming editorial feature with window and floor displays. Neither part of my job kept me busy, and as usual, not being busy worried me—especially when everyone else in editorial seemed to be working flat out. I confided to Hugh that I expected to be fired any day because I didn't have enough to do.

My other worry was not fitting into the ladylike ambiance of the office. Each day when Byrne arrived she would greet everyone personally and make sure we were all right, like a mother checking on her children. "They're all so *nice*," I used to wail to Hugh. "Hardly anyone ever says anything bitchy about anyone else." Of course that was far from true. There was a lot of tension—as there is in any office with creative, ambitious people. Keeping everyone happy and trying to personally deal with any signs of strain was Byrne's way of managing her almost all female staff.

And there were signs of strain. About a year before, Gerry Anglin had been commandeered from *Maclean's* by Floyd Chalmers, the dynamic president of Maclean Hunter, to be associate editor. Chalmers wanted *Chatelaine* to be run more like *Maclean's*. Gerry was an ex-newspaperman who had worked for the *Toronto Star* and then the *Maple Leaf*, a paper for the armed forces during the war. Genial and enthusiastic, he nevertheless must have been a jolt to the gentility of Byrne Hope Sanders's *Chatelaine*. The staff used to joke that he didn't need a telephone when he phoned in the downtown area—his voice was so loud that all he needed to do was open the window.

About three months after she hired me, Byrne resigned as editor. She and her brother, an advertising executive, were starting the Gallup poll in Canada. Chalmers immediately appointed Lotta Dempsey, who had been a feature writer for *Chatelaine* during the thirties, as editor.

In the dislocation that often occurs when a magazine era ends, the editorial staff seemed even more harassed and overworked than usual. I kept offering to take up some of the slack, and both Gerry and Lotta were more than willing to try me out. I wrote captions, headlines, and blurbs, and edited copy. I became so engrossed in what I was doing that I would stay late every night and work over weekends. Within six months, they decided to take me on as an editorial assistant.

I began doing rewrites and generally helping Gerry. He was an excellent teacher and I an eager pupil. Once again, I found myself being pressed to become a copyeditor. We would lunch at the Silver Rail, Old Angelo's, or the Purple Lantern in Chinatown—where you could get a meal and a martini for about 65 cents. Gerry would run on about the joys to be found in correcting someone else's bad research or meticulously polishing and sharpening someone else's disorderly, sloppy prose. I was even more stubbornly opposed to becoming a copyeditor than before. I loved magazine work. I was willing to do almost any job—except, to my mind, the totally uncreative task of copyediting.

I kept pushing to be allowed to write articles and Gerry finally agreed. My first piece was a filler on ice cream. Soon after that, Deirdre and I decided to take a bus trip to New Orleans, where Pops Volmer, another friend, was now living with her husband and a new baby. Gerry suggested I take notes and hire a professional photographer to shoot a few pictures while there. When I returned, I wrote a piece for the magazine about the delights and hazards of bus travel.

➤ In the fall of 1951 I moved into a small one-bedroom apartment in Parkdale. Apartments were so scarce that you had to know someone moving out to get one—which is exactly what I did. I still wasn't ready to marry. Although Hugh and I kept discussing it, every time we tried to settle on a date, we quarrelled—mostly initiated by me, I'm sure—and plans would be postponed again.

With little money and no furniture, I started buying second-hand pieces at auction sales and refurbishing them. A stripped down oak poker table with sawed-off legs became a coffee table. A dilapidated old wire-back chair I bought for $4 got a new lease on life when I re-covered it in black denim. My experiments in colour were less successful. I painted my bathroom what I had hoped would be a sophisticated taupe. It turned out to be a bilious khaki. After telling the whole office that it was so repulsive that I would have to board it up, I returned from lunch to find a mink-covered chamber pot sitting on my desk—a gift from Posy Boxer, *Chatelaine*'s fashion editor.

Rosemary Boxer was blond, bouncy, vivacious—and rich. She told me she had once purposely worn her "old" mink coat when she visited her millionaire father. He had immediately written a cheque for a new one. I kept the chamber pot on my coffee table for several months as a conversation piece, and then—fur being acceptable in those days—I made a hat out of it.

Lotta Dempsey was a dream boss—enthusiastic, full of ideas, generous, and open-minded—but she stayed as editor at *Chatelaine* for only a little more than a year. She much preferred writing to editing, and when the *Globe and Mail* offered her a feature column in 1952, she returned to her first love—newspapers.

Once again, Floyd Chalmers tapped the *Maclean's* staff, picking John Clare, the managing editor, to be *Chatelaine*'s editor. Clare had sold a number of fiction stories to American women's magazines, which probably convinced Chalmers that he had some qualifications for editing one. Clare and Anglin were charged with bringing to *Chatelaine* some of *Maclean's* success, as well as trying to find a new formula to improve *Chatelaine*'s sagging profits and circulation.

Having a male editor of a women's magazine was not unusual. In fact, North American women's magazines—with the exception of *Chatelaine* and its Canadian rival, *Canadian Home Journal*, which was edited by Mary Etta MacPherson—were all edited by men. However, in all the annals of publishing I doubt that there was a more unhappy and reluctant editor of a women's magazine than John Clare.

A gruff, pipe-smoking man, he had been a war correspondent, like most of the men at *Maclean's*. He could be a witty and polished raconteur when he chose, but much of the time he preferred to silently smoke his pipe and stare at people—a disconcerting habit that sent his new employees into spasms of nervous chatter to fill the heavy silences. As women, and used to Byrne's concerned nurturing, they expected something more than an occasional grunt in exchanges with an editor. Passing his office as he hunched over his typewriter pecking something out in his intent, two-fingered fashion, I often fondly thought he looked like a bear—a bear who could miraculously type.

Clare was bemused by Posy Boxer and the fashion department, and left them alone. Considering himself a gourmet—he liked his steak rare and lots of garlic in his pasta—he had strong ideas about features on food. He despised the fussiness of the recipes produced by Marie Holmes and her small staff in Chatelaine Institute.

That Christmas, the institute staff decided to do a little public relations. Decked in holly and singing carols, they toured the office dispensing gifts of cookies and punch. Clare happened to be in the art department. On hearing the cavalcade approaching, he barricaded himself behind its glass door. The carollers paused, then tried the door. He heaved violently back on it. They faltered, undecided on their course of action: they could see the outline of what was clearly the editor, like a behemoth behind the frosted glass. Finally, they quavered into song again and continued uneasily on their way.

We always had a farewell party when anyone on staff left. In Sanders's regime, it was tea or perhaps wine in Chatelaine Institute with a going-away present and speeches. Clare's idea of a party was in the *Maclean's* manner—a room at the King Edward Hotel with lots of booze and deli food supplied by the institute staff. On one occasion, the institute poured an entire bottle of gin into a watermelon and then drilled holes into it. Everyone was supposed to stick straws in the holes and drink. Clare was apoplectic at what was, to him, a shocking waste of good liquor.

In his better moods, he could be gentlemanly and good company. Professionally, he was an accomplished, graceful writer, and I learned a lot from him. But in the area that interested me the most—article ideas for *Chatelaine*—Clare and I might as well have been on different planets. I peppered him with suggestions that I thought appropriate for a women's magazine. I rarely even got a response. In my dealings with both Anglin and Clare, I continually hit what seemed to me colossal blind spots about what was going on in the minds and lives of their readers.

Gerry Anglin, who had a growing family, was far more open to ideas than Clare, who was married but childless. Anglin often came up with useful ideas about family travel and raising children. And he made one brilliant coup. He persuaded Dr. Marion Hilliard, his wife's obstetrician, to contribute her common-sense ideas on women's health and life in articles for *Chatelaine*. To ghost write the series and add that intimate, emotional touch that became her trademark, he hired June Callwood.

"Sex—a Woman's Greatest Hazard" and "Fatigue—a Woman's Greatest Enemy" were so popular that women kept their copies for years. "Menopause—a Woman's Greatest Blessing" broke all newsstand records up to that time. Generations of women had dreaded menopause as the beginning of the end of their lives. Now a doctor was assuring them that it was only a new phase, liberating them from pregnancy and child care, and signalling the start of many more years of good living.

Finally Clare and Anglin gave up trying to turn me into a copyeditor, and hired Elizabeth Reeves. Small, plump, and superbly adept at all writing skills, Elizabeth did exactly what Gerry had been talking about: she sat in her office, perfectly content to polish, correct, and enhance other people's work before it was set in type.

During the early 1950s, Chalmers and the top executives at Maclean Hunter constantly held up the *Ladies Home Journal* as the exemplar. It certainly was the most successful and profitable of all the women's magazines in North America. I considered it a relic from another era—the pre-war days when a few people lived graciously, and everyone else aspired to that lifestyle. Etiquette was still heavily emphasized. Table settings were far more important than food. Decorating articles assumed readers could afford to engage tradespeople to do the actual work. Any suggestion that every woman wasn't jubilantly happy as a housewife and mother was, like most other unseemly matters, simply not discussed.

In the real world, where I lived, all my friends were building their own furniture and doing their own decorating—as I was. Young people entertained much more casually than their parents. How food tasted was far more important than how it was served and with what china and silverware. Every mother slavishly followed Dr. Spock's advice, as if his book on baby care was a foolproof recipe for raising perfect children.

It seemed to me that far too much was expected of young married women of my generation—which is another reason I was so marriage-shy. If the marriage failed or the children turned out badly, all the blame fell on us. We hadn't been sexy enough or accomplished enough—as wives, mothers, hostesses, cooks, temptresses, and home decorators.

Better educated, and less inclined to be martyrs than their mothers, married women—in contrast to all the media propaganda—were frequently unhappy. John Clare's wife, for example, desperately wanted to work. She became so exasperated at one dinner party that she threw a plate of spaghetti at him. Finally he reluctantly agreed to "let" her take a job.

Usually wives didn't air these personal problems except among very close friends and relatives. Putting myself in their place, I realized that I would go mad with boredom and frustration at the effort to be the perfect, little hem-stitched housewife that the magazines, including *Chatelaine*, were urging me to be. I suggested we start an advice column. Although all the men on the magazine, including the art director and assistant art director, were married and all but Clare had children, they thought I was "sick" for implying that women like their wives might not be perfectly contented.

From time to time, I would be invited to a meeting to discuss some upcoming feature. Often the idea would be fairly superficial and involve photographing lots of beautiful women. I usually thought it stank, and as politely as possible said so. Clare would become so exasperated that he would threaten to fire me and hire "Sadie Glotz"—a fictitious character he frequently used to let me know I was completely replaceable.

To counter my opinion, Posy Boxer would be brought in. As a wife and mother of two children, Posy was thought to exemplify the "real" women of Canada. (I was fairly certain she believed no one read the magazine—with the exception of the fashion and beauty pages—but nerdy suburban housewives hunched over coffee in sloppy housecoats.)

On one of these occasions, Clare went to great pains to lay out all the arguments, starting with the negative points before he presented his own—and opposite—position. Posy, wanting to please and bored with the discussion, leaped in during his careful recitation of the negatives. Batting her huge lashes furiously in agreement, she exclaimed in her most supportive manner, "You're right! You're absolutely right!"

Clare was flabbergasted.

Gradually, in spite of how much I irritated Clare at times, I became the staff writer and general dogsbody. After all, I was there and willing to throw myself into anything that needed to be done. I wrote a waspish little piece about office politics. I planned and wrote a complete issue about the suburbs—the advantages—and hazards—of living in those split-level houses with picture windows.

Finally I was sent on an out-of-town assignment—to Nova Scotia on a free CNR train pass. In two weeks I did the research for stories on the life of a fisher wife in one of the outports; on a fine, pioneer newspaperwoman, then battling crippling arthritis; and on Halifax's most scandalous romance—that of the Duke of Kent, Queen Victoria's father, and his long-time mistress, Madame St. Laurent, who lived there in the nineteenth century.

Stan Furnival, the art director, became so excited about the picture possibilities of the fisher wife's story that he and a photographer flew to Nova Scotia. I don't know what they expected—perhaps some busty glamour girl in hip boots. When they saw a rather plump, middle-aged housewife in an apron, they returned, declaring I had missed the real story completely—her husband!

They had sheets of dramatic pictures of this rugged fisherman and his boat, and a few—barely enough to cover the story—of his wife. I reminded them that this was a women's magazine, and although readers might like to know the dangers the husband faced, they were far more interested in his wife's story.

The Duke of Kent saga was a great success, but Clare killed the story on the newspaperwoman. She was too old, he said. That broke her heart—and mine.

I then dreamed up a series I was certain would be a big hit with women—as well as a sure circulation builder. Calling it "The Women of Canada," I proposed that I visit all the major cities, and identify the female movers and shakers in each one, interview them, and have them photographed.

Everyone liked the idea. The art department saw it as a photo story in the style of *Look* and *Life*, the great post-war photo magazines. Paul Rockett, a trendy young photographer, was assigned to the job. To my dismay, by the time I boarded the CNR train for Winnipeg, my first destination, I had been manipulated into serving as Paul's secretary. I was to do all the preliminary work and set up the photography schedule before Paul flew in to do the pictures. There were to be captions, Furnival emphasized, but no story—art directors hate type except as convenient blocks of grey to set off the photographs.

By the time Rockett arrived, I had selected and interviewed the women and set up several options for the photo schedule, with a variety of possible backgrounds and situations. I found, for the first time, how stimulating it can be to work with another truly creative person. Whatever ideas I had for each photo, Paul always improved on them. We turned out to be a good team.

Once back in the office, I made sure the story of each woman contained so much interest that the captions had to be quite lengthy. Then, to give readers in other parts of the country some idea of what it was like to live in a prairie city, I insisted, to the disgust of the art department, on writing about Winnipeg, its history, and the influences that had shaped its women. The first article in the series was a great success, and I went on to write about Calgary, Vancouver, Regina, Hamilton, Ottawa, Montreal, and Halifax.

In 1955 Alberta and Saskatchewan were celebrating their fiftieth anniversaries as provinces. I again went west by train, this time to interview pioneer women who had settled what had been the North West Territories. Amazing old women with gnarled hands and half-fearful eyes told me how they had travelled by train to Winnipeg, then by coach or ox-cart following buffalo trails. They spoke of the incredible loneliness of life in tiny cabins far from civilization with no other woman for miles, of crops hailed out, of babies dying because there were no doctors. They described winters when the blizzards were so fierce that their husbands had to tie a rope from the house to the barn so that they would not lose their way back.

I coaxed them to trust me with precious old photos stored in their trunks and albums. The sepia photos showed pretty, hopeful young women in Victorian finery on the brink of the greatest adventure of their lives. Often standing beside them were their stern-looking young husbands and cherubic children.

Once again, I ran into trouble with the art department. Furnival, to his credit, tried to give work to promising newcomers. He had already assigned my story on pioneer women to a talented young artist called Harold Town. I knew Town and by 1953 owned one of his lithographs. He cut a highly eccentric figure in Toronto. Sharp, witty, and vulgar, he posed as a dandy in specially tailored suits with a cane, a tie pin, and a Victorian hat. According to Furnival, Town had not one but two mistresses—one in Toronto and the other on Centre Island.

To illustrate the story, Town produced a heavy black sketch of horror on the prairies, with a menacing native looming in the foreground. He had incorporated the title into his design, making it difficult to determine what the story was about. Furnival spread Town's illustration across a double page and vetoed all the pictures I had so painstakingly coaxed from the old women. Pictures would spoil the illustration, he insisted.

I dug in my heels and fought. Women didn't give a damn about Town's illustration, I argued. It was ugly, frightening, and off-putting. Readers would want to see how the old women had looked when they were young, like themselves, and they would be curious about the men they had married and the children they had borne. Arguing the case before Clare and Anglin, I won a partial victory: small pictures of the women were added.

In the mid-1950s the admirable and extremely capable Almeda Glassey, who had been Byrne Hope Sanders's right-hand woman, left *Chatelaine* for New York. I campaigned for her job as associate editor in charge of the departments. Clare hired a Canadian who had worked on *Town and Country* in New York instead. When she left in 1955, after scarcely a year, I finally got the job.

I was in charge of all the service departments—Chatelaine Institute (recipes, consumer research, and house care), under Marie Holmes, very much a grande dame and old enough to be my mother; fashion and beauty, under the irrepressible Posy Boxer and her equally striking, black-haired assistant, Eveleen Dollery; and crafts, under Wanda Nelles. Gardening, child care, and decorating were free-lanced—the latter to Catherine Fraser, the mother of John Fraser, who later became editor of *Saturday Night*.

It was my first taste of directing other people skilled in their own fields, helping them nurse ideas through photography, layout, and final-copy stages. I not only had to come up with ideas, but also keep the editors on track for *Chatelaine*'s audience—not, as some of them would have preferred, to satisfy the more exotic tastes of *Vogue* or *Gourmet* magazines' readerships.

Everyone had been writing her own copy. Those who were not writers by trade had been having "writer's block" over a few lines on casseroles or summer hair-dos. I solved the problem and speeded the process by completely taking over the copywriting. "Just give me the facts and I'll do the writing," I assured them. Posy, who had no pretensions to being a writer, was more than happy to hand me the job.

In 1956 Gerry Anglin left *Chatelaine* to become editor of *Canadian Homes and Gardens*, another Maclean Hunter publication. I replaced him as managing editor. At last I was in charge of what I really wanted to do—

assigning articles for the main body of the magazine. Soon after, Clare turned over to me the job of planning each issue, which had to be done four and five issues ahead of the publication date.

By this time, Clare's disaffection with *Chatelaine* was complete. He had developed a serious drinking problem. In the morning, he was hung over, grouchy, and difficult to talk to. By the afternoon—after a long, liquid lunch—he was more creative but often quite irrational.

About once a week, we would go out to lunch together. After he'd had two drinks, it would be possible to discuss future plans with him, but it was an ordeal. He insisted I match him drink for drink, although he must have weighed a good hundred pounds more than I. In those days I could hold my own—as most women in my business had to learn to do. After lunches with Clare, though, I always took a trip to the washroom, put my finger down my throat, and threw up: otherwise I would never have been able to go back to the office and function with any degree of efficiency.

I had a small circle of women friends, who were also single and career-minded. Besides Deirdre O'Connell, I regularly saw Helen Gougeon, the vivacious bilingual food editor of the newspaper supplement *Weekend*. Helen later married the playwright and author Joe Schull, had three children, and opened one of Canada's first kitchen shops with Deirdre. Joan Chalmers, Floyd Chalmers's daughter, was the art director of *Mayfair*, another Maclean Hunter magazine. Great fun and totally unstuffy, she never took advantage of her close relationship with the company's president. Once a week I lunched with Helen James, who was in charge of women's programming at the CBC—both CBC's radio show for women as well as its new afternoon TV show. Because she was articulate, well-informed, and wise, it was a great relief to mull over with her our various problems with male bosses and mostly female staff.

Although my relationship with Hugh continued, I still balked at marriage. Impatient with the delay, he had broken up with me after a couple of our quarrels, and even had a short relationship with another woman. We always drifted back together again. In 1955, on a trip to Europe with the Women's Press Club, I met his family. His mother couldn't understand why we hadn't married. Frankly, neither could I, except that I still dreaded that final step.

Hugh had moved to a much more promising job at the CBC, working for a producer in the drama department, where he had a distinguished career and eventually ended up as head of all arts and science programming. In the spring of 1956, he gave me an ultimatum: either we married or we parted for good. Even faced with this stark choice, I couldn't bring myself to agree to that decisive act. It had nothing to do with him, and everything to do with my own deep fear of losing my independence. We parted.

To raise the money to come to Canada, Hugh had sold one of his favourite possessions—a first edition of T. H. Lawrence's *Seven Pillars of Wisdom*. As a parting gift, I bought another copy and sent it to him.

Now thirty-five, I faced the serious possibility of never marrying. However, I still very much wanted children, and I started looking into the possibility of adopting. I found it was out of the question for a single woman in Canada. Even trying to adopt an abandoned child from a Third World country would have been extremely difficult.

A few friends were raising children alone, but it was out of necessity, never choice. While I firmly believe a man and a woman in a good egalitarian relationship provide the best environment for a child, I see nothing wrong with a single loving parent or a same-sex couple raising children. I do have some problems with women resorting to artificial insemination. What do you say to a child when he or she asks, as I did at the age of four, "Who is my father?" "I don't know" is an even worse answer than the one I received. Although I didn't particularly like my father, at least I knew who he was and, in time, had a chance to recognize and respect his good qualities and learn to live with his bad ones.

A few months after I broke off for the last time with Hugh, I was asked to go sailing by Jim Knight, a friend who worked for *Canadian Homes and Gardens*. The 38-foot yawl on which he crewed was a handsome craft, and there must have been at least ten people on board that night. The lake was as flat as a sheet of glass. I sat beside a Czechoslovak psychiatrist whose novel approach with women was to claim he could click the bones in his ears. He invited me to snuggle up to hear this phenomenon.

The owner of the boat, David Anderson, was a genial giant of a man. Tall, with greying curly black hair and glasses, he looked so normal that I immediately assumed he had to be married—probably with four children and a wife in some trendy suburb like Don Mills. That evening proved so uneventful and sailing so tame that I decided it was not for me.

The next week Jim phoned me from Kingston. He was once again sailing on David Anderson's boat, this time in the Bay of Quinte. Would I like to come down for a day? I had discovered that David was a bachelor and a lawyer. Jim had met him while working on his election campaign for the Ontario Liberals. Although David had put on a respectable show against his opponent—the sitting Tory member and minister of Education—he had lost.

Jim explained that David had a court case on Wednesday, and I would be able to get a ride with him that night. My immediate response was that I had too much to do and couldn't possibly take off sailing in the middle of the week. We left it that David would phone me in case I changed my mind.

That week the thermometer hit record highs. My office, facing south over Dundas Street with no air conditioning, was like a sauna. Realizing I wasn't getting much done, when David phoned, I jumped at the chance to get away. I told Clare I was taking a day off to go sailing and he growled, "Nobody ever gets back from sailing in one day." Without knowing much about sailing, I assured him I would be back on Friday.

On the two-hour drive to the Bay of Quinte, I discovered that David came from Prince Edward Island, where his father and brother still ran the family farm. His mother had been a schoolteacher, and she and his father had decided that every one of their six children would have a university education, though it meant sending them away to high school. The farm had been mortgaged to help put David, his four brothers, and his twin sister, Doris, through university.

He also told me that he came from a long line of bachelors. Four of his father's brothers had never married.

The wind was whipping across the bay the next morning, and David had everyone up at dawn. This time the sailing was exhilarating, totally different from that first placid trial run in Toronto's harbour. The boat heeled over beautifully, and David put me through the ultimate test—I cooked breakfast in the galley without complaining while he tacked—which meant every five minutes or so the boat lurched in the opposite direction. Everything would go flying if you didn't hang on to it. (Once I realized that it was possible to keep the boat on an even keel for cooking, I never put up with that again.)

I insisted on getting back to Toronto for the weekend, even though my plans were not all that exciting. As I said goodbye, I knew I very much wanted to see David again. We dated all that fall, did a lot of talking, and found that we had a great deal in common. I was attracted to his open, affable manner, his keen interest in politics, and his joyful approach to life. What particularly impressed me, though, was his openness to the idea of my having a career as well as children.

I considered it something of a miracle to have found someone so suitable after all my doubts about marriage. Having been foolish enough to have lost one good man, I was determined not to do it again. In March he proposed. I accepted and we set the date for May 24.

The following week, David told everyone he knew that he was getting married. Still racked by doubts, I only admitted I was engaged when people phoned me to check all the rumours—one was that David was marrying the now-divorced Posy Boxer! In the meantime, I heard that Hugh had met someone, and he married shortly before I did.

Soon after our engagement, I met Harold Town in an elevator full of executives from the ninth floor returning from lunch. "Hi, McCubbin," boomed Town. "I hear you got knocked up and have to get married!" I ignored this typical Town sally, but there was a deadly silence until, thankfully, I escaped on the sixth floor.

Just two weeks before my wedding, John Clare's doctor ordered him to take a job with less pressure. He was returning to *Maclean's*. I genuinely liked him, and was pleased for him, although certainly not unhappy to see him go.

Perhaps Clare had wanted me to succeed him, but I doubt it. He certainly had never mentioned the possibility, and I think he would have, if I were being groomed as his successor. Like all *Maclean's* editors, he considered women useful workers and researchers, not people who were given titles and actually ran things. No matter, I thought. I had been carrying the magazine for the past year, and everyone, including Chalmers and the publisher, Cy Laurin, knew it.

I was not even offered the job. Floyd Chalmers dropped into my office and casually told me that Gerry Anglin was going to be the new editor of *Chatelaine.*

My reaction was immediate. "Then I will resign."

"But why?" He was truly astonished.

"Because I have been carrying this magazine for the past year, and I know I would make a far better editor for a women's magazine than Gerry."

"But," said Chalmers—and I will never forget his exact words—"you are going to be married and you will become a hostess and a mother." (Even today the emphasis on "hostess" astonishes me.)

"I don't care," I replied. "I like Gerry, but I've worked for him, and I know I can edit this magazine better than he can." What I really meant, but didn't say, was that I was tired of running the magazine under a male editor, and I was not going to do it any longer. "Either I get the job or I'm leaving."

Chalmers was a man I greatly admired. Self-made, he had joined Maclean Hunter after the First World War, and by the time he was thirty was editor of the *Financial Post*. As president, he was the driving force in changing Maclean Hunter from a cautious, pragmatic company that published the *Financial Post* and dozens of small business magazines like *Sanitary Engineer* and *Canadian Grocer* into a company with world-wide interests and assets.

Later, as a philanthropist, he used his business acumen to help put the Canadian Opera Company and the Stratford Festival on solid financial footings, and he personally underwrote the opera *Louis Riel*. Fervently believing people like himself owed something to Canada, he set up the Chalmers Foundation for the Arts—one of Canada's largest and most important private foundations.

For a short period, this tall, handsome man played to the hilt the role of head of one of the largest publishing firms in North America. Arriving at the University Avenue door in a chauffeured Jaguar, he would stride into the building attired in a bowler hat and a pin-striped suit. As the last president of Maclean Hunter to come up through the editorial side of the business, he had more integrity and vision about what a publishing company should be than any other boss I ever worked for.

Nevertheless, although he liked women—and women certainly liked him—he was awkward with them. Because he was always probing and contentious in his personal relations, I rarely had a conversation with him during which we could agree on very much at all. Above all, he was a gentleman of the old school. He respected me as a talented woman, but it never crossed his mind that given the opportunity, I would not prefer to drop everything to further the career of a husband. I think he best summed up his attitude to women after I had won a writing award. As he presented it to me in front of the whole company, he remarked, "What I like about Doris is that she looks like a woman, acts like a lady, and works like a dog."

If Chalmers was taken aback by my reaction, I was equally perplexed by David's attitude. Although he had encouraged me to believe he supported the idea that women had the right to have a career, and couples should share the raising of children, faced with the actual possibility, he was not nearly so positive. He couldn't understand why, since we were marrying— and he presumed that was more important than any job—I couldn't just continue doing what I had been doing. Why did I have to be editor—or quit? He had expected me to work for at least a year or two so that we could buy a house and get settled. In fact, never having been much of a saver himself, he actually needed me to work for a while.

I tried to explain how impossible the situation was for me. Then I gave him what I think was a reasonable alternative: I was willing to quit and free-lance. I had again saved my share of a good down payment on a house. It was up to him to come up with his share. As a well-established writer, I knew I could earn a respectable living, and, with my biological clock ticking away, we could get on with having a family. If I stayed at *Chatelaine*, it would only be as editor.

I thought then, and I think now, that it was a reasonable decision. Worried about our financial situation, and concerned that I might resent leaving *Chatelaine*, David reluctantly agreed to my becoming editor: by this time the company, not wanting to lose me, had grudgingly offered me the job.

And so in the spring of 1957, against almost everyone's wishes, I became editor of *Chatelaine*. The company put a codicil in the agreement. I could have the job, but I would still be called managing editor, at least for the time being. The message was clear: if you get pregnant, everything goes back on the table.

CHAPTER NINE

Having Babies the Company Way

David and I were married in the late afternoon of May 24 in the United Church. I would have preferred what is now common practice—a do-it-yourself ceremony held in a private home—but in 1957 the only alternative to a church wedding was a bleak little ritual at City Hall.

Our wedding must have seemed a strange affair to some of the guests. We had planned to invite only a few very close friends to the ceremony, to be followed by a large reception at the Toronto Women's Press Club. I asked only Helen James, Deirdre O'Connell, and my bridesmaid, Joan Chalmers. My gregarious husband-to-be started with a small list but kept adding more and more people. We ended up with only two on the bride's side of the church and about thirty on the groom's side.

Our parents were not present. Because David's parents were teetotallers, he argued, "If your parents come, my parents will insist on coming, and we won't be able to serve any liquor." I agreed that a party without liquor would have been ridiculous, given our circle of friends. Today I can't imagine why I went along with this bizarre suggestion. We were in our mid-thirties and had been running our own lives for years. Later, when I met David's parents, they didn't strike me as people who would arbitrarily impose their views on anyone.

Nevertheless, I phoned Mama and explained that we would be leaving immediately after the ceremony for a honeymoon in Mexico, and it would be much more sensible if she came for a longer visit when we returned. It was a decision I have always regretted. Of course my mother wanted to attend the wedding of her only daughter. I believe I hurt her deeply by suggesting otherwise.

Finding a place to live was the next problem. I wanted to move into one of the new high rises then going up all over the city. David couldn't abide them. Since he owned no furniture, he wanted to rent a furnished house, but after dragging me off to see a couple of musty suburban relics where some elderly soul had just died, I protested, "I break out in a rash when I move out of the downtown core."

We advertised and found a charming little red-brick house on McMurrich Street, which couldn't have been more central—a block west of Yonge just above Davenport. It was one of a group of row houses built by Jesse Ketchum for his factory workers in the nineteenth century. We were enchanted with the tiny iron fireplaces in each room, the original pine floors, and big old-fashioned windows. A kitchen had been tacked onto the back, and a coal furnace occupied the basement, replacing the original scullery. We had the floors sanded and polyurethaned and the whole house painted fresh, bright colours. On viewing our treasure, David's partner, Richard Roberts, remarked gloomily, "It looks like the kind of house lawyers move into when they are disbarred."

Right up until the actual afternoon of the wedding, I had been too busy with arrangements to be nervous. When I began to dress, I could hardly get my shoes on the right feet. By the time the limousine arrived to take me to the church, I was catatonic—and the walk down the aisle was the longest I had ever taken. Although any reference to my "obeying" David had been removed from the vows, I didn't need the minister's fearsome eyebrows and solemn words to impress on me what a grave step I was taking. When it came time to put on the ring, it was too small, and David barely managed to push it on. We giggled nervously at each other in the limousine all the way to the reception.

My finger was turning blue and our first priority that evening was removing the wedding ring. When we left for Mexico the next morning, David sported a shiny wedding band, but I, having spurned an engagement diamond, wore no ring at all. I was finally legitimate and never looked more like a woman having an affair.

The night before, we had phoned both sets of parents. My mother's comments to David amused us hugely. "I'm so happy," she told him. "Now Doris has someone to look after her." I don't think she understood, even to her dying day, that what I wanted more than anything was to be able to look after myself and make sure that every other woman in the world could do the same.

After my anxiety about the wedding, the honeymoon was remarkably relaxed, except for one incident. At the resort in Taxco, we stayed in a small cottage, where a huge black tarantula joined us during the night. In the morning, I saw it, screamed and, like a traditional bride, called on David to kill it. He wisely suggested we vacate the room as quickly as possible and report the intruder. Two men came, looked at the spider, and left immediately. They returned with the owner and an assistant and all of them began to argue. Finally, a large matronly woman arrived with a sack and a broom. She dropped the sack on the spider and smacked it with the broom several times, then strode off, ending the matter.

After we returned from our honeymoon, my new husband sank into a deep depression that I could only interpret at the time as a severe aversion to married life.

David had set the wedding date to ensure we would be back in time to vote in the federal election on June 10. For the Liberals, it was a disaster: Louis St. Laurent's government lost its majority, and the Progressive Conservatives under John Diefenbaker formed the government. I couldn't believe that anyone could take politics seriously enough to become depressed over it. However, David, who believed the Liberals would be out of power for years, certainly had. It wasn't until after what became known as the Kingston Conference the following fall that David regained his usual buoyancy. At the conference, David, Keith Davey, Royce Frith, and Dan Lang—all, except David, later appointed to the Senate—began the process of rebuilding the party in Ontario. He and Dan Lang set out to scour the province for new people to run, and in the next election both Ontario and Toronto voted Liberal.

I remember the days living on McMurrich Street with great fondness. Of course there were problems. I was organized, and David, like many bachelors, was disorganized and hated planning ahead. He liked to decide at four o'clock in the afternoon to invite twenty people home. I, being responsible for the food and the state of the house, discouraged such spontaneity.

Nor could we agree about money. As a partner in a small law firm, David enjoyed a good but irregular income and disliked bookkeeping. Having lived all my life knowing exactly what money I had and where it was being spent, I insisted on a budget. After three consecutive evenings trying to work one out, we gave up. Instead, he bought all the groceries and paid the taxes, hydro, and water. I paid for everything else—my own expenses, the furniture, any renovating and decorating, and later, the household help and the children's expenses. It wasn't a solution I would recommend to anyone else. Although we roughly paid the same amount of money, each of us believed he or she carried the major share.

Soon after we met, David had told me solemnly that he had been a coeliac as a child, and as a consequence, his growth had been stunted. I found this comment, by a six-foot-three giant, hilarious. It soon became clear, though, that this early experience had left him nervous about his health, and that we had completely different attitudes to being sick. I had been raised in a family with a father who considered illness a personal affront to his own robust health and lineage, and my Christian Scientist mother believed that it was mostly in your head. While David was for the most part strong and healthy, he was always expecting to be sick. I soon learned that a goodly dose of tender loving care on my part was far more important than any medicine in getting him back on his feet. It was a role I never did play well, and grew to resent.

In spite of these differences, we greatly enjoyed each other's company, and I think we were generally good for each other. I was a workaholic. David, on the other hand, worked hard at what interested him and thoroughly enjoyed relaxing, which I needed to learn how to do. And he was far less critical than I. Although I was the movie freak, and would often have to coax him inside a theatre, once there he invariably had a much better time than I did.

His amiable and gregarious nature drew people to him. He was always bringing home new acquaintances, and we entertained a great deal. He persuaded me to buy more flamboyant clothes. I talked him—a big, handsome man—into buying better, more classic clothing. After we married, we threw out all his socks and gave away thirty cheap T-shirts that no longer fitted.

I learned to drive his car and immediately bashed in a fender—an act he took with remarkable sanguinity. The following year, we decided to buy a new car. Because I couldn't abide any of the North American models with their protruding fins and torpedo-like bumpers, we began to look at imports and bought one of the first Citroëns in Canada. Revolutionary for its time, the Citroën so startled other drivers they almost ran off the road. Once, as we approached a filling station near Stratford, the owner was so taken aback by our strange-looking car that he ran inside and closed up for the day.

The following March, I discovered I was pregnant. I was delighted but well aware of the maternity rule at Maclean Hunter: at five months, women had to resign. However, because the magazine was doing well by this time, and I planned to continue working, a new approach had to be worked out for me. The executives—all men, of course—decided I would take six weeks off—four weeks before the baby was born and two weeks after.

As I was not engaged in physically strenuous work, I believed I could easily work right up to the baby's due date. I wanted all the time off after the birth. Getting my pregnant self out of sight was far more important to the company, though, than accommodating me and the baby. I didn't press the argument then, realizing how far they were already stretching company rules.

David wanted one of his male friends to be my obstetrician and the birth to take place in Toronto General Hospital. I was adamant that Marion Hilliard be my doctor and the baby be born at Women's College Hospital, which was staffed entirely by women and had a fine reputation, particularly in obstetrics. David went along with my plans but said in all seriousness, "If you are having any difficulty during the birth, I will get you out of there and over to Toronto General." I told him in no uncertain terms that the last thing I needed to do in the middle of delivering a baby was to change hospitals.

I was devastated when Marion Hilliard was diagnosed with cancer and later that spring died—she had become a real friend. Another excellent doctor, Sheila Hill, helped with the delivery.

At that time, many women were rebelling against the overuse of drugs while they were in labour and were refusing anaesthetics. Although we had run several articles in *Chatelaine* on the subject of natural childbirth, I had no time to take any of the courses. Once the actual delivery started, it seemed only natural to breathe deeply and reserve my strength for the next push. The birth itself was one of the most painful, yet exhilarating, experiences of my life. Having been rather a duffer at sports, I remember thinking with wonder and surprise, I was made to do this, and I'm quite good at it!

On November 19, 1958, after ten hours of labour and nine days after my thirty-seventh birthday, I gave birth to a healthy ten-pound baby boy. We called him Peter David, and like all mothers I fell in love with him instantly. I don't think there is anything quite like the warm, almost freshly baked smell of a newborn. I spent hours watching him and examining his tiny toes and fingers, the brave way he tried to hold up his little head, and the peremptory manner he moved his mouth around—like an MGM lion cub searching for food.

On the second day, without any warning, I was overcome by a severe case of post-partum blues. I couldn't stop crying and I didn't know why—except that I felt profoundly sad about bringing this perfect, wondrous little creature into an imperfect, deeply flawed world. Later, when David appeared, I vehemently told him, "We've got to have another one." He was naturally astonished—we had already agreed to have more than one child. "I couldn't stand it if anything happened to him" was my only explanation.

I stayed in the hospital almost a week, which was standard practice in those days. In talking to other patients, I realized how many women looked forward to those few days when they could enjoy some respite from the duties at home. I'm not surprised by recent reports that our current custom of sending mothers home after a couple of days short-changes both the baby and the mother.

Having a baby while holding down a job was so unusual then that some of the myths about me are still repeated. It was rumoured that I corrected page proofs on my way to the delivery room! Not true—although I did work for *Chatelaine* at home before Peter was born. The staff was small and overworked, and there really was no one to replace me. I kept in touch with everyone by telephone, and Joan Chalmers, who by this time was my art director, delivered material to be read every day after work and picked it up the next morning. Meetings that I needed to attend were held in my living room. This regimen continued while I was in the hospital—except for the meetings—and during the two weeks after Peter was born, while I was at home.

Like other healthy women, I fully expected that I would be back to normal the minute we left the hospital. I quickly realized how fragile a woman can feel after a birth and how enormous the responsibility can be. Once home, I would have liked nothing more than six months at least—not two weeks—to get accustomed to the profound changes in my life.

Today in Canada women are given anywhere from the minimum of eighteen weeks to six months' maternity leave after the birth of a child. Many countries do much better than that—almost a year's leave with close to full pay, the option of staying home for two more years without pay, and a guarantee of the same job on the mother's return to work. In some European countries, the partner automatically gets ten days off at the time of the birth, and either parent can take the longer leave.

In Canada and the United States, having babies is barely accommodated by society. Both countries have more women working outside the home than almost any other industrialized country, and both pay an inordinate amount of lip service to "family values." Yet, until 1993, the U.S. had no federal law granting women maternity leave—even today they get only six weeks off, without pay.

If every young Canadian had to serve in the army for two years—as they do in countries like Israel—we would think it only right that they be given special training and assistance to help them return to the work force afterwards. Having a baby is an even greater service to the country, but companies penalize mothers: taking away their jobs, seniority, and even dismissing them if they can get away with it, which, in spite of the law, they often do.

Once home, I was busier than ever. Besides work from the office, there was a long list of new tasks: sterilizing bottles, making formula, bathing the baby, and doing the laundry—we had no diaper service. Because it was November, I also had to stoke the furnace. David had announced that the upcoming weekend was his last chance to go duck hunting. In retrospect, I think I should have told him to bloody well stay home and help me, but always independent, I rather grumpily told him to go. Although I ran a magazine with a staff of close to twenty people, that weekend I felt completely swamped. Peter and I managed to get through, of course, but I remember settling down with a pile of manuscripts at night with immense relief: here was a task I knew I could do.

Determined to find the best care possible for my small son, I offered $40 a week in my advertisement—almost twice the going rate in those days—for a woman to come in each day to look after him. For two days, the phone rang off the hook, and after interviewing more than twenty women, I chose Mabel Saunders, a short red-haired Scot who had been highly recommended by someone I knew. She proved to be a wonderful, dependable, loving woman who stayed with my children until the last one was in school.

At first, I was afraid she would supplant me, but that never happened.

My children instinctively knew I was their mother, and "Nana" was their baby-sitter. It's true that I wasn't home every day when they came back from nursery school to report what they had done. But I don't think it ever hurt them to describe everything to Nana first, then repeat it later to me and David, and to realize that three people, rather than two, were deeply interested in everything that happened to them.

After Peter was born, our little house seemed far too small to accommodate all the baby paraphernalia we had collected. We started looking for a bigger place, and bought a three-storey brick house on a corner lot in Rosedale in the spring of 1959. Built in 1906, and owned for years by the same family, the house had had little done to it. Like many young people, we renovated it from top to bottom, installed a new kitchen and powder room, and turned one of the five bedrooms into a den. We also made mistakes: one was tearing out an old pantry to make a breakfast nook. The thin pantry walls had been built with a purpose—to keep food cold—and it was always chilly.

My mother had visited us soon after we moved into McMurrich Street. Although she was not impressed by that funny little house, the Rosedale home did win her approval. What pleased her even more was David's boat, on which she proved to be a good sailor. She nonchalantly braced her sensible walking brogues against the opposite seat when the boat heeled over, as if she had been doing it all her life. After she returned to Calgary, she kept requesting a picture of the boat. I couldn't imagine why—until it finally hit me. Mama, modest to a fault, never boasted about any of her children. I had long been an embarrassment to her—as the only unmarried daughter in her knitting group. A picture of David's "yacht" would be convincing proof that I had finally, though belatedly, entered the world of respectable and successfully married women.

The following year, as planned, I became pregnant again. This time I told no one at Maclean Hunter, but as my condition became more and more apparent, I could imagine the consternation in the ninth-floor executive offices. When I was about six months' pregnant, Floyd Chalmers suddenly appeared, looking like a thunder cloud. He made a few attempts at small talk—a skill he had never bothered perfecting, and one he clearly didn't enjoy. All the time his eyes roamed the room, looking at the ceiling, the floor, my Dictaphone, my in basket—everything except me.

Finally, from under his bristling eyebrows, he shot me a look and asked, "When are you going home?"

"I am going home the day after I have this baby."

"Well, when are you going to have the baby?" he demanded.

"I'm not going to tell you," I replied.

I pointed out that I had worked from home all through the last four weeks of my first pregnancy at great inconvenience to the staff and myself. Because I was not in any physical danger as a magazine editor, I intended to carry on until I had the baby, then spend at least two weeks at home before coming back to work.

He sat stewing for a few tense minutes while I told him that I planned to arrive at the office late and leave late to avoid being too conspicuous. After I assured him I would not be having the baby in the lobby, he reluctantly went along with my plans.

Joan Chalmers, who, no doubt, helped persuade her father we women knew what we were doing, picked me up and took me home every day in her red MG. It became more and more of a tight fit as the months went by. When Stephen Robert weighed in at almost eleven pounds on April 13, 1961, I could understand why.

For a woman of that time, I was earning a high salary. In addition to Mrs. Saunders, I was able to hire a weekly cleaning woman, but I needed some live-in help as well. In my advertisement for a live-in baby-sitter, I offered free room and board in exchange for baby-sitting at night when we were out, and one afternoon over the weekend. Our first live-in baby-sitter, Chris Hjorth, stayed with us for three years and became a good family friend.

By the summer of 1963, when my third baby was born, the old Maclean Hunter policy of forcing pregnant women to quit had long gone.

On July 31, the baby was overdue. I looked at my calendar for the next day to find it full of meetings I didn't particularly want to attend, as well as people I didn't want to see. At lunch I went out, bought a bottle of castor oil, and that night took a good dose of it. The next morning at five o'clock, I began to have labour pains and barely made it to the hospital for the birth of my third son. Although I had had my heart set on a girl, the fact that the baby was another boy mattered not at all once they laid him in my arms.

For several months, our third son had no name. I suggested numerous possibilities to David, and both grandmothers sent long lists of their own.

David seemed unable to agree to any of them. When he was indecisive, it usually meant he knew what he wanted wasn't what I wanted. Rather than discuss it, he would stall until, exasperated with waiting, I told him to have it his way, and that's exactly what happened. After receiving a second letter from the provincial registrar with the barely concealed implication that I was a delinquent mother (probably sitting around in beer parlours indifferent to the naming of my child), I flung the letter at David. "Name him whatever you want—Ezekial, even!"

He immediately sprang up, rushed upstairs, and came down with the form filled in. The baby was named Mitchell Richard after Mitchell Sharp, the Liberal cabinet minister, and Richard Roberts, David's partner. Although I admired Mitchell Sharp's integrity in public office, I would never have named a baby after him, and I heartily disliked my husband's partner.

As an editor and the mother of small children, I had to put up with quite a bit of personal and public abuse. The first time I met Laura Sabia, the well-known feminist, we were on a panel together. Although I was clearly pregnant, she had the audacity to state that mothers with small children should be home looking after them. I politely told her and the audience, composed mostly of well-to-do women who seemed to agree with her, that such decisions were the responsibility of the women concerned and their families—not society as a whole. Many women, I pointed out, had to work outside the home. Why, I asked later in an editorial, was nursery school considered an enriching experience for the children of well-to-do, stay-at-home mothers while day care was much maligned? The answer, of course, was that society didn't want to pay for good, publicly supported nursery schools for the children of working mothers.

At a party or after a speech I would occasionally be backed into a corner by a complete stranger. "Why aren't you home looking after your children?" she would snarl. I realized that personal problems and individual frustrations drove these women to attack someone they hardly knew.

The "right" of women with children to work outside the home was a controversy that raged in the press all through the fifties, sixties, and even the seventies. The irony is that women have worked to help support their families all through history. Before the Industrial Revolution, they toiled on farms alongside their husbands, milking cows, looking after chickens, weaving fabric, sewing clothes, cooking and, above all, producing large numbers of children to provide workers for the farm. Even after the Industrial Revolution, at least 25 per cent of mostly poor women worked outside the home out of necessity.

In post-war Canada, Laura Sabia, who became a good friend, was simply articulating the conventional wisdom of the day. Working mothers like me were "bad" mothers.

The status quo was, of course, reinforced in the schools. In an interview during which I expressed concern about the erratic spelling of one of my sons, the principal assured me it didn't matter. "When he grows up, he will be an executive, and he will have a secretary who can spell." Taken aback, I told him I didn't approve of girls who were good at spelling always having to work for males who hadn't bothered to learn.

On another occasion, I received a call from Stephen's Grade 4 teacher, asking me to use my influence to persuade a male reporter to talk to the class about journalism. I pointed out that I was a journalist and would happily talk about my job, but she firmly said she would prefer a male. Feeling somewhat cowed, I actually did ask a friend of mine to talk to the class. After he refused, saying he thought the idea was ridiculous, I phoned the teacher and she finally agreed to settle for me. Armed with colour separations, page proofs, and even lead print, I eagerly descended on the school, thinking, At last I am going to impress my son!

Throughout my speech, two little boys regarded me sceptically, and when the time came for questions, one of them said, "That magazine of yours—it isn't very big, is it?"

I replied that it was the biggest magazine in Canada.

The other one piped up, "But you're not really the boss!"

I took great pleasure in telling that little male chauvinist that I was, indeed, the boss.

With the children in school, I needed a housekeeper rather than a nanny. With great sadness, we said goodbye to Mabel Saunders, although we kept in touch until she died. I began the search for a reliable live-in person. One I hired turned out to be a secret drinker who raided the liquor cabinet. Another tippler came reeling down the stairs just as I was leaving for Halifax on a business trip.

What I needed, of course, was what every successful man I knew at that time took for granted—a wife. Men with far fewer professional responsibilities than mine had wives to look after all the things I still did myself. As a working woman, I needed what we still don't have enough of in Canada today—good supervised day care and after-school care for children.

In an editorial for *Chatelaine*, I lamented the fact that it was easy to find a top secretary, but tough to find someone to look after my home and children. I said quite honestly that of the two jobs, child care was more important to me. My secretary was so insulted at even being compared to a housekeeper that she stormed into my office and quit on the spot.

I remember lunching with a man who ran a much smaller magazine than mine. "My job is so pressured," he told me, "that when I get home at night, my wife has a double martini waiting for me. She keeps the kids away until we've had a nice gourmet dinner. Once I've unwound enough, I see them before they go to bed."

My life was markedly different. When I got home, my household help would reel off the day's events. One of the boys had thrown a toy car in the toilet, blocking it. Another was running a fever and might be coming down with measles. And we were out of milk. Whatever the office worries, they disappeared as I changed gears and coped with a fresh set of problems.

David, in spite of our pre-marriage conversations, had been raised in a household with a strict division of labour between men and women. Although typical of his generation, he did try to help. He took over the grocery shopping, which always resulted in an oversupply of pickled herring, Worcestershire sauce, olives, and steak. (Never mind, he did it.) He looked after house repairs, and when the children were older, he supervised breakfast. All the rest was up to me.

Being human, he took advantage of the situation. While an extra salary allowed him to spend far more time at politics than he ordinarily would have been able to manage, he complained from time to time about how much other wives did for their husbands—laying out their clothes, running all the errands, and entertaining clients. (In fact, between his political and professional commitments and my own widening circle of friends and acquaintances, we entertained and were entertained several times a month.)

His contribution to getting us out of the house to go sailing would be to sit in the car honking the horn. Once I asked him to help the boys wash their hands and faces and get dressed while I prepared the food for a day's sail. When I got into the car, I turned to see three darling but filthy little faces and the strangest assortment of clothes imaginable.

Life was seldom the way it was supposed to be in *Chatelaine*—as I frequently reminded readers in my editorials. It wasn't easy back then—and it still isn't easy. Any woman who combines a career and raising a family has to have an ample supply of energy. I was lucky in that department, having never required more than four or five hours' sleep. I always knew that no matter how tired I might be at bedtime, I would wake up early the next morning—or even in the middle of the night—and be completely recharged.

Another big factor, of course, is a partner who is willing to shoulder half the work. Today, although statistics indicate women do far more than half the work in the home, a more enlightened generation of men make this goal more possible.

Like most working mothers, I carried a full load of guilt. I made sure I was home most nights to have dinner with the boys and put them to bed, complete with bedtime stories. It seemed to me then—as it must to many women at the same stage of life—that everything was moving too fast: at times I felt I'd mounted a roller coaster and was desperately trying to hang on.

I anguished over the fact that I wasn't home making ingenious Hallowe'en costumes. At the spring fair there was a parade of children wheeling their decorated bicycles, which some mothers had worked on for weeks. My kids decorated their own bikes with the crepe paper, cardboard, and glue I had supplied. I thought their inventions were quite original, but they didn't stand a chance against the full-time moms.

On reflection, I gave my children the leeway I had never had as a child to express themselves through hobbies, art, or music. They were encouraged to build anything they wanted, including a huge, multi-roomed doghouse in the back yard. It was very impressive—although our multi-pedigreed dog shunned it. Later on Peter cut a hole in his closet door to convert it into an office, and put his bed on stilts to make more room for his fish tanks and drum set. They were also allowed to keep frogs, mice, and gerbils. They all learned to skate, ski, swim, and play tennis. I think I probably overwhelmed them with lessons in anything that temporarily interested them. Some lessons—art for one, guitar and drum for another—worked, just as others failed.

At times, guilt caused me to lose my perspective and common sense. We had enrolled Peter in the Institute of Child Study, a renowned nursery school. At that time, it was like getting your child accepted into Harvard. But Peter and the institute didn't hit it off at all. I visited the school several times, and although it had been advanced twenty years earlier, I thought it rather rigid then. Why should Peter be a butterfly when he wanted to be a wolf? But who was I to challenge this eminent institution?

My wise old mother brought me to my senses. "I don't understand the problem. Peter doesn't like the school, and neither do you, so why are you keeping him there?" We took him out and found another less prestigious nursery school, where he got along fine.

The boys all learned to cook, iron, and clean up after themselves—as my brothers had. Later when Mitchell craved homemade pies, cakes, and bread like those his grandmother made, I explained to him that I had never been able to make passable pie crust and had no interest in becoming a bread baker. With the aid of a cookbook, he learned to make better pies than I ever could.

One day, Stephen pointed out that the *Moby Dick* pattern on his bedroom curtains—I had lovingly run them up on my sewing machine before he was born—were not suitable for a young man approaching puberty. I went downtown with him to choose other curtains, but we couldn't find anything to fit the oddly sized windows in our old house. Knowing he had taken sewing at school, I had a sudden inspiration. "If you want new curtains, why can't you make them yourself?" He chose material he liked, and after buying lining, headings, and rings, I sat him down at the dining-room table one Saturday afternoon while I worked upstairs. Whenever he got stuck, he called for help. At the end of the day he had new curtains, exactly the way he wanted them.

In general, I loved my life, but at times I longed for just a few minutes for myself. David always claimed that I would go anywhere at any time to give a speech—an observation that had some truth in it, and I told him why. It meant that for twenty-four hours I had no responsibilities for anything or anybody else.

Finally, I hit on a brilliant idea I highly recommend to other women. Every Saturday afternoon, I hired a baby-sitter and disappeared for three hours, sometimes just to wander around the art galleries, sometimes to see a movie, sometimes to simply walk and browse. What was most important to me was that no one knew where I was—no one could reach me—not my office, and not even my family. It gave me the psychological break I needed.

Though I had no idea where David was for hours at a time, or when he would be back, he was certain I was having an affair. I laughed hysterically at the idea. "I haven't time to have a lover," I assured him.

To counteract our rather hectic schedule, it was my idea to build a cottage in Prince Edward Island, close to the Anderson family farm. From my first sight of those wide, almost empty, white beaches, I had been thrilled by the thought of children exploring the endless treasures served up every day by the ocean—navy blue mussels with their pearly interiors, frilled pale green seaweed, tangles of brackish rope, wood so soft and wave worn that it felt like satin, and battered lobster traps and bottles.

My younger brothers were both married with children and working overseas—John an executive in an American oil company and Jim an engineer in Pakistan on the Colombo Plan. I saw the cottage as a haven where we could all meet but be close to the wonderfully warm Anderson clan. The family farm still had chickens, pigs, cows, and even a horse. My mother-in-law baked fresh bread and rolls every day, as well as keeping us supplied with homemade cookies and pies. My incomparable sister-in-law, David's twin sister, also called Doris, cleaned the cottage and stocked the fridge every year before we arrived.

Three of David's brothers had left the island—Robert was a heart specialist in Halifax, Allan taught biology at Laval in Quebec City, and Ken had a business in Kingston. They often came back to PEI with their families in the summer. With Don's four children on the farm, there were many cousins about the same age. We played tug-of-war and volleyball and staged races on the beach—I always came last in the mothers' race. The children had wild water fights in an anchored rubber dinghy that we had bought at an army-surplus store.

At night we played baseball at the farm. Everyone from the smallest child who could hold a bat to the oldest adult took part. Back at the cottage, we read by a log fire, toasted marshmallows, and often stayed up till all hours trying to finish a jigsaw puzzle. The cottage became a sanctuary and, to this day, many of us go back every year.

The sixties had even been charitable to my parents. Although my

TOP LEFT: *Joseph Laycock, my ambitious grandfather, on the eve of his departure for Canada.*

ABOVE: *My twenty-year-old grandmother, Ann Leigh, just before her marriage.*

LEFT: *My mother, Rebecca Laycock, posing as a cowgirl at sixteen.*

ABOVE: *My father, Thomas McCubbin, on leave during the First World War. He's seen here with his sisters, Agnes and Janet.*

RIGHT: *My first photo opportunity, with Fred pushing and Reg holding me. Even at that early age, I seem to be viewing the world with scepticism.*

ABOVE: The proud occupant of my first apartment, with mostly hand-made furniture.

LEFT: Off to Europe in the fall of 1949, determined to crack the popular magazine short-story market.

After travelling around the British Isles, I posed with my friend and road companion, Vera Boysyk, for publicity shots taken for BBC-TV's "In Town Tonight." Jimmy Stewart was the other guest the night we appeared.

My wedding to David Anderson, May 24, 1957.

Paul Rockett and I mug for the camera while working on "The Women of Canada" series for Chatelaine *in 1954.*

Biking with my three sons (left to right): Peter, ten; Stephen, eight; and Mitchell, six.

Receiving the Order of Canada in 1973 with a magnificently attired Stephen.

Accepting the Persons Award from Governor General Ray Hnatyshyn in 1991.

A meeting with fellow feminists at the Women's Centre in Singapore, 1991.

Feminist friends. Left to right: Kay Sigurjonsson, me, Pat Hacker, and Kay Macpherson.

mother sorely missed her two sisters who had died, she greatly enjoyed her grandchildren when they came to visit. My father had retired in 1956. Mama still owned their small house, but they worried constantly about having enough money to look after themselves in old age. Any serious illness would have wiped out their savings, and they dreaded being a "burden on our children." When Canada brought in Old Age Security in 1952 and then medicare, two more grateful people would have been hard to find, especially later when my father was hospitalized twice for ulcers and a heart condition.

Then, after all the years Father had expected his ship to come in, it finally did in 1966. I returned from a trip to Germany to be greeted by a long-distance call from my thrifty mother, who never phoned other than in emergencies. I assumed that my father, who had been in the hospital, had died. Not at all. He had won $60,000 in the Irish Sweepstakes. They had been featured on the front page of the Calgary *Herald* and interviewed on TV and radio.

Mama immediately wanted to take a trip, but everyone thought my father was too frail. However, a few months later he went off on a spree with his Canadian Legion buddies and came home late at night none the worse for wear. The next morning she told him that if he was well enough to get drunk and stay out all night, he was well enough to take a trip back to the Old Country. She booked the tickets that day.

My brother John was living in London with his family. He met their plane with a limousine and showed them the city in style. Then they flew to Scotland, where Father hired a bus to chauffeur all the McCubbin clan on a tour of all his old boyhood haunts.

After a couple of weeks in Scotland, they planned to leave for Tockholes, where Mama would visit her own mother's birthplace. As she got up from a chair after lunch one day, she collapsed and died immediately.

During the period after her death, my Scottish relatives were wonderfully kind and sympathetic. Father had decided, even before John and I arrived, that Mama should be cremated so that he could take her ashes back to Calgary. I agreed, but felt a terrible need to see her once more and mourn beside her open coffin, tell her how much I loved her, and what she had meant to me. That was not possible—the coffin was already closed. Even today, as I write about it thirty years later, my eyes fill with tears.

In the past, I had often thought about what I would do should one of my parents die. I knew if my mother were left on her own, she could look after herself quite happily with the help of her wide circle of friends and relatives. If she died first, however, I planned to finally tell my father what I thought of him, then never see him again. When I arrived in Scotland, he turned to me so needily and trustingly—as the only woman left in his family—that I couldn't possibly do that to this pathetic old man.

When my father returned to Canada, he and my uncle Don, Aunt Annie's husband and a widower, tried batching it together, but it didn't work out. He even tried to fill the yawning silence left by the absence of my mother's weekly letters. He would send me one page, half filled with his crabbed handwriting, describing the weather, the political situation in Alberta, and the state of the garden. Then, as an afterthought, he would add a note at the bottom—which often blew my mind. "Don is getting married," he wrote in a postscript to one letter. Not a word about the bride, the date, the circumstances, or how my seventy-eight-year-old uncle had met her!

He insisted I come out to Calgary to sort through my mother's things, which I did. It was a heart-breaking ordeal going through all the gifts we had sent her—things that she had put away "for good" and never used—satin slippers, an eiderdown, silk scarves, and all kinds of electrical appliances.

On the second trip home, I finally realized what my father really wanted me to do—approach Eva, my mother's niece, and ask her to come and look after him. He could never have done it himself because they thoroughly disliked each other. She was a retired schoolteacher, and a deeply religious, born-again Baptist. He was an unrepentant atheist, and a drunk from time to time, now being besieged by people who wanted to help him spend his money, including several gold-diggers of indeterminate age and obvious ambition. At least he had the sense to realize he needed a good woman like Eva to look after him. I met her, and—bless her heart—in spite of her distaste for the job, she agreed to take it on. "Beckie [my mother] would have wanted me to," she said simply.

They were a strange pair. Eva insisted on long prayers before each meal. As she was saying them, Father, like a bad schoolboy, would mutter protests under his breath. Every two or three weeks, he would go out and tie one on, which shocked and offended her. Once he passed out in their only bathroom, and unable to either move or wake him, Eva had to use an improvised chamber pot for the rest of the night.

The arrangement was not a long one. By March 1968 he was back in the Belcher hospital for war veterans because of an obstruction in his bowel. I flew to Calgary to see him and talk to the doctors. His black hair, now completely white, was as fine as a baby's. Even the flannelette pyjamas my mother had made for him seemed several sizes too big and heavy on his shrunken arms. But his eyes burned as fiercely blue as ever. Typically, he was grumbling at the staff. "Every time they have a spare needle they don't know what to do with, they come in here and jab it into me!"

As I bent over him to kiss him goodbye the night before the operation, he told me, "You were always great at sports, dear." It was an odd comment, but I understood. It was the closest he could ever come to telling me he regretted anything about our relationship. My father survived the operation but died in the recovery room.

My older brothers and I arranged the funeral, since John was now in Libya and Jim still in Pakistan. Father had grudgingly said he liked the hospital padre—"for a priest"—and I asked him to conduct the service. As I listened to the long biblical quotations and threats about the damnation awaiting people like my father, I knew I had failed him once again. I half expected him to sit up in the middle of the service and demand that "this old geezer immediately cease his waving and ranting."

After the minister finished, four grizzled veterans from the First World War marched up the aisle and placed a single poppy on the coffin. It was a ceremony for Red Chevrons—veterans who, like my father, had joined up in 1914. The old men looked awkward, even apologetic, yet it was by far the most moving moment in the ceremony.

He left his money to be divided among his children and stepchildren as well as other relatives. It seemed sad, after all their years of hardship and struggle, that those two old people had had so little time to enjoy that belated windfall.

CHAPTER TEN

How We Changed a Magazine— and Women

As I look back on my life, I see that my timing could certainly have been improved on. During that first year of adjusting to marriage, followed by Peter's birth, I went through the trauma of a totally different kind of birth—a complete makeover of *Chatelaine*.

All through the 1950s, *Chatelaine* and its chief rival, *Canadian Home Journal*, lost money. Our biggest problem was the flood of American women's magazines that inundated Canada every month. Because these magazines were filled with many of the same ads *Chatelaine* carried, U.S. branch-plant firms in Canada saw no reason to advertise in a Canadian magazine.

The second problem—shared by all magazines—was the arrival of television. It was gobbling up many of the advertising dollars that had previously gone into print media.

The third problem was the presence in Canada of the two most successful publications in the world, *Time* and *Reader's Digest*. Their so-called Canadian editions directly competed with Canadian magazines for advertising. By the time I took over *Chatelaine*, they were scooping up close to 60 per cent of all the advertising dollars that supported magazines in Canada.

In 1957 Maclean Hunter hired an American consultant to determine whether a women's magazine could survive in Canada at all. The answer was a cautious yes, provided that we put out a more exciting, future-oriented publication. At that point, the company bought *Canadian Home Journal*, already foundering—a move that bumped up *Chatelaine*'s circulation to more than half a million.

Even as a lowly editorial assistant, I had been itching to make changes to *Chatelaine*. Now, with the go-ahead from management, we redesigned everything—content, cover, logo, type, and even the letters page— renamed "The Last Word Is Yours." As a reward for all my hard work, one month before Peter was born I was officially made editor.

Instead of making *Chatelaine* ape *Ladies Home Journal*, as management was pressing me to do, I had other plans. I am sure they would never have approved of my plans—had they known about them in advance. Fortunately, they concentrated on the growing circulation figures and the profits. I doubt that they read the magazine's contents carefully at all. By the time they were aware of the radical changes I had made, the circulation was climbing, and we were Maclean Hunter's chief moneymaker in the magazine division.

I knew that no matter how much we pumped up the magazine visually, we could never compete with the big, glossy U.S. women's magazines—by comparison *Chatelaine* looked thin and anaemic. They could run sixteen full-colour pages of fashion shots; at the most, we could afford to run four. They had seventy or more people on staff; I had fewer than twenty. And there was nothing I could do about it.

With a population ten times larger than Canada's and more than equal access to our readers through subscriptions and newsstands, U.S. magazines not only had a lot more money to spend, but they also dominated our newsstands by a ratio of twenty to one—right here in our own country. Because the newsstands were owned and run by Curtis Publishing, the owner of *Ladies Home Journal*, it was difficult to even find *Chatelaine* on them. For years, anytime I or members of the staff was near a magazine kiosk, we furtively moved *Chatelaine* from its obscure position on the back rack to centre front.

In order to compete in such an unfair climate, I devised a twofold strategy: first, *Chatelaine* would be as Canadian as possible—the one thing U.S. magazines couldn't be. We pushed B.C. apples, Atlantic salmon, saskatoon berries, and Quebec maple syrup. Wherever possible in fashion and decorating stories, we interviewed Canadian personalities, used different regions of Canada as backdrops, and promoted the crafts and recipes of new Canadians.

We commissioned several two- and three-part series featuring famous Canadian families—the Masseys, the Molsons, the Eatons, the Vaniers, the ranching Cross family of Alberta, and the coal-mining Dunsmuirs of British Columbia. We played up our own celebrities: Juliette, Marg Osborne, Maureen Forrester, Sylvia and Ian Tyson, as well as women painters, musicians, and politicians, and popular male entertainers and artists. We rarely used American personalities. Once we ran a picture of Elizabeth Taylor on the cover with a small story inside. In spite of good sales, we received a bagful of angry letters from readers complaining about demeaning *Chatelaine* by writing about a "trollop."

By far the most radical change I made was to double the number of articles. Merely giving Canadian women more content along the conventional lines of the U.S. women's magazines would have been futile, no matter how decked out we were with maple leaves. I planned to do what no American magazine dared—give my readers something serious to think about, something to shake them up a little. I not only wanted life to change for Canadian women, I also had definite ideas about the direction the transformation should take. However, I knew I had to move carefully and bring my readers along with me every step of the way.

It was never my intention to produce a magazine for an elite group of women. My main job was to provide what every successful women's magazine has always supplied—up-to-date information on cooking, child care, fashion, and beauty—a kind of trade journal for new generations of females facing the same, but ever-changing, tasks most of us have to learn. I was determined to give my readers a lot more mental grist for their $2 subscription or the 15 cents they paid for a newsstand copy.

I believed that, like my mother, most women were idealistic and hardworking. In my opinion, most were also far too obsequious, trusting, uninformed about public affairs, and romantic for their own good. Mama, for all her common sense, her ability to cope with adversity, and her own experience with men, still believed, to her dying day, that the right man would have solved all her problems. An avid reader of the precursers of Harlequin romances, she baffled me.

I never believed those fairy tales. I never felt any affinity for those passive, beautiful creatures, Snow White and Sleeping Beauty, who lay around in comas waiting for some prince to stumble upon them and make life begin. Nor could I understand those Feeble Fannies in movies who stood by screaming while two men fought over them as if they were trophies to be carried off by the victor. Why didn't they have the wits to find a rock or a two-by-four and hit the man they didn't want over the head?

I was convinced that there was a whole new generation of younger women that *Chatelaine* should be reaching. I met them frequently—most were bright homemakers, many with a university education. Some might have gone into law, medicine, engineering, advanced physics, or philosophy. Instead, they poured all their energies into being perfect wives and mothers. They passionately wanted—as I did—to give their children a richer life with more opportunities than they had had. Armed with the "right" books and the latest information, they believed they couldn't possibly fail at mothering—or gourmet cooking, interior decorating, or keeping their marriage intact. Had I married earlier, I might have been one of them.

No wonder when some of them realized they were working to advance mediocre and often errant husbands, and fretting and badgering quite average, though much cosseted, children, they became self-critical and deeply frustrated. Why wasn't the formula for being a perfect wife working better, they asked.

Talking to them, I realized that traditional women's magazines weren't even touching them. They proudly told me, "Of course, I never read women's magazines." That stung me because they were exactly the kind of women I wanted *Chatelaine* to attract.

At the time, there were no studies on women much more profound than their preferences in baking powder or sink cleansers. All I had to go on was what every good editor must have—gut instinct. To make sure I wasn't merely imposing my own opinions on my readers, I read their letters carefully and replied personally to each one. Those letters helped me a great deal by providing me with a key to the hearts and minds of my audience.

One of my first changes was to reinstate the editorial, which John Clare had dropped. I saw it as a direct link to my readers, a platform to set the tone of the magazine and explore contemporary, and often controversial, issues. After my first editorial—a tribute to Marion Hilliard—my second was a call for more women in Parliament. In 1958 only two seats in the House of Commons were occupied by women, compared with almost 10 per cent of the seats in some European parliaments.

Gradually, my editorials took a more emphatic position as *Chatelaine* became outspokenly feminist. Some readers wrote to complain that I was turning a "nice, wholesome, Canadian magazine into a feminist rag." About every fourth or fifth month, just to remind them I shared their daily concerns, I resorted to humour, often about my own defects as a homemaker or sometimes about the joys of being a mother.

We frequently involved our readers in the magazine. A regular column called "What's New with You" encouraged them to send in news—a kind of national bulletin board for women—out of which we developed several features with a special Canadian spin. For years we also ran an ad, "Tell Us Your Story," asking our readers to write in with true stories from their own lives. Often, they arrived hand-written on lined scribbler paper. Although the writing lacked polish, the feeling in those stories was genuine and frequently heart-rending. Almost all of them had to be extensively rewritten by our staff.

In fact, we ran a kind of correspondence course for aspiring Canadian writers. At that time, the staff members of most U.S. magazines didn't even read the slush pile—unsolicited manuscripts that came, as we used to say, over the transom. We did, never knowing what unpolished gem of Canadiana might be discovered. In 1971 forty-eight stories in *Chatelaine* were written by people who had never before been published in a national publication.

It soon became obvious to me that many of our readers shared a common problem—frustration. With the advent of the Pill, they were having smaller families. With children in school and time on their hands, many were bored and longed to get a job. They wanted money to pay for ballet or music lessons for their children, or a larger house, or their children's university tuition. But husbands often considered a working wife a reflection on their masculinity. "No wife of mine is going out to work!" was a common rallying cry.

Providing our readers with information about the workplace was as relevant, in my opinion, as providing them with standard women's magazine fare such as "Whip up These Hearty Cold-Day Casseroles," and "16 Easy-Care Summer Hair-do's." We began to run articles such as "70 Best Jobs for Women Going Back to Work." We compared part-time and full-time occupations, told them where to get training, and how to fill out a job application. We ran recipes and fashion stories slanted towards working women, and tips on how to inveigle household help from husbands and children. An article on home university courses brought in more than one thousand inquiries.

In 1960, to combat the obsessive message that women were delinquent if everything from the front doorknob to the garbage pail wasn't pristine, we published "Housework Is a Part-time Job," written by a former staffer, Eileen Morris. Because the story set off a raging debate among our readers, we frequently returned to its topic in later articles. Sometimes we had men switch jobs with their wives, which always resulted in a lively story. Husbands cut the housework down to basics—and were still bored and felt overworked. Wives who went off to an office felt liberated and guilty.

Housework and working outside the home were current topics of the day, but in the late 1950s there were some subjects people rarely spoke about, including wife battering, child abuse, and sexual discrimination. If they surfaced, the implication always was that the woman involved—not society—had failed. My plan was to explore some of these untouchable subjects.

In 1959 I plunged in to tackle a subject that threatened to get me fired and the magazine closed down—and still rages on nearly forty years later. It seemed ridiculous to me that in Canada, where social workers could be legally prosecuted for giving out information about birth control, women had no legal access to abortion. Every year many hundreds died at the hands of illegal back-street abortionists.

We took what I considered an extremely cautious position on such an explosive subject, asking only that abortion be made legally available to women under three specific circumstances: if the woman's life was in danger, in cases of rape or incest, and if the woman knew she was carrying a grossly defective fetus. We stressed that people who did not believe in abortion under any circumstances had every right to follow the dictates of their own religion and conscience.

As soon as the issue hit the newsstands, Sheila Kieran, a free-lance writer who was then married to a Catholic, called me. "Good for you! But when the church sees that article, the roof is going to fall in on you!" she warned. She was right. Almost immediately we were inundated with phone calls threatening not only to cancel subscriptions but to have me fired and the magazine run out of business. Management, of course, was very perturbed. So, frankly, was I.

But I thought I knew my readers. I published some of the most virulent letters on our letters page. In response, we began to receive letters from women who supported our position, asking, "Who are these people trying to force their opinions and beliefs on everyone else?"

For the next two years the debate raged on, with letters continuing to pour in. A powerful campaign had obviously been mounted against *Chatelaine.* Many letters from the same parish were so slavishly similar that even spelling mistakes and grammatical errors had been copied.

We did lose some subscriptions, but we gained many more. Women were beginning to question why such sensitive concerns involving women were always decided by men. For the next twenty years, I continued to run articles on the issue of choice. In 1969 a new law was finally passed that allowed legal abortions, although only if the woman's life was threatened. The decision to perform an abortion was made by a board of three doctors. We attacked the law immediately as unfair and unworkable. Twenty years later, the Supreme Court of Canada struck it down as unlawful under the Charter of Rights and Freedoms. Until then, one-third of all Canadian women had no access to abortion because their area's hospital boards refused to allow the procedure to be performed. Even today women in Prince Edward Island have to leave their province to get a legal abortion.

In 1960 we ran the first article in North America on battered babies. With a new baby myself, I was horrified to read in the paper, at least once a week, about a tiny child scalded to death or battered by one of its parents. These brief stories were usually tucked in the corner of a back page. Why, I wondered, did we have laws to protect animals from abuse but seemed to think parents had a right to do whatever they wanted with defenceless children?

I called in Dorothy Sangster, a seasoned free-lance writer, and put her on the story. She came back a few days later to tell me that there was no story: the Children's Aid had reported that such cases were rare. The real problem—and the story they wanted her to write about—was "maternal deprivation," the dangers to children when mothers went out to work.

Chatelaine had already run that story. In fact, dozens of research studies in the next ten years tried to link working mothers with every ill in society—from drunken husbands to delinquent kids—none with any success. Theoretically, I was one of these "bad" mothers, and I was growing weary listening to the arguments.

I insisted Dorothy dig further. She did, and when her battered-baby story was published, it brought a howl of rage from our readers. They simply would not believe such atrocities were taking place in Canadian homes. I was accused of being a sensationalist. Readers again threatened to cancel subscriptions.

We had been too quick off the mark—two years later every magazine in North America, including *Chatelaine*, was running stories on battered babies. Over the next ten years, laws were passed to try to protect these tiny victims.

I was learning that real social change is rarely the result of a single article. Every cause we tackled had to be revisited year after year, each time with a fresh approach, new information, and enough innovation to help dislodge some of society's deeply held convictions hampering the progress of women. Gradually opinions were modified, women's groups began to lobby, and change finally came about.

Canada's antiquated system of divorce was a subject we tackled as early as 1961 in an article called "The Hypocrisy of Our Divorce Laws." When I became editor, the only grounds for divorce in Canada was adultery. In Quebec and Newfoundland, the law was even more restrictive: you couldn't get a divorce without a decree passed by the *House of Commons*. Only rich people—which meant mostly men—could afford to divorce. Few women had enough money to support themselves, let alone sue for divorce.

Well-to-do men often divorced their wives and remarried, usually to younger women. The first wife was generally awarded custody of the children, a meagre settlement for herself, and some child support—if she could collect it. If she were rash enough to have a relationship with another man while receiving alimony, she risked losing all financial support—and custody of her children. This archaic post-marriage chastity belt was accepted as right and proper by most of society.

Men, according to the conventions of the time, were expected to "fool around." As they had done for centuries, some kept mistresses and never bothered to tidy up a situation that short-changed both the women in their lives. The wife put on a brave front. The mistress lived in the shadows and in hope. But any woman who looked for a more rewarding relationship for whatever reason—an impotent, violent, or absent husband, or a husband who was incarcerated, or as a forcibly chaste divorced wife—was censured.

On the other hand, some spouses would not accept that long-gone partners living in another relationship were never going to return. Couples wanting to marry but unable to obtain a legal Canadian divorce often got a divorce in the U.S., followed by a quick marriage. Neither was legally recognized in Canada, but it was an attempt to legitimatize the relationship.

I became aware of how ridiculous this situation could be when *Chatelaine* was threatened with a libel suit. No editor wants the expense and time-consuming bother of libel suits, so we went to a great deal of trouble checking the accuracy of stories in order to avoid them. There was no way we could have anticipated this particular action.

We had run a profile on a popular woman radio hostess. I immediately received a letter suing us for libel. The first wife of the hostess's husband had never agreed to a divorce—and claimed the article was damaging to her as his legal wife—even though, by this time, the couple had been married for years and had four teenage children! When I phoned the hostess, she said, "I'll take care of it," and I heard no more about the suit. However, the incident convinced me that our divorce laws needed a thorough overhaul, and we continued to run articles all through the sixties and seventies.

Change came in 1968 when Pierre Trudeau, as minister of Justice, in keeping with his famous dictum, "The government has no business in the bedrooms of the nation," liberalized the law. The Divorce Act has been overhauled several times since. Today divorce is legal with the consent of both parties after one year, and in three years if one spouse opposes it.

It's hard to believe today, but thirty years ago most people, including many women, accepted the fact that women were paid one-third less than men for doing exactly the same job. Society's attitude was that men were the breadwinners, while women worked for "pin money." I was well aware that the *Chatelaine* staff, including me, were paid considerably less than *Maclean's* editors. Unlike most women, though, I resented this fact.

In 1962 we ran "All Canadians Are Equal except Women" by Christina McCall. To dramatize the difference in wages, we featured photographs of male and female social workers, retail clerks, office staff, and accountants with attached salary tags. In each case, the man was paid substantially more for performing the same job.

New laws were eventually passed in the 1960s, granting women "equal pay for equal work." Employers got around it by having men do some small extra task—for example, locking up after work—to entitle them to more pay. In the 1970s, laws were tightened up by granting women equal pay for "work of equal value." Even today, however, employers still manage to discriminate and cases are still difficult to prove.

The average gap in earnings between men and women in Canada is now around 72 per cent—far below most industrialized countries, with the exception of the U.S. Even when salaries are equal, women's progress up the corporate ladder is much slower than men's—only 2 per cent of top corporation jobs are held by women. In fact, any field that women dominate—nursing, social work, child care—is considered less valuable, and paid less, than jobs held mainly by men and requiring far less education and skill. Up to the 1996 Canadian census, all the hours of work in the home were never measured or recognized in the GNP.

When I first became editor, only 5 per cent of doctors and lawyers, and fewer than 2 per cent of engineers were women. In 1962 we ran "70 Jobs with a Future for Girls." By the 1970s, after we'd run articles on the subject for a decade, the numbers of young women in law, medicine, and business administration began to increase dramatically. Today, half of all medical and law students are women. In some faculties, such as veterinary science and pharmacy, women actually outnumber men.

All through the late fifties and sixties, we continued to publish groundbreaking feminist articles: on Canada's two-faced stance on child care—floods of promises and a trickle of money; the inadequacy of both money and enforcement in child support, and its fallout—ever-increasing numbers of children being raised in poverty. We ran articles on lesbianism, women's prisons, and our patriarchal churches, classrooms, and unions. We explored what could be done about sexual harassment on the job, battering in the home, and the lack of support for women in both sports and the arts.

The first time I put the word "sex" on a *Chatelaine* cover in the early sixties, a Maclean Hunter director was so shocked that he came down to my office and almost tearfully begged me to remove it. I didn't, of course, because like the royal family back then, and money today, it sold issues. In the mid-sixties, when we ran an article based on a Kinsey Report figure that said one in four married women didn't enjoy sex, our readers were outraged—not because the number was so high, but because we dared talk about enjoying sex in a family magazine at all! Some readers burned their copies of *Chatelaine*, some cancelled their subscriptions, and others hid the issue from their teenagers.

By the late sixties, we were regularly running articles telling our readers it was possible to have a lot more fun in bed. The subject continued to shock some of them, but we persisted. Occasionally, I would realize we had gone too far and would pull back, only to return to it about six months later. However, when Helen Gurley Brown ran a nude pin-up of Burt Reynolds in *Cosmopolitan* and two dozen prominent Canadian men offered to pose nude for *Chatelaine*, I balked, knowing my audience would, too.

In 1966, Laura Sabia, then president of the University Women's Clubs of Canada, and Margaret Hyndman, one of Toronto's few practising women lawyers, were agitating for a Royal Commission on the Status of Women. I immediately wrote an editorial and published an article in support of it. Urged on by Judy La Marsh, the only woman cabinet minister, Prime Minister Lester Pearson set up the Royal Commission in 1967.

Chatelaine published a questionnaire, which took at least three hours to answer, asking our readers what they wanted from such a commission. More than 11,000 women replied. I wasn't a bit surprised—after all the proselytizing we had done over the years—at their requests: subsidized child care, birth-control clinics, more liberal abortion and divorce laws, equal pay and more opportunity at work. We tabulated the results, and I presented a formal brief to the commission, which was chaired by Florence Bird, a well-known journalist and radio commentator. With her keen insight and sense of fairness, she made a splendid head for a royal commission on women.

At first the media treated the hearings as a colossal joke. However, as they continued, it became less and less possible to write jocular copy about women's firsthand accounts of living on welfare, family incest, rape, and the ludicrous situation of needing a husband's written permission to assent to a child's emergency operation or to get a library card! We responded with Christina McCall's "What's So Funny about the Royal Commission on Women?" and followed up with coverage of the commission's deliberations as well as its final report.

We also explored aspects of Canadian society that were not directly linked to women. Aware of the looming dissatisfaction of Quebec as early as 1960, we hired a young French-Canadian journalist, the future premier René Lévesque, to write "What Does Quebec Want?" We followed up that article every two years with another on the same subject.

In 1961 we first exposed some of the appalling conditions in nursing homes for old people. Then in 1965 I persuaded a former nurse, Tori Salter, to take a job in some of the most notorious homes and write about what she found. As a result of her piece, three Ontario nursing homes were closed. Later on we ran an article entitled "Where to Grow Old in Canada" and rated each province on how well it looked after its seniors.

One day I received a letter from a woman in a mental institution in Nova Scotia, claiming she had been falsely incarcerated by relatives thirty years before. Something about the author's literate style convinced me to send a writer to investigate. The writer discovered that in the 1930s people could indeed be institutionalized by relatives for quite minor eccentricities. We ran an article exposing the practice, and our informant was later released.

With a burgeoning population of new immigrants, all through the 1960s we tackled prejudice with articles such as "What Would You Do If They Moved onto Your Street?" We ran articles on mixed marriages and tried to show our readers the changing face of Canada in our service articles.

In 1962 we ran "The Forgotten Canadians," about the discontent among our native population. In 1968 an entire issue was devoted to aboriginal people, their customs, and their demands for self-government. The tough, hard-hitting writer of the main article was Barbara Frum.

Occasionally we ran articles critical of the country itself. One, in 1960, was called "Why I Left Canada" and was written by Mordecai Richler. It was typical of what was to become one of his staple themes—deriding Canada as a cultural and intellectual backwater.

To help the growing number of Canadians moving about the country, we rated Canadian cities on their livability, comparing schools, housing, recreation, the cost of living, and the price of a bag of groceries. In a similar way, we graded schools in an article called "The 65 Best Public Schools in Canada."

One story almost earned us a legal injunction, which would have meant no copies of the edition containing the article could be distributed. Eva-Lis Wuorio, who had worked on *Maclean's*, was living on the Isle of Sark off the coast of England. She suggested a two-part as-told-to autobiography of Fiorenza Drew, the wife of the former premier of Ontario, George Drew, then Canada's High Commissioner in London. The first of two parts appeared in the March 1963 issue. It was a glitzy account of Fiorenza Drew's privileged, cultured upbringing, and her engagement and marriage to a rising young politician. In it, George Drew, whom I had always regarded as pompous and humourless, appeared quite human and even possibly attractive.

Immediately after the first article appeared, I received a cable from Mrs. Drew ordering me not to publish the second. I wired back that this was impossible: she had already okayed it and the presses were about to roll. The first cable was followed by a second one from George Drew himself to Floyd Chalmers, who was away at the time, threatening an injunction if we published the second part of the story.

My publisher, Cy Laurin, and I phoned George Drew. Drew would talk only to Cy, and when I tried to explain our position, he shouted, as though addressing a subaltern in the army, "You be quiet!" If I had had the final say, I would have run the article and dared him to try to stop us. But Cy agreed to pull it.

When the story got out, I was deluged with requests for a copy of what people assumed was a scandalous article. There was nothing in part two, of course, that couldn't have been published in the *United Church Observer*. No hot gossip, no skeletons in the closet. Everyone was mystified until the rumour broke that George Drew might be named the next governor general of Canada. He didn't want the article to appear because he wished to play down his partisan and highly controversial political career.

When Chalmers came back, he dropped in to see me and told me confidentially, "George Drew has always been a fool. He did himself more harm by trying to cancel the article than if he'd let it run." I agreed with him.

To explain the absence of the second article on Fiorenza Drew's innocuous story, I published this statement: "Readers will wonder why the second half of Fiorenza Drew's autobiography is not in this issue. Her husband threatened to put an injunction on *Chatelaine* if we ran it. There are some stories for which we are prepared to run the risk of an injunction. But the story of Fiorenza Drew's marriage to George Drew, who was once a premier of Ontario and is now High Commissioner in London, is not one of them."

Drew immediately sent a cable to Chalmers threatening to sue *Chatelaine* and me for contempt. Chalmers showed me the cable but took care of it himself, and I heard no more about it. Mr. Drew never did become governor general of Canada.

Floyd Chalmers did intervene on one other occasion—a profile of

Nora Michener, wife of Roland Michener, who had been named governor general of Canada. She asked to see the copy. I told her it was our practice never to show stories to profile subjects, although I would give her a list of facts to check if she wished. She went over my head to Chalmers, a great friend of the Micheners. Breaking his own rule, he asked to see the article. I doubt that he passed it on to Mrs. Michener, but he asked me to remove the fact that she had once been the cooking editor of *Canadian Home and Gardens*, a former Maclean Hunter publication. I removed it but thought its omission made her sound a lot less interesting.

We once got into trouble with the Canadian National Telegraph system. I had wanted to publish an excerpt from Mordecai Richler's *St. Urbain's Horseman*, but he had sold all the good parts to U.S. magazines. When Richler heard about our reservations, he turned up at the office, looking as though he had slept in his clothes—which he had, after drinking all night with Jack McClelland. He pointed out a good little piece in the book about Jewish kids at Christmas, and I bought it.

After Richler returned to England, we tried to send a cable with some changes we had made—mostly deletions of at least two dozen four-letter words. Canadian National refused to transmit the "shits" and "cunts," which meant I had to get up in the middle of the night and sleepily read all the deleted swear words to him over the phone.

Our readers often accused us of being too solemn—and we were. Although jokes and gibes were commonplace around the office, little of the hilarity made it into the pages of *Chatelaine*. One of our favourite pastimes was to think up great cover lines to sell issues. One prescient title I remember was "Is Prince Charles Fit to Rule?" However, publishing this kind of humour in *Chatelaine* was discouraging—some readers always took it seriously. I once ran a self-deprecating piece called "I'm a Terrible Housewife" by Phyllis Lee Peterson, and dozens of people wrote in with earnest suggestions to help her do better!

One day, though, I received a truly funny piece—almost a book—about growing up in Winnipeg. It was too long for *Chatelaine*, but I suggested the author send it to a book publisher. She did—and *True Confections* won the Stephen Leacock Medal for humour. Her name was Sondra Gotlieb. An accomplished Ottawa hostess and cook—and no feminist—she later wrote several articles for *Chatelaine* about food and wines, which were turned into books—the best provinces in which to buy wines, the best Greasy Spoons, the best gourmet restaurants, and the best family restaurants in Canada.

In 1961, to balance the strong feminist line I was taking in the editorials and in many articles, I started the Mrs. Chatelaine Contest. Readers from all over Canada were invited to write and tell us about themselves. Our questionnaire asked them all about their lives, from their budgets and how they fed their families to their community work and philosophy of life. The rewards were a trip abroad for the grand-prize winner, and runner-up prizes for provincial winners.

Thousands of women wrote to us every year. In addition to sending us the details of their lives in letters, they sent snapshots, poems, cookies, tapes, and even songs. Reading those letters always gave us a lift—and a yearly jolt of reality. We needed to be reminded that most of our readers cooked simply, dressed conservatively, decorated their homes modestly, and made the family their first priority. I believe the contest kept us more closely in touch with our readers than anything else we ever did.

Most important, though, it gave the women who wrote us a chance to sit back and think about their own busy lives. Every year I would get several hilarious letters from women who spoofed the contest. They would tell us what terrible housekeepers they were and how much they scorned the paragon who usually won the contest. Many other women wrote to say what a boost it had been—to take time out to write about themselves and what they had accomplished.

To pay for the initial contest that first year, my publisher insisted I turn it into a beauty makeover. Because the winner was to come to Toronto for the makeover, I sent Eveleen Dollery, the beauty editor, out to Saskatchewan just before Christmas to check that our finalist was who she said she was. When she returned, she reported with some concern, "The woman is okay, but I don't know what we're going to do about the husband."

"Why?" I asked, in alarm, expecting her to tell me he was a falling-down drunk or worse.

"His skin!" she exclaimed, her eyes widening. "It's terrible—all rough. He's going to have to wear pancake make-up."

Believing the man had some serious skin condition, I explained to Eveleen that no farmer from Saskatchewan was going to put on pancake make-up for any high-falutin magazine from the East. I suggested we keep him in the background for photos with the family and hope for the best.

Part of the prize was a trip to Europe, and the couple dropped in to see me en route. The husband, an ordinary farmer with weathered skin, looked perfectly normal to me—in fact, quite handsome. His wife gave me a piece of her mind about the makeover. "I didn't enter this contest to be turned into a model," she told me, and I agreed with her. From then on we cut out the makeover. The contest changed as the years went on, eventually including single mothers.

Another big success was our yearly budget issue, which we ran in January after all the fuss and expenditure of Christmas was over. We usually chose a typical family who were having trouble with money. Our consultants showed them how they could handle their finances better, from grocery shopping to the mortgage. The editors worked wonders overhauling tired wardrobes, suggesting more nutritious meals, and sprucing up drab rooms.

By the mid-1960s, considering all the subjects we had covered, I was galled that *Chatelaine* was still not included in the *Canadian Periodical Index* in Ottawa. In answer to repeated requests, the executive director—a woman—wrote back disdainfully that *Chatelaine* didn't qualify because the bulk of the magazine consisted of "beauty notes and recipes." Finally, in frustration, I resorted to blackmail. The next time I was asked to publicize *Library Week*, I replied that until libraries recognized *Chatelaine*'s usefulness for more than just publicity, we would give libraries no more coverage in the magazine. Our articles were finally indexed.

One of the most rewarding aspects of being a magazine editor is working with gifted people. My strategy was to surround myself at *Chatelaine* with the very best I could find. I expected them to challenge and push me, just as I challenged our readers. They rarely needed pushing themselves, however. More often I had to rein them in—they had far more exotic ideas about who our typical reader was than I did. I would become uneasy with fashions that were too expensive or recipes that had too many ingredients or took too long to make.

Each one of the talented and knowledgeable people I recruited cared as passionately about what he or she did as I did about the magazine as a whole. Not only were they hard-working and dedicated, but they were also witty, supportive, and wonderfully sardonic—as well as temperamental and wildly impractical at times.

I brought together a staff few magazines have been able to assemble in Canada. At a time when only two magazines—*Women's Day* and *Cosmopolitan*—had women editors, *Chatelaine*'s masthead was almost entirely filled with women's names. One reason I was able to attract such exceptional people was the scarcity of good magazine jobs for women in Canada. The other was the flexible hours I was willing to give them. Secretaries could come in late and leave early to accommodate school-age children. Writers could work at home. Some women with families worked part-time and took longer holidays. These unconventional changes caused almost no disruption in our work, which is why I have never been able to understand our national nine-to-five obsession, resulting in rush hours and so much inconvenience to workers and their families.

Unlike Byrne Hope Sanders, I could not have been accused of "mothering" the staff. It wasn't my style, and in the perilous financial state of Canadian magazines at the time, we were more like comrades under siege, proudly in charge of our own little feminist beachhead. In later years, visiting journalism students would marvel on how hard everyone worked. Unlike *Maclean's* editors, we almost never trooped off together for lunch. In our precious noonhours everyone had family errands or other, non-magazine women friends to meet.

My first managing editor was Keith Knowlton, a quiet, well-read bachelor, who penned memos and corrected copy in an elegant script. When he left, Jean Wright took over as my right-hand woman. A recruit from *Maclean's*, she had replaced Elizabeth Reeves in our copy department in 1953, a job I had enormous difficulty prying her away from. First I persuaded her to take over the service departments, then I asked her to become managing editor. Small, dark, and perceptive, Jean allowed nothing to escape either her sharp eye or her black pencil.

Merle Shain, a glamorous TV performer, newspaper columnist, and author of a best-selling book on men and love, was one of several women who ran the service departments. Another was Marjorie Harris, who today edits her own gardening magazine and writes gardening books.

Elaine Collett, my second director of the Chatelaine Institute—and more familiar to our readers than Betty Crocker—produced thousands of tasty recipes, geared to the timetable and budget of the average homemaker. The annual "Family Favorites Contest," which asked readers to submit their own specialities for prizes, became so gargantuan, with 7,000 entries in 1967, that we finally had to kill it.

I think I drove elegant, ageless Vivian Wilcox, our fashion editor, a bit mad with my insistence on gearing features to our readers—with such mundane offerings as "How to Sew a Complete Spring Wardrobe for $64.73." And I once counted up the total number of hours a woman was expected to spend on improving her neck—fourteen a week. I sent the copy back to Eveleen Dollery with a request to come back down to earth.

We always had to photograph features months in advance. Every winter the art director, fashion editor, two models, and a photographer—generally the urbane former model Beverley Rockett—would wing off to some sunny spot like Mexico or Spain to shoot all our spring fashion features as well as some covers. I didn't care about the wild escapades—some are still being talked about—as long as they didn't get in trouble with the police and stayed within the budget—which they rarely did.

Houses featured in our decorating articles also had to be photographed months in advance. One year our decorating editor, Alan Campaigne, tied leaves to a tree to simulate spring as the temperature hovered around ten below zero. Another decorating editor, Barbara Reynolds, defined another aspect of the job when she described herself as "a cleaning lady with a hat on."

In searching for article ideas, I put out as wide a net as possible. Often some excruciatingly boring piece of research in an academic journal would spark an article idea. I scanned at least fifty magazines and journals each month from *Vogue* and *Elle* to *Harper's*, the *Village Voice*, the *Georgia Straight*, and all the feminist magazines as they began to appear in the seventies.

Anyone on staff and our regular free-lance writers were encouraged to come up with ideas for our article meetings held about once every two months. I routed articles, fiction, and my own editorials around to staff members for their frank opinions. And they were frank. In fact, some of the wisest and wittiest comments were penned by our quiet, unassuming copyeditor, Barbara West.

We usually had only one staff writer, and some of the best women in the country wrote for *Chatelaine*. Jeannine Locke, who later was hired by the *Telegram* and then became a CBC producer, was one of them. Christina McCall, who came over from *Maclean's* because she felt we could give her more scope, wrote many of our most analytical articles on women's issues in the 1960s. When she moved to Ottawa, she wrote a book column for us and later a monthly column called "It's Your World." In the latter, she would untangle some complicated situation in national or international affairs in just one page. That column was used by schools all over the country. After she left, I could never find anyone to do it half as well. I was not surprised when she later won the Governor General's Literary Award for *Grits*, her book on the Liberal party.

Mollie Gillen, an Australian writer who had married a Canadian during the war, returned to writing after her children were raised. With her meticulous love of research, she would have made an outstanding history professor. Instead, she turned her mind and skill to writing many groundbreaking articles for *Chatelaine*. Her piece on L. M. Montgomery was later expanded into a book. It is still the best biography of the famous author of *Anne of Green Gables*.

For years I tried to get Michele Landsberg, a newspaper writer, to write for *Chatelaine*, but with three small children, she had no time. In 1972, after the NDP in Ontario, led by her husband, Stephen Lewis, had been defeated, she phoned her former paper, the conservative *Globe and Mail*, and asked for her old job back. Clark Davey, the managing editor, laughingly suggested she apply for a job on the *Don Mills Mirror*, a suburban weekly. In desperation she phoned me. I had no job but told her to come in. I gave her a desk and kept her busy free-lancing until I could take her on staff.

During the seventies, Michele's rigorous mind and passionate prose produced many outstanding articles, including a blisteringly critical survey of women's and children's TV programs, and a story on male-dominated unions. The only subject I was leery of giving her was the one closest to her heart—motherhood. I once told this wonderful, expansive woman, "You write about mothering so intensely and with such dedication you make every other woman in the country feel guilty!"

With a small staff, I always depended heavily on a large bank of professional writers to fill the pages of *Chatelaine*. In the past many distinguished names had appeared, including those of Stephen Leacock, Pearl Buck, and Gabrielle Roy. During my own time, we added Margaret Laurence, Marian Engel, Alice Munro, Jane Rule, Margaret Mead, Knowlton Nash, Roger Lemelin, Robert Thomas Allen, Yves Thériault, and Mavor Moore.

In the dwindling market for magazine-article writers, *Chatelaine* used many of the same people who worked for *Maclean's*. Bob Fulford, guru of the arts and later long-time editor of *Saturday Night* magazine, once wrote a women's guide to the law for me. (Earlier he had bombed when I asked him to find out if there was an embryonic women's movement in Canada. He found no evidence of it at all.) Jack (of-all-writing-trades) Batten, who started his career as a lawyer, was such a skilled writer that I kept him busy with one assignment after another as long as I was editor.

At first I had to coax some of the top women writers like June Callwood to work for *Chatelaine*—they much preferred by-lines in the more prestigious *Maclean's*. Later I kept June busy—as soon as one article came in, I assigned another. In fact, we had a co-operative arrangement. She often called on me for support for her many causes.

Many media stars in Canada wrote their first magazine articles for *Chatelaine*. The glamorous hostess of "Adrienne Clarkson Presents" on CBC TV once wrote our book column. *Chatelaine* actually discovered Barbara Frum. As a young suburban housewife married to a dentist, she sent us an article on child care—a subject we had done to death. Struck by the quality of her writing, I asked her to come in and tried her on another assignment. I kept her busy until the CBC hired her, first on radio as hostess of "As It Happens" and then on TV's "The Journal."

Sheila Kieran was a voice on the telephone whose by-line I had noticed frequently in *Liberty* magazine. Although she was keen to write for *Chatelaine*, I was dubious. She had seven children, and in my mind's eye I saw a harassed nursery-rhyme woman-in-the-shoe. When I met her, however, she was considerably more substantial in person and in the range of her interests and passions. She became a regular and colourful writer for *Chatelaine* for many years.

Erna Paris was a single mother precariously trying to support two small children when I discovered her. I kept her busy until I left *Chatelaine* and she began to write scholarly but extremely readable books.

Other regular free-lancers were Cathie Breslin, Constance Mungall,

Sonia Sinclair, and a collection of writers from all across the country—
Helen Porter in Newfoundland, Lisa Hobbs, Simma Holt, and Shirley
Wright d'Estrube in Vancouver.

On his trips back to Canada, that rare bird Roloff Beny always paid
Chatelaine a visit to display his photographic wares. A native of Medicine
Hat, Alberta, he flaunted being gay, and was often dressed in a silk suit
designed by Scassi. To produce his handsome coffee-table books, he made
the most of his connections with people such as the Shah of Iran and
Indira Gandhi.

To go with Beny's photographs of his famous friends—the Duke and
Duchess of Windsor, John Huston, Marlene Dietrich, or Vivian Leigh—we
also had to have some kind of story. His own accounts were embarrass-
ingly laudatory, and a staff writer would always have to winnow his purple
prose to create a sketchy piece on life in the fast lane. I usually scheduled
Beny's pieces—as well as our twice-a-year stories on the royal family—to
spice up an issue that seemed soggy with scalloped potatoes and cures for
children's colds.

The writer and publicist Fiona McCall kept insisting I meet her psychiatrist—a woman she thought should be writing for *Chatelaine*. I finally
agreed. When I arrived at the restaurant where we were to have dinner, Dr.
Mary McEwan and I recognized each other immediately. Years before, our
husbands had insisted that we meet. The evening had been a total bust—
the men had talked law and politics while we sat in numbed silence. But
that night I realized Fiona was right. This witty woman, full of common-
sense advice, was a modern-day Marion Hilliard. After she began writing
a very successful column for *Chatelaine*, she and I became firm friends
until her untimely death.

When I took over as editor, *Chatelaine* was buying most of its fiction
from U.S. agents. Although *Maclean's* and *Saturday Night* had run fiction
in the past, by the 1960s so few Canadian magazines were carrying fiction
that authors rarely wrote popular-magazine short stories at all.

As a subscriber to several small Canadian literary magazines, I was
impressed by the growing number of women fiction writers. What really fired
me up to "Canadianize" our fiction, though, was the launch of Alice Munro's
first book of short stories, *Dance of the Happy Shades,* in 1968.
I was invited to the press party and was incensed to read in the book's

promotional material, "None of these stories was published by *Chatelaine*." The idea of a Canadian author, and a woman, boasting about not writing for *Chatelaine* deeply bothered me. And I was determined to change it. (I also pointed out to Munro at the time that she hadn't sent any of her stories to us.)

I began to woo Canadian fiction writers—in some cases by commissioning stories. By 1970 I was confident enough to declare that we were going to run nothing but Canadian fiction from then on, and I sent out letters requesting stories to every fiction writer in Canada. I must confess that the effort was only partly successful. We did publish stories by Margaret Laurence, Claire Martin, Marie-Claire Blais—and Alice Munro—but we also published some strange fiction for a mainstream magazine. Canadian writers, I found, tended to write moody, morose tales. I was guiltily aware that many of our readers, tired after a long day and looking for a little light escape, would not find it in *Chatelaine* some months. One story I particularly remember—and regret publishing at all— was about a deeply disturbed child who locked herself in the bathroom and cut off the head of her dog!

One day Breda Harding, our long-time receptionist, called to tell me that Jacqueline Susann's husband was waiting to see me. At the time Susann's steamy sex-in-high-places novels topped the best-seller lists in North America. Her husband was her manager and promoter. I told Breda to explain that I was too busy to see him. I didn't even suggest he meet with someone else.

A few minutes later, she appeared at my door. "It's actually Mordecai Richler," she said.

"Well, tell him to come right in." Richler shambled in, looking slightly embarrassed that as a high-profile American agent, he couldn't get in the door, but as a Canadian writer, he had direct access.

Dealing with writers was easy. In the end, they had to produce an article that satisfied the editors, or they had to rewrite it. Illustrators and photographers were a little more difficult. I believed as passionately about supporting Canadian artists and photographers as I did fiction writers but resented not getting what we had paid for. This sometimes resulted in heated arguments with the art department. (I think I was hard on art directors because there was a fair turnover—five men and two women in my twenty years as editor.)

Many top illustrators worked for us—Jimmy Hill, Wally Stepoff, Heather Hill, and among the photographers, Bert Bell, John Siebert, and Paul Rockett. Most were men, and a few looked down on *Chatelaine*, taking the attitude that we should be happy with whatever they deigned to give us, in spite of our clear instructions.

I particularly remember one fiction piece about a widow travelling out West by train with her two children. She meets a widower, and by the time they reach Regina, romance is blooming like a prairie crocus in spring. The art department asked an artist who had just returned from Mexico to provide an illustration for the story. Imagine my dismay when the artwork came back featuring dark-haired Mexican children and their mother sitting barefoot in what looked like a pigsty!

Male photographers, on the other hand, always wanted to put a little sex into their pictures. A photographer assigned to shoot a promising young violinist would come back with a photograph showing enough cleavage to satisfy *Playboy*. When all we wanted was a straightforward photo of a cardigan for our crafts department, I would get a picture of the model rising from a rumpled bed! One photograph of a naked baby girl was positioned so that she was spread-eagled across the page. The art director—a man—saw nothing exploitive about it. "She's only a baby!" he remonstrated when I insisted it be changed.

Because *Chatelaine*'s staff was small, I not only wrote editorials but also a movie column, some book reviews, and the occasional article. And in my first ten years as editor, in addition to redesigning and redirecting *Chatelaine*, I supervised the launch of three more magazines—the French edition, *Châtelaine*, *Miss Chatelaine*, and *Hostess*.

In order to publicize *Chatelaine* and connect with my readers in person, I gave at least two or three speeches a month throughout the sixties and seventies. Not all of them were successful. Sometimes the woman who was supposed to thank me used the time to deliver a spirited rebuttal of everything I had said. I was frequently challenged about my low-key but insistent feminist message. I was confronted on religion: was I a Christian or not? And I was frequently berated for "undermining the family."

At Timothy Eaton Memorial Church in Toronto, the woman introducing me mentioned that I had three young children, bringing a gasp from the audience. My well-to-do audience laughed at my jokes but sat poker-faced through my prediction that more and more women would be joining the workforce in the future, and that it was foolish to educate men and women equally, but use only the talents and abilities of the men.

I was impatient when capable women did things poorly—ran sloppy meetings or stumbled over procedure and then smilingly excused themselves because they were "only women." Even as late as the early 1970s, when I flew out to speak to a western women's conference, the woman who met the plane kept enthusing about "the really good speaker" they had lined up for the final dinner—not me, but a man, of course. I'm sure she didn't mean to be tactless, but I was clearly second class.

The opening session was delayed until Premier Edward Shreyer arrived—three-quarters of an hour late. He told the women they were doing important work in the home, and added that they should argue with anyone with whom they didn't agree—this obviously aimed at me. He left to a standing ovation for turning up at all.

At the banquet the "really good speaker" turned out to be a newspaperman with a lot of funny jokes—all at the expense of women. His audience clapped and laughed good-naturedly, though every second comment was an insult to them. He ended by saying that men shouldn't listen to any more complaining from women because, like slaves, they really enjoyed working on the plantation. He received a standing ovation!

One of the least attractive parts of my job was attending promotion receptions. The advertising department was always pressing editors to attend these events, especially when advertisers were promoting a new product. Because they usually took place after work when I wanted to get home, I resented them. I would put in an appearance, if I couldn't persuade another member of the staff to be there.

At one promotion for soft drinks in cans, we had to listen to a series of inane commercials followed by a man with a flip chart, a flashlight, and endless statistics on teenage consumption of soft drinks. When one sceptical journalist pointed out that according to the stats, there were more teenagers consuming pop than teenagers in the population, it threw the presenter into a wild frenzy of scrabbling through a file as thick as the Toronto telephone directory. As we left, we were given a record of the commercials and a seventy-page book of stats to take home!

Through the sixties and seventies, I was asked more and more frequently to serve as the "token" woman on committees, radio programs, TV panels, and boards of such institutions as York University. Because I was the first woman to breach some of these previously all-male bastions, it was something of a trial. It wasn't that the men didn't try to make me feel welcome—if anything they were excessively polite, greeting my entrance at one meeting by knocking over several chairs in their eagerness to get to their feet. As the speakers droned on, I would find my companions staring at me curiously as though I were some rare species of bird. They always paid polite attention when I spoke but rarely heard what I was saying. Many of them, ignoring my point, picked up on the remarks of the last male speaker—or even credited him with my arguments. Their lingo, bristling with militaristic and sports terms—right in the ball park . . . run it up the flag pole . . . blast them out of the bunker—unintentionally excluded women.

I was often numbingly bored as, one after the other, they reaffirmed what the most important man had said—again and again. At such times I would do what they undoubtedly were doing to me—I mentally undressed the more attractive ones. But I was probably kinder than they were—I left their boxer shorts on. In time the awkwardness would ease, when other women were added to the group.

I felt sorry for the men at those meetings—they competed so fiercely with each other and seemed to feel so much was at stake. Younger men cosied up to older, more powerful men who could help them, far more obsequiously than any woman would dare. Their nervousness was revealed in giveaway tics—pulling their ears, tearing the flesh around their nails, and obsessively drumming their fingers on their knees.

Needless to say, the Old Boys' Club was supportive of its own members, not women. In 1969, when Judy La Marsh, former minister of Health, left politics, no Toronto firm was interested in hiring her. This was in stark contrast to the eager offers other lesser male ministers received. She opened a law practice in her home town, Niagara-on-the-Lake, and became a part-time lecturer at York University—a common-enough practice for ex-politicians. To my dismay, at the next meeting of the York board, several of my fellow members objected strenuously to even that minuscule appointment.

In addition to excluding women from important positions, some men simply assumed sexual harassment was a perk of being boss—whether it involved gross and demeaning comments, nude pictures on the wall, or sleeping privileges. Women either put up with the conditions, tried to jolly the men out of it, or left the job. Every single woman I knew had been propositioned at some time, mostly by married men. It gave us a somewhat sleazy view of the men and their marriages.

Dubarry Campeau, a masterful, witty journalist and conversationalist, cut a rather bizarre figure with her flowing garments, pop-eyed gaze, and twitching mouth. Having lost her hair to illness, she wore a rather ratty wig, long after excellent wigs were available. Her husband, Cyrille, head of *Time* magazine's Canadian bureau, was a persistent womanizer. One night when he turned his attention to me, Dubarry drawled, "You might as well give in, darling. He'll get his way in the end." He didn't. That attitude was not unusual for women with wayward husbands—either shut your eyes to their humiliating behaviour or try to turn it into a joke.

Women speakers were a rarity at predominantly male meetings. I remember an advertising and sales club luncheon at the Royal York Hotel at which a top female executive from New York spoke—and was the sole woman at the head table. She gave a spirited, witty talk: advertising for women had to change, she told her mostly male audience. Sexist advertising using half-clad bimbos to flog everything from cars to men's cologne was increasingly offensive to young women. The men stirred uncomfortably. Not much has changed in the interim. Today's sexist advertising is often more overt and more pervasive.

Years after the women's movement was well established, I would be challenged regularly for running fashion and beauty articles and for the sexist ads in *Chatelaine*. I always explained that magazines depend on ads for their revenue. As an editor, I always went directly to the publisher if I thought an ad was going to offend our readers, and in some cases the ads were rejected and in others changes were made. Because most of our ads were made up in the U.S., we had little influence over them. My advice to women was to write directly to the president or the advertising manager of the offending company. Even a dozen letters from customers have an impact: if their highly expensive ads are turning buyers against products, advertisers want to know about it.

When I took over *Chatelaine,* the circulation was 480,000. By the end of the 1960s, the magazine was being read by 1.8 million women—one of every three in Canada. No magazine in the U.S. had anything like that penetration. A comparable American magazine would have had to have 16 million readers. The biggest, *Ladies Home Journal,* had only 7 million.

In 1970, out of curiosity, I counted up the requests for information we received in one month, and it came to more than 7,000. As time went on, we were asked more frequently for permission to reprint articles for home and school use, study groups, and reprints in books.

During most of the 1960s, *Chatelaine* continued to make money, while *Maclean's* and *Saturday Night* sank deeper and deeper into the red. I regularly lunched with Bob Fulford, Gerry Anglin, and Pierre Berton, who, like most people in the industry, believed with some justification that magazines in Canada could well go under. Gerry Anglin, then back at *Maclean's,* once remarked, "I don't know what you dames are doing right, but I sure hope you keep on doing it!"

Even Ralph Allen, *Maclean's* legendary editor and a rather shy man in the presence of women, used to phone me from time to time and say, "I'm a kept man. How about taking me out to lunch?"

What we had "done right"—besides putting out a good solid magazine with lots of Canadian content—was, through *Chatelaine,* help launch in North America the second stage of the women's movement.

I first became aware of this when an American, Elizabeth Drew, a fine writer and shrewd political commentator in the *New Yorker,* came to see me. She had discovered some copies of *Chatelaine* and wanted to meet its editor. I remember our conversation about feminism vividly. It was like Livingstone meeting Stanley in the depths of Africa, or a whooping crane meeting, for the first time, another whooping crane.

The next evidence that we might indeed be in the avant-garde of a new movement came in 1963, when we received a set of galleys for a new book being released in New York. I gave them to Jean Wright to read. She sent them back with a memo: "We've run most of this stuff in *Chatelaine.* In any case, it's far too American, and it's not very well written."

That book was *The Feminine Mystique* by Betty Friedan, which has always been credited as launching the women's movement in North America. *Chatelaine* probably missed the scoop of the century, but Jean was right—we had published stories on many of the topics in Friedan's book. One of the best sections in *The Feminine Mystique* was her severe criticism of American women's magazines. Betty Friedan, of course, had never laid eyes on *Chatelaine*.

By the 1970s, consciousness-raising groups were forming far faster than Tupperware parties. The first women's centres were opened on opposite ends of the country, in British Columbia and Newfoundland. New, brave little magazines and provocative books began to appear. Sit-ins and lobbies were staged, and a whole spectrum of feminist political positions were hotly debated. Soon both federal and provincial governments responded by setting up advisory councils and dribbling out money for women to hold conferences—and hopefully be pacified. The women's movement in Canada—with a big boost from *Chatelaine* and an enormous amount of work on the part of many women and some men—had been well and truly launched.

As for *Chatelaine*, it was something of a miracle to have survived, made a profit, and more than doubled the circulation—at a time when every other magazine in Canada was in trouble. Even more remarkably, we did it when even the big U.S. women's magazines had begun to falter.

In the mid-1960s *McCall's* magazine displaced *Ladies Home Journal* as the top American women's magazine, then it, too, began to run into trouble. A well-known journalist, Shana Alexander, was brought in. She banished food, fashion, and decorating sections, concentrated on articles—and failed disastrously. Only *Cosmopolitan*, by then under Helen Gurley Brown, was an outstanding success. The author of *Sex and the Single Girl* had turned it into the female counterpart of the immensely successful *Playboy*, and it became a handbook for single women bent on catching a man.

By 1970 U.S. women were so dissatisfied with their magazines that an eleven-hour sit-in was staged outside the offices of *Ladies Home Journal*. The rebellious crowd threatened to take over the magazine and publish an entire issue with articles on consciousness raising, having a baby, and women at work.

According to a recent five hundred-page thesis on the women's magazine industry during the fifties and sixties written by Valerie Korinek at the University of Toronto, everything the protesters planned to publish had appeared in *Chatelaine* years before. Even when the revolutionary feminist magazine *Ms.* was launched in 1972, most of its topics—family politics, domestic violence, abortion, women's health, women and religion, incest, drugs, poverty, and lesbianism—had been covered in *Chatelaine* a good ten years before.

Korinek says, "Canadian feminism during the sixties . . . had an unofficial leader in *Chatelaine*'s editor. Through her monthly editorials, readers across the country were given an education on all the key issues of second-wave feminism."

CHAPTER ELEVEN

Down Below the Glass Ceiling

By the late 1960s, I had been editing *Chatelaine* for a dozen years and had done most of the things I wanted to do with it. Although I still found fresh causes to take up, innovative stories to assign, and talented new people to write them, I realized more and more that I had to rev myself up to do my job.

Even though *Chatelaine* was Maclean Hunter's moneymaker, we always played Cinderella to the crown prince, *Maclean's*—which, by this time, leaked money. Its editors enjoyed more lavish expense accounts, and in a company where salaries were a closely guarded secret, I strongly suspected my yearly salary of $23,000 was paltry compared with that of the editor of *Maclean's*. Moreover, it was still an annual hassle to pry even meagre raises for my staff out of the publisher, Lloyd Hodgkinson.

Pride in the company's flagship magazine on the part of Chalmers and Hunter was all that kept *Maclean's* alive—that and the money *Chatelaine* continued to make. In fact, if we had stopped making a profit, Maclean Hunter might have given up on magazines altogether and the entire consumer magazine industry in Canada would have gone under. At least once that I know of during those years, the company rescued *Saturday Night*, a rival publication, by writing off its printing bill at the MH plant.

Maclean Hunter was no longer solely a Canadian publishing firm. It was deeply into cable, radio, television, trade shows, and business forms, and had offices all over the U.S. and Europe. With cable the fastest-growing moneymaker, an increasing number of the company's top executives came from broadcasting. Rather than publishers and editors, they were accountants and MBAs.

There were two jobs in the company that I wanted. They were not only logical moves for a successful editor, but would also give me the kind of challenge I needed. One of them was publisher of *Chatelaine*, should Lloyd Hodgkinson be elevated to another job or leave. The other was the editorship of *Maclean's*.

Although most publishers in the company had come up through the sales side, Ralph Allen of *Maclean's* and Paul Deacon of the *Financial Post*, as well as several business magazine editors, had moved into the publisher's chair by way of editorial. I thought I could do either of the two jobs I coveted and had already let Hodgkinson and Chalmers know my objectives.

To expand my knowledge of the magazine business, I had become acquainted with several editors in New York and London, England, particularly Geraldine Rhoads, editor of *Women's Day*. Through her, I had joined the American Association of Magazine Editors and regularly attended its annual meeting. I was struck by how well American editors and publishers worked together: the latter were particularly useful in alerting editors to trends in both publishing and advertising.

I met with my publisher, the advertising manager, and our promotion people as often as they wanted to see me, but seldom felt I learned much from them. Nor did it seem to me that we were on the same track. Our sales staff rarely read the articles. My usefulness was solely as a source of information on upcoming beauty, food, fashion, and decorating features that could be used to sell ads. Although we gave them this information months in advance of publication, they always wanted more—more details, names of manufacturers being featured, help from editors. I thought that method of selling advertising space short-sighted back then, and I still think so.

I was keenly aware that a healthy advertising picture meant more editorial space, but every year we ran dubious promotions to try to help the sales staff, long after they had ceased to generate many ads. In one annual furniture campaign, we built and furnished five houses across the country, and ran as many as sixteen editorial pages—for a total of three to four pages of advertising. Any suggestion that this sales strategy needed rethinking was rejected: I was always told next year would be better.

I genuinely liked many of our sales staff—all men; however, I realized they had little interest in what *Chatelaine* was trying to do for its readers. Indeed, a succession of advertising managers didn't seem to know their magazine's readership at all. I remember sitting with one of them while he griped about how tough his job was. "There's a lot of advertising going into travel these days," he complained, "but of course women don't travel." Astounded, I told him the young single women on our staff had more time and money to travel than most couples. Even when married people travelled, it was often the woman who made the decisions. "If you want travel editorial, I can give it to you," I told him. "And it's a subject our readers will welcome." I immediately set up a travel column and planned some features.

When I thought of some of our salesmen representing *Chatelaine*, I cringed. Their idea of a witty conversational opening was a sexist joke, and not even my frostiest response made the slightest dent in their programmed patter. At one advertising conference, our sales staff put up a big sign over the door of *Chatelaine*'s suite: The Ladies Room—which they thought wildly amusing.

Lloyd Hodgkinson frequently complained that the growing number of young women buyers of ad space were among the salesmen's toughest sells. I would point out how out of touch and downright offensive some of our men must have seemed, with their "Hi, sweetheart" approach, to bright young female executives.

"Why don't you hire some women?" I would ask.

"There are no women experienced enough to sell *Chatelaine*," he would tell me solemnly.

I felt we were missing all kinds of advertising opportunities. Little specialty shops were opening across the country, and American magazines were running pages of small mail-order ads offering merchandise from similar stores. When I suggested our advertising department go after that business, I was told, "The salesmen aren't interested. Not enough money in those little ads." And this from a staff that was supposed to be desperate!

"Then hire a woman," I urged. "She'll go after those ads and more than pay for her salary." It was never done. In fact, it wasn't until *Ms.* magazine was launched with its all-women staff that women cracked the hallowed profession of selling ad space. Saleswomen on *Ms.* proved so good at it that other magazines kept stealing them away.

Lloyd Hodgkinson and I had a long and productive association, but not what I would call a close or trusting one. Short and slight in stature, with a moustache, he was always cheerful. I admired his optimism, his bouncy salesman's capacity for going back tirelessly again and again to make his pitch—no matter how bored or difficult the customer might be.

We didn't get off to a great start. Before he joined *Chatelaine*, he had been publisher of its rival, the *Canadian Home Journal*. When it was about to fold, I knew he regularly passed information on to Cy Laurin, the publisher at *Chatelaine*. It earned him a job as advertising manager of *Chatelaine*, and when Cy left, Lloyd became publisher.

Like many salesmen, he was a hustler, always trying to make a buck. His methods, though, were often expedient and short-sighted. Just before *Canadian Home Journal* folded, he persuaded the editor to run a beauty feature tied in with one particular advertiser. It proved to be the magazine's death-knell. In the magazine business, you can't do a favour for one advertiser without having twenty more demanding the same concessions. In no time, readers have the feeling they are reading an advertising brochure, not a magazine.

Lloyd was always trying to pressure me to do something similar in *Chatelaine*. Giving an advertiser a special break would usually involve asking the beauty editor to write something to be used in an ad, or letting the advertiser use material from our editorial. I always refused, but in all our years together he never stopped trying. I thought this sales strategy was so suicidal that I sometimes wondered whether he was just amusing himself on a slow—for him—morning while he tested his advertising skills on me.

He would drop in and spend as long as an hour trying to soften me up. (Once, to impress me, he told me he was reading his way through the *Encyclopedia Britannica*!) Sometimes I grew so bored that I almost fell asleep; in fact, I could have dozed off without missing a thing, because just before his "pitch" he always gave himself away. His throat would tighten, and I knew I had to wake up and watch for his hidden agenda. It was a game, but a time-wasting one on a busy work day.

One memorable battle concerned advertising supplements; they are small booklet inserts that read like editorial, although they are clearly marked "advertising" and are produced by advertising agencies. In 1969, both *Maclean's* and *Weekend* magazines started running supplements. Lloyd and Bruce Drane, the publisher of *Miss Chatelaine*, saw them as a bonanza— as I did—provided that our editors were not involved in writing the copy.

Lloyd spent hours arguing that writing advertising supplements was no different from telling readers where to buy the clothes we featured in our fashion pages. I said there was all the difference in the world: one was an editorial service that every magazine provides for its readers, while the other obliterated the line dividing advertising and editorial.

This battle raged on through several stormy meetings in my office, and the showdown came at our monthly planning conference before the company's top executives. Lloyd claimed that many magazines were using editors to write advertising supplements. I had spent most of a day going through every major magazine in North America without finding a single example of this practice—and said so. Incensed, he ran out of the boardroom, declaring that he would return with proof. The meeting ended before he came back. A couple of days later, Donald Hunter, who was the president of the company and a majority shareholder, gave me a victory sign as he was driving into the company garage.

That, however, wasn't the end of it. I had just been forced to let the editor of *Miss Chatelaine* go for incompetence. Soon after, I received a memo from Lloyd: he had talked to the young woman and thought she should be given another chance. Because the supplements were to run in *Miss Chatelaine*, I suspected he had talked her into running them if he gave her her job back. Furious at this kind of interference, I had it out with him, and the editor left.

His next scheme was to publish books. He told me he had hired a man called "Cap" Leahy and that Leahy would be dropping in to see me. A few days later, a short, aggressive man walked unannounced into my office, and proceeded to tell me that I had better get along with him because in no time I would be working for him. It wasn't an auspicious start, and his ideas turned out to be no better than his manners.

Leahy expected to use *Chatelaine* material in books he would sell by mail. When I asked him who was going to do all the work, he said he expected my editors to do it. When I pointed out that my tiny staff was already overworked and had put in hundreds of hours producing books and booklets already, he suggested paying them $300 to $500 a book. Any profit from the sales of the books was, of course, to go to his department. I had grave doubts that this bumptious man would put out a quality product and hated the idea of anything second rate being sold under *Chatelaine*'s name.

I confronted Lloyd about my doubts, and he assured me that Cap was "a great guy, perhaps a little rough about the edges," but he would do a good job. That year we did produce a diet book, which Lloyd soon asserted had sold 8,500 copies. Leahy started pushing for a beauty book, an astrology book, and even selling some junky-looking jewellery through the magazine. Fortunately, a couple of months later, Gordon Rumgay, the circulation manager, reported that only 1,800 diet books had actually been sold—not nearly enough to pay for Leahy's operation. Rumgay thought Leahy and his ideas were duds, and soon after Leahy left the firm.

Then came *Chatelaine*'s foray into television. One February morning in 1970, Hodgkinson and I were summoned to the office of Don Campbell, who headed MH's broadcasting division. I had first met him soon after he joined the company in 1957. A sunburned young man in shirt-sleeves, he arrived at my office door bearing a clipboard. The company was putting up a new building, which would incorporate the original structure, on the corner of Dundas and University. He informed me that the *Chatelaine* offices would be in the old building. (*Maclean's*, of course, was going into the new building.) To save money, none of the *Chatelaine* offices would have doors. I argued vigorously that *Chatelaine* not only had to be in the new building but that its writers had to concentrate on what they were doing and needed doors. He listened to me, went away, and later assigned us offices in the new building—with doors.

That morning in his office, Campbell had two $25,000 black-and-white TV cameras sitting on his desk. "This is the future," he told us, patting them. "I want TV shows for cable, and *Chatelaine* is the logical place to start." Maclean Hunter, along with other cable companies, was being pressed by the Canadian Radio-television and Telecommunications Commission to produce "Canadian content," and *Chatelaine* seemed a natural resource to mine.

I liked the idea of promoting the magazine through television, but not in a Mickey Mouse way. Because one in three Canadian women already read *Chatelaine*, I saw no advantage in being featured in an amateurish third-rate TV show on cable. Besides, TV was soaking up advertising dollars that had previously gone into magazines, and I wondered why we were giving away our talents to a rival.

About a month later, a young man appeared fresh from the engineering side of Bell Canada, and introduced himself as our producer. He began by telling me cable was going to put magazines out of business completely. Once again, *Chatelaine*'s editors were expected to work on this new enterprise free of charge. When I took our visitor around the office to meet them, he was surprised—as most people were—at how small the staff was. He behaved like an impresario auditioning starlets, his dissatisfied expression telling us clearly that we were not "making it." We did produce a few cable shows in a small studio in the Toronto suburb of Rexdale, but it took hours of time and did nothing to enhance the magazine.

A year later, Michael Hind Smith, who had held several executive positions at CBC, was hired to produce TV shows using the *Chatelaine* name. Because professionals were involved, this operation had my full support. Working with the filmmakers Allan King and Beryl Fox, we spent many long hours on a proposal with General Foods in mind as sponsor. I thought the final script was bland, as did King and Fox, but General Foods found it far too controversial and a whole year's work came to nothing.

Frustrated with all these energy-draining proposals, I remember commiserating with Jean Wright, my managing editor, that we were being treated like a herd of cows to be milked dry. I was sure some of the schemes might have worked if I had been given a minimum budget and been allowed to come up with my own ideas of what might appeal to our readers and make money at the same time. Unfortunately, the business minds running the company didn't trust creative people—particularly women.

In 1968, the editorship of *Maclean's* began to seem like a possibility, even for me.

I had watched *Maclean's* deteriorate from its position as the magazine every journalist in Canada wanted to work for, to the basket case of Maclean Hunter. Ralph Allen, its successful long-time editor, had left in 1960. Blair Fraser, the magazine's Ottawa political correspondent, was brought in on an interim basis for two years. When he went back to his Ottawa beat, Ken Lefolii became editor, with Peter Gzowski as managing editor. During their short tenure, they ran the magazine like Ben Hecht's *Front Page*. Everyone who worked there at the time now fondly describes that era—along with the Ralph Allen years—as an Olympian period in the magazine's history. It was also a time when the magazine ran up record financial penalties at the plant for late copy and attracted a record number of lawsuits. This, of course, did not go down well in a cautious firm like Maclean Hunter.

In 1968, Donald Hunter became chairman of the board and president. Ron McEachern, former editor and publisher of the highly profitable

Financial Post, was put in charge of the magazine division. His special assignment was to resuscitate *Maclean's* and find a solution to the corrosive presence of *Time* and *Reader's Digest* in Canada.

A short, nattily dressed man, with a beaky nose and an abrupt and explosive manner, McEachern was brilliant but erratic. Even in a profession with more than its share of eccentrics, stories about his management style astonished journalists. He had been known to rip an entire issue of a magazine up in front of its editor. When Peter Newman was a reporter on the *Post*, and received a better job offer, he told McEachern he was about to quit. McEachern, instead of asking this able and talented young man if anything could be done to induce him to stay, simply asked, "When?"

In his new position, McEachern immediately saved some money by turning *Maclean's* from a bi-monthly to a monthly and reducing its page size. He objected to the overtime costs and lawsuits, and under his hectoring management style, Lefolii and most of the staff finally walked out en masse.

Borden Spears, a highly respected former managing editor of the *Toronto Star*, then working on the *Financial Post*, was ordered to take over as editor. Spears certainly did not want the job, but he did what he was told. Less than a year later, in early 1969, McEachern hired Charles Templeton, the charismatic ex-evangelist and TV personality, as editor. Spears was demoted to managing editor.

It was rumoured that Templeton was getting $45,000 a year, stock options, a guarantee of half his pension if he retired early, as well as a company car. The day after the Templeton announcement, McEachern appeared in my office and offered me a car and a membership in a rather stuffy club that he belonged to. I wanted neither and rightly suspected I was being given this unusual windfall because my salary at $23,000 was so shockingly small compared with Templeton's—after all, he was a novice in the magazine business. (The story all over town that night was that after hearing about Templeton's appointment, I had stormed into McEachern's office and he had handed me the keys to a Cadillac.)

I told McEachern I wanted more authority and opportunity in the company and more money. When I asked about the lavish Templeton package, he denied everything, then offered me a large colour TV set with a remote control. This I accepted on behalf of my sons! Claiming he had no control over my salary, he suggested I talk to Lloyd Hodgkinson.

When I tackled Lloyd about a raise, I got the usual runaround. He scoffed at the money Templeton was supposed to be making and went into his usual spiel about tough times, claiming the magazine couldn't afford a substantial raise that year. (Selling one four-colour page of advertising would have provided a $10,000 raise for me.) He asked me to wait until June to see how the profit picture for spring was shaping up. He also reminded me that I, along with other senior executives, had been allowed to buy stock before the company went public in 1965. It proved to be an excellent investment; however, like everyone else, I had paid for it myself and doubted that other executives, Lloyd included, were expected to take a substantially lower salary as a consequence.

That afternoon I received hand-written approval from McEachern: "*Chatelaine* is by far the best run editorial operation here, but the rumours about T. are not true."

Three months after Borden Spears had been asked to stay on, he was fired at age fifty-six, with only three months' severance pay. He immediately called me and offered to take me out to lunch. A gracious, discreet, much-respected man, he spent our lunch telling me what a contemptible company he thought Maclean Hunter was. He asked me how much I was earning, and when I told him $23,000, he said he had been getting $35,000.

I marched right back to the office and confronted Lloyd Hodgkinson with this interesting piece of information. He finally promised to give me a raise of $7,000 in June.

In August 1969, with rumours flying all over the publishing community that Templeton was about to quit after little more than six months, Ron McEachern invited me to lunch at his club. I took this to mean that I was at last being considered for the job. I was not foolish enough to believe that under ordinary circumstances I would ever be offered the editorship of *Maclean's*. But for a decade, the magazine had been in trouble, with editors coming and going as if through a revolving door. In fact, every male journalist in Canada believed he might be offered the job. In these circumstances, it seemed just possible that I—as the most successful magazine editor in Canada—might finally be considered a candidate for the position, in spite of my sex.

McEachern's interviewing technique was as outlandish as the man himself. As we worked our way through two martinis, gazpacho, and a salad, he told me he had once slept with two women at once. One, he added, was now married to a member of the House of Lords in England. He also confided that he had once tried heroin.

Perhaps he was trying to shock me or to discover whether, as a woman, I lived too sheltered a life for the rarefied world of sex, dope, and general magazines. (Because I had spent many long hours listening to male colleagues, nothing he said could possibly have shocked me.) Or perhaps he was just trying to impress me with what an adventuresome bon vivant he was!

He then went on to tell me what I already knew: *Chatelaine* made money, *Maclean's* lost money. The company was considering folding the French version of *Maclean's* and cutting back on the budget for the French edition of *Chatelaine*. I also managed to find out that *Hostess*, a giveaway project dreamed up by Hodgkinson, had lost about $1.5 million in its short life—which didn't surprise me.

I realized he was coming to the pitch when he began to squirm, working his mouth as though ingesting a prune. "What would you do with *Maclean's* yellow pages if you were editor?" he suddenly demanded.

Although his question wasn't a job offer, I grabbed it anyway. I told him I thought the short, newsy upfront section was useful, but it was too much of a grab bag of information on different topics. The pages needed a sharper focus, harder-working titles to catch the reader's attention, and a less gimmicky layout. I added that I had some other ideas for the magazine as a whole, to make it more relevant. McEachern reacted enthusiastically, asking me to prepare a memo for him as quickly as possible.

For the next few days, I worked hard on the memo. I suggested that *Maclean's* needed a much broader focus. The magazine was too "Toronto" in its outlook and writing. It used too few writers from around the country, was too parochial, and not analytical enough about national and international affairs. I sent the memo to McEachern and received an ecstatic memo back from him.

A few days later, he dropped into my office for a chat about the present—and past—*Maclean's* staff. He was extremely critical and had little good to say about anyone—even such icons as Ralph Allen and Pierre Berton. He also mentioned that he might ask Mitchell Sharp to take over the *Financial Post*, a bizarre idea if there ever was one. Sharp, a cautious, skilled politician and bureaucrat, had no experience in publishing at all.

Some days later, I had lunch with Bob Fulford, and he told me he was backing his long-time friend Peter Gzowski for the *Maclean's* job. "Of course, if you were a man, with your success at *Chatelaine*, there would be no question that you would get it yourself," he had added tactfully.

Jean Wright, who had worked on *Maclean's*, told me bluntly that I would be crazy to take the job, with a staff full of male chauvinists of mediocre talent all hankering for the editorship. She said *Maclean's* never promoted women, and its editors repeatedly demonstrated that they considered women underlings fit only to do research and service jobs. McEachern, in her opinion, was almost certifiable.

Not even my husband was encouraging. "Look," he said, in what he believed was his most considerate manner, "you're getting close to menopause, you know. Perhaps you should start thinking about slowing down."

On Friday, September 12, Templeton resigned and I expected a call. There was nothing but silence. The following Monday at a planning conference, McEachern seemed unusually buoyant. Afterwards he took me aside and told me his version of the story. He claimed he and Templeton had been getting along fine, then, "Bang!" he said, smashing his fist into his hand. I asked him about my memo. He said he had turned it over to Templeton and told him to call me.

Templeton, of course, hadn't called. My memo had been used as part of McEachern's strategy to force him to resign. By bullying him into quitting, McEachern had saved the company the severance pay Templeton had negotiated. I asked McEachern for an interview about the *Maclean's* editorship, and he assured me he would be getting back to me soon.

A short time later, I bumped into Gerry Brander, publisher of *Maclean's*. Up to that point, he had had very little to do with hiring *Maclean's* editors, so I was surprised when he cheerfully told me—as though he were giving me good news—that he was going to hire Peter Gzowski as editor. I angrily asked him if he had seen my memo. He had never even heard of it. Furthermore, he seemed quite startled when I told him that I had been led to believe I was a candidate. "I heard you didn't want it!" he said.

"Where did you get that information?"

"On the street," he replied, whatever that meant.

I asked him for an interview, and he dropped into my office the next day—not, I realized, the way serious prospects for an important job are treated. Nevertheless, I gave him a strong pitch. After it, Brander explained why he was going to hire Gzowski: when most of the staff had staged a mass walkout with Lefolii, Gzowski had stayed behind to put out the magazine. He also said he thought Gzowski was a changed man—no longer the young hothead who had run up thousands of dollars of overtime printing at the plant and cost the company so much in lawsuits.

He went on to give me his overview of the magazine business. *Chatelaine* Brander described as a big "paper mill," as though we could fill it with almost any twaddle and money would just flow in. I pointed out that during the fifties, under three previous editors, *Chatelaine*—not *Maclean's*—had been the sick magazine of the company. His reply was to tell me he had to leave for a meeting and would look at my memo. As he left my office, he suggested we have lunch someday.

On October 3, I heard a news announcement had confirmed Gzowski as editor, with Phil Sykes, previously with the Toronto *Telegram*, as managing editor. I phoned Brander, who hadn't even had the grace to get back to me, and asked how the decision had been made. "The main objection to you," he said candidly, "is not that you're a woman, but that you can't represent the company publicly. And we're not sure what—as a woman—you might do in the future."

I asked what possible reason there could be for my not being able to represent the company publicly—except that I was a woman. I gave more speeches and appeared on more panels and television programs than almost any other editor in the company. What did they mean by implying I couldn't handle the job because of my family commitments, when I had reorganized *Chatelaine* and launched several other magazines and books while my children were still small? Now that my sons were in school, I had more time and needed more challenge. He muttered again about "lunch."

Infuriated at the abominable way I had been treated, I was ready to take an axe to the executive floor. Instead, I invited Jean, my long-suffering managing editor, out for a drink and ranted away for at least an hour. The next day I wrote Gzowski a note—something about the "best man" winning. I received a nice reply, in which he said he thought I would have been a good choice too, "but God knows this company has made it clear in so many ways already that it just won't practice what a great many of your editorials have preached. I'd offer to buy you a drink on it if I wasn't afraid you'd think (probably correctly) that I was trying to pick your brains. The hell with it, let's have a drink anyway. The man pays. P.G."

I didn't expect him to call and he didn't.

About the same time, a note from McEachern landed on my desk: "I don't know your real feelings about the settlement at *Maclean's*. But I very much hope you have no regrets. The *Maclean's* job will be a success only for the person who pours everything into it. The thing needs an awful lot of fix to have relevance for the seventies. I think your private and personal life deserves time to flourish. And if *Chatelaine* now takes less than your all, I think that's the way it ought to be. I am a horrible example of one who for too long poured everything into my job. Now on the verge of retirement I realize I hardly exist as a private person. Don't you do that to yourself. Ron."

In December 1969 at the annual Eaton party for the press, I ran into Gerry Anglin, who was working at the *Star Weekly*. In the presence of my husband and Gerry Brander, he began to enthuse about what a great job he thought Gzowski would do. I suppose I should have smiled sweetly and agreed with him, but I didn't feel like it and exploded. I reminded him that when he was on staff at *Maclean's* he had been treated like a has-been by both Gzowski and Lefolii—a fact that had irritated me and should have enraged him. I added that his comments were just another example of how well the Old Boys' Club stuck together. Anglin, Brander, and their wives, along with David, acted as though I had dropped my drawers in the middle of the floor.

Within weeks, I heard that Gzowski was getting a lot of editorial interference from McEachern. Five months later, on April 27, I received a call, this time from Donald Hunter himself, asking me to come to his office. He informed me that Gzowski had resigned and he and McEachern were finally considering me for the editorship of *Maclean's*. I told him I had wanted the job for some time, but with the magazine's record of five editors in less than two years, I was beginning to have some reservations about editorial interference and how permanent the job was likely to be. He suggested I join him and McEachern for lunch.

Back in my office, I immediately called Gzowski, Hodgkinson, Brander, and Gordon Rumgay, the company's circulation manager. An exhausted and dejected Gzowski told me he had resigned for a number of reasons. An article by Mordecai Richler, with the usual complement of four-letter words, had been vetoed by McEachern even after it had been cleaned up. McEachern had also decreed that certain writers he didn't like were not to be used. Gzowski's advice to me, if I took on the job, was "to look around for something else and not plan on staying long."

Gordon Rumgay said he thought *Maclean's* was going to take a long time to turn around and advised me not to touch it. Brander's report was that McEachern had meddled with everything Gzowski considered important, then added that half the staff—still almost entirely male—would probably walk out if I became editor. Hodgkinson said the company couldn't fold *Maclean's*, because it would have to repay more than $1 million in unserviced subscriptions.

On Tuesday over lunch at the University Club, McEachern assured me he had left Gzowski alone, but in the next breath admitted that he had objected to several stories and had vetoed the Richler piece. I told Hunter and McEachern that I couldn't possibly operate—nor could any other editor—if I had to be constantly looking over my shoulder and trying to second-guess someone else.

I assured them that there was no job I wanted more than *Maclean's*. However, because I would be relinquishing a very secure job with a secure pension, I would need some guarantee of decent severance pay, should I too be forced to resign. I pointed out that if I had to quit, my pension would be negligible. (Today, after twenty-six years working at Maclean Hunter, it's only $10,000 a year.) The severance package would be an assurance of good faith on both our parts, and a guarantee that I would be able to operate with reasonable freedom from interference.

Both men appeared to be shocked. They apparently thought I would be so grateful to even be considered that I would take the job without any protection at all against either interference or financial loss. In fact, Hunter objected at once, saying that a contract for severance pay would be an incentive for me to quit. I asked him why I would do such a thing—since I had more at stake than almost anyone else. With a career and reputation based solely on my work at *Chatelaine*, I wanted more than anything else to prove I could successfully edit a general interest magazine. Until I did, nothing but intolerable working conditions would make me quit.

We parted. They said they would get back to me in a few days with a counterproposal. I spent the rest of the day and most of the night thinking about *Maclean's* and going over my plans for it. Once again, I was completely fired up about its possibilities.

On Wednesday I heard that Phil Sykes, managing editor of *Maclean's*, was trying to organize a strike by the staff if he wasn't made editor.

A few hours later, I met with Hunter and McEachern again. As they talked about their vision of *Maclean's*, I began to realize why they were now approaching me. They wanted a much less controversial magazine— more of a lifestyle one that would generate advertising with articles on checkers, golf, and other "soft" features. I explained that *Chatelaine's* success could not be traced to its service features, no matter how much credit Lloyd Hodgkinson attributed to them. *Chatelaine* had succeeded because I was willing to take on tough, controversial subjects—abortion, divorce, wife battering, and family-law reform. These topics had caught the attention of readers and built circulation. For *Maclean's* to succeed, it would have to tackle equally difficult subjects—the possibility of Quebec separating, the future of the CBC, native unrest.

I then decided to go further than I ever had in appeasing a publisher. I offered to submit controversial material to McEachern ahead of time so that we could work out any problems and avoid the vetoes that had plagued past editors. That was a big concession and, considering McEachern's penchant for interfering, a considerable risk. But I truly wanted the job.

The upshot of the meeting was that they agreed to those terms, but we were still stuck on the financial arrangements. They were willing to offer me only $35,000—slightly more than I was then being paid. If I quit or was fired, they would consider half pay for a short period. I wanted at least full pay for a year. The meeting ended with McEachern's taking my arm and accompanying me out the door. "I know you think I'm a son of a bitch, but I'm the best friend you ever had," he said, which did little to reassure me.

The next day, I sent Hunter a memo assuring him once again that I wanted the position. As a concession, I shortened the severance packet from a year to nine months. That's how desperately I wanted to be editor of *Maclean's*. He called me back to say he had read my memo and would get back to me the next day.

Friday after lunch, I heard that the staff of *Maclean's* had met with Hunter. That night at a party at Anna Porter's, then editorial director of McClelland and Stewart, I talked to Charles Templeton, who told me his salary at *Maclean's* had been not $45,000 but $53,000. He said McEachern interfered at least a dozen times a day. Nor did he have anything good to say about the staff, most of whom he considered lazy and unprofessional. He wagered the magazine would fold within a year.

Over the next few days, although I continued to work on plans for *Maclean's*, I heard nothing from Hunter. I called. No reply. After almost a week, on May 6, I heard through the grapevine that Sykes had been appointed editor. On May 7 it was announced in the *Telegram*.

I phoned Hunter again. He said they had appointed Sykes because the whole staff had threatened to walk out if they hadn't. I was called to McEachern's office, where he was sitting in the darkened room, his glasses as usual perched on top of his head. He was smoking furiously. "I assume you've read the papers?" he asked with a wry smile. I said I had. "We decided to settle for peace this time around." He added that the staff were "acting like undergraduates" but things weren't settled. They were "just on ice."

Later that day, Hodgkinson dropped into my office to say he thought McEachern should be fired, Hunter should be made chairman of the board, Donald Campbell, by then executive vice-president, should be made president, and he, Lloyd, should get McEachern's job. He suggested that if that happened, I would be made editor of *Maclean's*.

Mid-week, I had lunch with Bob Fulford, who thought Gzowski's mistake was in not firing everyone when he first took over. Later that week, Alan Edmunds, a *Maclean's* writer, told me confidentially that he and Sykes would have quit if I had been given the editorship. This, of course, would not have bothered me, but it did surprise me. I had considered him a friend.

In June, Brander came to my office and said he thought Sykes would last about three months. To my astonishment, I was also paid a visit by the advertising manager of *Maclean's*, Ken Stewart, who prided himself on being an incorrigible male chauvinist. In the past he had always gone out of his way to refer to my husband as Mr. McCubbin, although I had dropped my maiden name years before. (Of course he never did it in David's presence.) That day, he began the conversation by telling me ingenuously that he wasn't against feminists but truly believed a woman's place was in the home.

He admitted that three hundred pages of advertising a year rolled into *Maclean's* on good will alone, without the sales staff lifting a finger, and that it wasn't enough to make a profit. As he left, he added he was supporting me for the editor's job—a statement I very much doubted. Nevertheless, the fact that Stewart was in my office making conciliatory remarks at all meant that I was still a possible candidate for the *Maclean's* job.

At this point, I was beginning to doubt I even wanted the damned thing. It was clear that McEachern would always be an interfering boss, and that Hunter expected me to work for much less pay and protection than he was willing to give a man. I also fervently believed *Maclean's* had to broaden its outlook to succeed, which would require the kind of rigorous journalism Hunter and McEachern did not seem to want.

In September, McEachern resigned and Don Campbell became president. Once again Brander came in for a talk. He told me I wasn't given the job on the last round because McEachern didn't think I would be able to get along with him. I didn't disagree. Hodgkinson, in his usual buoyant manner, was sure he was going to get McEachern's job. Apparently, he was boasting around town that he and I were the best magazine team in North America. Although this surprised me, considering all the set-tos we'd had in the past, I reasoned that it was a good selling point in his pitch to replace McEachern.

Early in November, I had a meeting with Campbell and gave him a short history of my negotiations with the company. I told him that I was still very much interested in *Maclean's*. About the same time, Peter Newman informed me at a dinner we were both attending that he was considering the *Maclean's* job. I realized immediately that my chances of becoming editor of *Maclean's* would drop drastically with Newman in the picture.

Floyd Chalmers, now honorary chairman of the board, told me later that month that he had recommended me as a director on Maclean Hunter's board. He added that in his opinion I was indispensable to *Chatelaine*, which was carrying the magazine division. As an afterthought, he confirmed that Peter Newman was being considered for the *Maclean's* job. He doubted Hodgkinson would be given McEachern's job because he had got the company into "too many projects that lost money."

Early in December, Campbell asked me for my ideas on *Maclean's*, saying they were toying with the idea of making it a controlled-circulation magazine—a giveaway. I suspected Hodgkinson was pushing the concept and, once again, had the feeling I was being considered because the company wanted a magazine with lots of "soft" subjects to attract advertising. Perhaps I should have encouraged the scheme, but the possibility of a great national magazine, and a voice Canada still very much needed, ending up as a pamphlet flogging merchandise sickened me. I told him flatly that I believed such a plan would make a travesty of the company's flagship magazine. I added that such an act would do both the magazine and the company incalculable harm. I sent him another memo with my plans for *Maclean's*, and we met again just before Christmas. He was still pushing the giveaway idea.

By this time, the talk all over town was that I would be given the *Maclean's* job only if Newman didn't take it. Privately, I knew that was true. My standard reply, however, was "I have always been the backup—after every other male in Canada who can read or write has been asked."

After Christmas, Hodgkinson informed me that he had been working flat out on plans for *Maclean's* over the holidays. He asked for my editorial ideas—and in the next breath told me he had been talking to Newman. I didn't even bother to reply, and I certainly didn't send him my notes. Instead, I made a pitch for the publisher's job at *Chatelaine* if he should be moved to *Maclean's* as publisher with Newman as editor.

Hodgkinson was appointed publisher of *Maclean's* early in January 1971, but no publisher was named for *Chatelaine*. Instead, Archie Gardner, *Chatelaine's* advertising manager, and I were to report to Campbell. In February, Peter Newman was made editor of *Maclean's*—the sixth in thirty months. He was given a five-year contract with an assurance of no interference.

For the public record, I have always said I was not offered the job at *Maclean's*. It saved me going into all the machinations, that, until now, I haven't wanted to divulge. I believe to this day that I could have put out a fine magazine—the one I dreamed of all that year. I have always regretted never being given the opportunity to prove it.

Over the course of a year I had been led to believe, on at least three occasions, that the *Maclean's* editorship was within my grasp. It turned out that I could have the job only if I were willing to abandon any idea of putting out a lively, provocative magazine relevant to the times. What I was offered each time was the job of gutting *Maclean's* in favour of a life-style magazine.

And I was expected to do it at a lower salary and without the protections other editors had been offered. Once it was clear to management that I wanted to put out a different kind of publication, they always chose a man.

In the fall of 1973, Archie Gardner died suddenly of a heart attack. Rather than appoint me, Hodgkinson became publisher of both magazines. *Chatelaine* continued to make money, but by the next fall, the number of ads started to slump in a softening market. Because Hodgkinson was spending most of his time on *Maclean's*, Bruce Drane, the publisher of *Miss Chatelaine*, was made publisher of *Chatelaine*.

Years after I had left the magazine, I bumped into Lloyd. As usual, we greeted each other cordially and then he said, "Do you know why I didn't make you publisher?"

"No, but I certainly would like to know."

"Because you would have been too hard on the salesmen," he replied resolutely.

"You're damn right," I said. "I would have fired most of them and replaced them with women."

In 1976, Donna Scott, who had been personnel director of Maclean Hunter, was made publisher of *Miss Chatelaine*. She asked for my help, and I met with her frequently. On the basis of my advice, she hired Keitha Maclean, a brilliant writer and editor, to supervise the changeover of *Miss Chatelaine* from a teenage magazine to *Flare*, a young-adult magazine designed to appeal to baby boomers.

Flare was a great success for Donna Scott, although she had had almost no previous experience on either the editorial or advertising side of a magazine. Today several magazines, including *Chatelaine*, have women publishers, and many women across the country are fine salespeople.

There was probably another reason I didn't get the publisher's job. All during the time the negotiations about the *Maclean's* and *Chatelaine* positions were taking place, I had been at cross-purposes with the company over an entirely different matter. In fact, at one point the situation was so bad that Lloyd Hodgkinson suggested I quit, and I, for the first time, told him exactly what I thought of him as a publisher.

The flashpoint for this raw and unfortunate confrontation was not our different personalities, or money, or an advertising campaign, not even the future of *Maclean's*, but the ever-festering question of *Time* and *Reader's Digest*.

Since the early 1950s, the two American magazines had been in Canada competing for advertising against Canadian publications, with devastating results. *Time* spent only 2 per cent of its total editorial cost on a meagre four pages of Canadian content, yet it had the effrontery to call the edition sold here "Canadian." The rest of the magazine was imported for free from its American edition. By contrast, Canadian magazines produced all their content from scratch. It had been highly profitable for both U.S. magazines. *Time*, for example, had an editorial staff of twenty-eight people—for four pages—far larger than that of either *Chatelaine* or *Maclean's*.

No other country in the world had allowed its periodical press to be ravished this way. The death toll among Canadian magazines had been catastrophic. In 1948, there had been nine major national magazines— *Maclean's*, *Chatelaine*, *Canadian Home Journal*, *National Home Monthly*, *New Liberty*, *Saturday Night*, *Canadian Homes and Gardens*, *Mayfair*, and *La Revue Moderne*. Twenty-two years later, with the two U.S. intruders scooping 60 per cent of the advertising for consumer magazines in Canada, only *Chatelaine*, *Maclean's*, and *Saturday Night* were left. Because *Time* and *Reader's Digest* were not cutting into newspaper revenues, the daily press presented the issue as a matter of "freedom of the press" and supported the two American publications. In fact, Canadians were perfectly free to buy U.S. magazines by subscription or on any newsstand, where they crowded out our own magazines twenty to one.

In 1961 a Royal Commission, chaired by the distinguished journalist Grattan O'Leary, had recommended that *Time* and *Reader's Digest* be forced to become true Canadian magazines or be disallowed from competing for Canadian advertising. He also predicted that if nothing was done (at least twenty more U.S. magazines were hoping to enter Canada under the same lucrative conditions), not only would there be no Canadian consumer magazines left but even business publications would be threatened.

The Conservative government of the day took no action, fearing the U.S. would cancel a major aircraft contract. When the Liberals came to power, that great nationalist Walter Gordon, then minister of Finance, passed a law in 1955 declaring publications had to be 75 per cent Canadian owned to compete for Canadian advertising. However, Henry Luce, the owner of *Time*, pressured the U.S. government into threatening cancellation of the highly lucrative auto pact with Canada if *Time* and *Reader's Digest* were not exempted. Gordon had to back down. It was a bitter blow to him—and to Canadian magazines.

In the winter of 1969 my old friend Keith Davey, now a senator, set up a Senate Committee on Mass Media. When Lloyd Hodgkinson showed me the brief he had prepared, it emphasized *Chatelaine*'s food, fashion, and decorating service sections, with the articles barely mentioned. I suggested that a Canadian commission would surely be looking for Canadian content, and perhaps he should put more emphasis on our articles. He apparently seemed to think the best strategy was to make the magazine sound as bland as possible.

His reasoning soon became clear. I knew that after the O'Leary commission, Maclean Hunter had made a truce with *Time* and *Reader's Digest*. To my dismay, the company under the direction of Hunter and McEachern now planned to argue before the Davey committee that we needed *Time* and *Reader's Digest* in order to maintain a viable magazine industry in Canada. This seemed particularly spineless to me, in view of the fact that this would probably be our last chance to rid Canada of the two international giants.

By now the *Toronto Star* and other Canadian papers were on our side. The *Star* was also calling for a National Press Council before which members of the public could take media grievances. Maclean Hunter was going to oppose it. Why, I asked, were we in bed with *Time* and *Reader's Digest*, when we finally had the support of the daily press? I warned Hodgkinson that if I were questioned, I was not going to take the company position.

When we arrived at the committee hearings in Ottawa, Grattan O'Leary was speaking. This grand old icon of Canadian journalism completely reversed himself, saying there wasn't a single Canadian magazine worth saving and that *Time* was doing a fine job. The fact that his son-in-law was now working for *Time* might have coloured his perceptions, but it was a disheartening performance from the former fiery nationalist.

The next day, Hodgkinson argued before the commission that the advertisers were "tired of dating the same girl"—meaning *Chatelaine*. This was his reason for supporting *Time* and *Reader's Digest* in Canada. When my turn came, most of the press had left. Keith Davey, who knew perfectly well what I thought of the U.S. publications, but fearing I would be fired, didn't ask me for my opinion about them. Instead, Senator Harry Hayes, who was a rancher, informed me kindly that he read *Chatelaine* in the bathroom, and asked me what I thought about selected breeding!

Back in Toronto, Martin Goodman, managing editor of the *Toronto Star*, queried me about the company's position. I told him I didn't agree with it, and that I was willing to be quoted. In the *Star* story that appeared following our conversation, I said a high mortality among magazines had always been normal, but in a healthy magazine climate new magazines always replaced old, tired publications. In Canada that wasn't happening, nor was it possible.

I went on to say I was completely confident that we had plenty of talent to support a flourishing Canadian magazine industry. What we needed was a level playing field. "Out of business expediency we've co-operated with *Time* and *Reader's Digest* in the Magazine Advertising Bureau, but as an editor I don't feel obligated to say—after twenty-three years of those two magazines raping the Canadian magazine industry—that I've enjoyed it."

I sent a memo to Hodgkinson alerting him to the interview. In his reply, he admonished me that the last time we had taken on *Time* and *Reader's Digest* we had lost $2 million in advertising from American companies. I wrote back, suggesting he make a list of those companies and send it to Keith Davey and the press, but received no reply.

Later that spring, Keith told me he was going to recommend that *Time* and *Reader's Digest* be deprived of their special status, and asked me for a statement to be incorporated in his report. I sent him one making these points: the job of Canadian magazines is to deal with national and regional issues that affect all Canadians, as well as to interpret different parts of Canada to one another; as a binding force, magazines are as vital to a country as railways, radio, and TV; Canada was certainly capable of supporting a vigorous magazine industry, but not with the continued crippling presence of *Time* and *Reader's Digest*. I added that the statement was my personal opinion, not that of Maclean Hunter.

In 1970, when Don Campbell became president, I was very encouraged when he told me he disagreed with the stand Maclean Hunter had taken before the Davey committee. In the next two years, the company lobbied several people in Ottawa—as did *Time* and *Reader's Digest*—although the two U.S. magazines had a lot more money to spend, of course.

By August of 1974, with another election safely behind it, the Liberal government finally announced that it was going to move on *Time* and *Reader's Digest*. I spent much of that year appearing on panels on the subject, and not surprisingly, in the spring of 1975, I was the only person from Maclean Hunter to be asked to appear before the parliamentary committee in the fall. Campbell, Hodgkinson, and Peter Newman, now also on the board, were shocked. At the next board meeting, an entire hour was taken up discussing my appearing. Two members actually suggested I beg off sick. Only Floyd Chalmers thought I would do a good job.

By the June board meeting, their attitude seemed to have mellowed: the board suggested I write an editorial about the situation facing Canadian magazines and get some public feedback. I did, taking care to send a copy to Don Campbell. The editorial was vetoed by Bruce Drane, my publisher, and later by Hodgkinson, who had been absent at the board meeting. They said it would hurt *Chatelaine* with advertisers. When I pointed out that I would have to phone Senator Davey to let him know the editorial had been vetoed, Hodgkinson burst out, "Why don't you quit?"

Without even thinking I replied, "Why don't you fire me?"

At that point, he calmed down and accused me of "harpooning" him while he was out of town. I was angry too and pointed out that I had been asked to write the editorial. I couldn't refrain from adding that *Chatelaine* had been his major success story among a number of flops—and that it had been a success before he arrived on the scene as publisher. I also said I deeply resented continually having to defend the magazine's integrity, which I considered was his job as publisher. I was dissatisfied as well with the niggardly way the *Chatelaine* staff and I had been paid and treated over the years.

In all my long years of association with him, it was the closest Hodgkinson and I had ever come to a personal fight. We were like two people caught up in a workable but not very compatible marriage, and we both realized we had gone too far—and we both backed down.

At the next board meeting, I began to understand why Hodgkinson was so disturbed. Not only was *Maclean's* still bleeding red ink at the rate of $1.25 million that year, but two other enterprises Lloyd had persuaded the company to invest in were in so much trouble that they had to be sold. Campbell had moved a man in from accounting to help Hodgkinson straighten out the books. After the meeting, Campbell gave me a lift in his chauffeured car and told me the company might have to get rid of the whole magazine division—with the exception of *Chatelaine*.

By September, Hodgkinson and Campbell had managed to get themselves on the list to appear along with me before the parliamentary committee. Hodgkinson's instructions from the board were clear: he was to explain—with no equivocation—that Maclean Hunter was experiencing severe financial problems in its magazine division and that the government's legislation was sorely needed.

In October, Bruce Drane suddenly forbade me to speak out publicly on *Time* and *Reader's Digest*. I told him that as far as I was concerned, Campbell was directing the company's policy before the parliamentary committee, and until I heard from him, I was going to continue as usual. I also pointed out that having to explain to the next journalist who phoned me that I was now gagged on the subject would certainly get us on the front page of every paper in the country.

Before the hearing, both Drane and Hodgkinson went over my brief, tearing it apart. Not being writers, neither was helpful in explaining what they objected to. They seemed to want me to perform some verbal contortion in which I would both support the legislation and throw a bouquet at *Time* and *Reader's Digest* for having helped the industry over the years! It was a declaration I could see both of them being perfectly capable of making, but I would have cut my throat before uttering such a statement. Drane finally said if I presented my brief as it stood, he would resign, which didn't perturb me one whit, of course.

In the end, with some nudging from Hodgkinson, Campbell asked me to remove all references to *Time* and *Reader's Digest*, as though the two magazines were not the point of the legislation! All this time both American magazines deluged the public with ads fighting the legislation. *Reader's Digest*'s large Canadian staff was featured in a full-page newspaper spread as victims if the legislation went through. Sheila Kieran organized a retaliatory ad with a much longer list of Canadian writers who supported the legislation.

When we arrived at the hearings in Ottawa on November 25, Ed Zimmerman, president of *Reader's Digest*, was making his presentation. Far from the mild pap Maclean Hunter was about to present, his statement expressed considerable rage, as he ranted about "rabid nationalists who make me want to vomit," glaring at me all the while.

When my turn came, although my brief had had all its teeth pulled, I managed to make the point that there was no future for magazines in Canada unless some action was taken.

Bill C-58 was finally passed in 1975. To operate in Canada, magazines had to be 75 per cent Canadian owned and have 80 per cent substantially different editorial content from any foreign parent magazine's. Canadian advertisers who placed ads in American magazines that did not meet those conditions could not claim their advertising expenses as tax deductions.

Reader's Digest, which, to its credit, had always been much more responsive than *Time*, met the new conditions. *Time*, arrogant as always, immediately killed its Canadian edition and to this day sells advertising at reduced rates—and still makes a handsome profit.

In the meantime, Maclean Hunter decided to turn *Maclean's* into a bi-monthly news magazine. I never thought this was a particularly good idea, and argued against it at board meetings. I thought the concept of a news magazine had been brilliant back in 1932, when Henry Luce first thought of it, but in the age of television, radio, and tabloids, news magazines—especially bi-monthly ones—seemed archaic. It wasn't until 1979 that *Maclean's* finally changed from a bi-monthly to a weekly. All told, it took fifteen years and the accomplished Bob Lewis, its present editor, to finally put it in the black.

Although Maclean Hunter's business-oriented management had always been a reluctant and certainly never a heroic champion of Canadian magazines, without MH the Canadian magazine industry would certainly have disappeared altogether. Today the company has ten consumer magazines—all, including *Chatelaine* (at least under Mildred Istona's editorship), heavily consumer-and-advertising oriented—and totally bland.

However, more than four hundred other magazines now flourish in Canada, surely proof that Bill C-58 was needed and a clear vindication for persisting in that long, discouraging fight. And the fight continues—*Sports Illustrated*, another magazine in the Time-Warner complex, was almost successful recently in making an end run around Bill C-58. Its case is still being contested. If it wins, a flood of other American magazines will surely follow.

Vigilance is still the price Canadians must pay for being the closest neighbour to the largest English-speaking country in the world. Ninety-five per cent of all movies shown in Canada are American, as are two-thirds of all books, and four out of five magazines. With the huge American bookstore chains threatening to open in Canada, our book-publishing industry is more imperilled than ever. It could be reduced to a handful of Canadian authors writing for and being marketed through branch plants of large U.S. firms.

As early as 1971, it was clear to me that there was no future for me any-where in the company except in the job I had been doing for fifteen years. The logical move would have been to start looking around for something else to do. With so few magazines in Canada, there was no place to go. Public relations and advertising had never appealed to me. Although I was a close friend of Ross MacLean's, the legendary television producer of "Tabloid" and "This Hour Has Seven Days," I was not a television type—not young enough, pretty enough, and much too opinionated.

I might have considered moving to New York where the magazine busi-ness was much more volatile and editors frequently changed jobs. By that time, though, a crisis, far more serious than any problems involving my career, was taking place in my life.

CHAPTER TWELVE

Life as a Single Parent

To me, one of David Anderson's greatest attractions was his genial, happy-go-lucky nature, so different from that of my difficult, explosive father. He adored our three sons but balked at disciplining them. Worse was that although he refused to make rules for them himself, he constantly subverted mine. I was tired of playing the heavy in a family of three boys, and my disagreements with their father had begun to affect the children adversely. After a long, anguishing year meeting with family counsellors and psychiatrists, David and I separated in early 1972.

The next six months were difficult as I agonized over whether I had done the right thing, half hoped we could still patch things up, and fretted at the thought of raising three young males—aged thirteen, eleven, and nine—by myself. As each month passed, though, I became more and more convinced that if parents can't agree, children are far better off under the care and consistent direction of one of them. And I was lucky. Financially independent, I had none of the all-too-common monetary difficulties that keep women locked in unhappy marriages.

Over the years at *Chatelaine*, we had often written about the need for reform of our divorce laws and child-support system, but 1973 was the year the plight of divorced women would hit the headlines with far more dramatic results than could ever be accomplished by a magazine article.

Irene Murdoch, an Alberta farm wife, had worked alongside her husband for more than twenty-five years, herding cattle, branding, and tending the ranch for long periods while he was away—and of course raising the children and looking after the house. When her husband decided he wanted to marry a younger woman and kicked her off the premises, her jaw broken in two places, this plucky woman took her case to court, claiming half the assets of the ranch.

The Alberta Supreme Court awarded her no assets at all and only a measly $200 a month support. Undaunted, she appealed to the Supreme Court of Canada, where she again lost. According to the learned judges, all her toil over the years only added up to "the work done by any ranch wife." This decision meant that no matter how much work a wife put into a family business, she was not entitled to a single penny of its assets after a divorce.

The Supreme Court ruling sent shock waves through Canadian households, bringing about fundamental reform that would benefit all Canadian women—though not Murdoch herself. Gradually, family law changed province by province. Today marriage is regarded as a partnership: when the partnership breaks down, the assets both partners have worked to amass—personal and professional—are divided evenly.

Under the old law, I probably would have been awarded the house and some child support. David and I divorced a good two years before Ontario's Family Law Act was passed in 1975, but we behaved as though it was already in effect. We had all our assets evaluated and divided the total down the middle. As I was the parent who would remain in the house with the children, I sold some of my Maclean Hunter stock to buy out his share of the house.

When it came to child support, I, like every other woman in Canada, got badly short-changed. My problem was not that of three-quarters of single mothers today—that my ex-husband refused to pay, or was in arrears with his child support. My problem was taxes. When my lawyer explained the income-tax laws regarding child support, I settled for minimum support—only $390 a month for the three boys. David, as a lawyer, could easily have paid much more, but whatever he gave me would have been added to my income and heavily taxed. On the other hand, he could claim everything he paid in child support as a tax deduction. (That law, which was grossly unfair to women, was only changed in 1996.) Instead, David and I agreed to split the costs of the big expenses of raising children: dental bills, camp, university education, and the like.

After the divorce, feeling the children needed stability and consistency, I stuck with my job at *Chatelaine* for another five years.

It wasn't until the second summer after our separation, when my sons were away for a month with their father, that I began to relax a little and feel less like a mother and more like a woman again. Alone for the first time in years at age fifty-two, I enjoyed a freedom I had almost forgotten. I jumped in the pool one night with all my clothes on, just because I felt like it. I dated a few men, and even slept with one of them. And to give myself new interests and to meet new people, I increased my after-work activities.

In 1974 I joined the board of the Canadian Film Development Corporation, the predecessor of Telefilm Canada. Our job was to try to fan the fragile flames of movie production in Canada. Gratien Gelinas, the French-Canadian playwright, was chair, and Michael Spencer, formerly of the National Film Board, was executive director. Our meetings were often hilarious: at one summer gathering of the board and English- and French-Canadian filmmakers, Gelinas wore only a bikini and a crocheted hat. Periodically, he would rise and dance with rage about filmmaking conditions in Canada. English-born Spencer, on the other hand, would sit—clad all in khaki topped by a Baden-Powell–style hat—like a long-suffering custodian of British values in a dreary outpost of the empire. At our regular meetings, we spent a lot of time mulling over scripts and projects, trying to decide which tiny grants should be allotted to what writers and filmmakers.

The real problem was starkly simple—and unsolvable: how can our audiences see Canadian films when the two big theatre chains are completely controlled by American distributors who regard Canada as just another marketing region of the U.S.? Even with voluntary promises from Odeon and Famous Players that they would provide a small amount of time to show Canadian movies, we had no method of enforcement. Most theatre owners showed Canadian films only in the "dead" times when attendance is seasonally low. We were like mice trying to bell two large cats.

When I replaced Signy Eaton as the only woman on the board of York University, I immediately managed to offend the chairman by actually speaking at my very first meeting. Apparently my predecessor had been much more quiet and ladylike. Subsequently, given the job of finding another woman to add to the board, I put forward my friend Barbara Frum. The board black-balled her as "too controversial." Undeterred, I presented ten more names, from which they picked another great friend, Adrienne Clarkson.

About the same time, I joined the Littering Control Council of Ontario. It had been formed to try to deal with the mounting numbers of non-returnable bottles and cans. I soon realized, if I hadn't grasped the fact before, how difficult it is to bring about even quite obvious changes in society if strong commercial forces choose to block them. After two years of meetings and all kinds of obfuscation from members of the industry, the only action taken was an educational campaign paid for by the taxpayer, which urged the public to be tidy in public places!

By far the most controversial board I sat on was the Tri-Lateral Commission. Probably it attracted so much conjecture about its so-called sinister intentions because it was founded by David Rockefeller, president of the Chase Manhattan Bank, and because several of its members ended up in high-powered positions in Jimmy Carter's government.

In the early 1970s, Rockefeller became convinced that there was a need for a closer dialogue between the West and the Japanese. The Tri-Lateral Commission was made up of thirty members each from Europe, the U.S., and Japan, with an additional ten from Canada. Most of the people from the first three groups were hand picked from top industrial, academic, and government leaders—for example, Giovanni Agnelli, president of Fiat in Italy; Garret Fitzgerald, future prime minister of Ireland; and Henry Kissinger, former U.S. secretary of state. One of the few women on it was Mary Robinson, who later became president of Ireland.

Our small Canadian contingent was selected in a typically Canadian fashion. All the usual bases—geographical, business, labour, French, English plus a token woman—me—were covered. At various times it included the ex-cabinet ministers Jean Luc Pepin, Mitchell Sharp, Donald Macdonald, Gordon Fairweather, as well as businessmen such as Alan Hockin from the Toronto Dominion Bank. The very capable Peter Dobell and his small parliamentary staff did all the administrative work.

In New York, at my first meeting in the fall of 1973, at breakfast I sat across from the governor of Georgia, a short, fair-haired man with a dazzling smile who introduced himself as Jimmy Carter. I noticed him particularly because he puckishly asked one speaker who had posed a long, bewildering question, "Would you repeat that, please?" At a subsequent meeting in Tokyo, he was busily shaking every hand in sight and telling everyone he was running for the presidency of the United States. Because the Tri-Lateral Commission was weighted heavily with Republicans, he was not taken very seriously. However, when he did become president, he dipped into its membership for more than twenty key appointments in his Democratic government, among them Walter Mondale, who later ran for the presidency himself; Caspar Weingarten, secretary of Defense; and

Zbigniew Brzezinski, the brilliant but hawkish secretary of the commission, who later became Carter's national security adviser.

Most of the commission's papers had a decidedly right-wing slant on subjects discussed at such gatherings: the governance of democracies, global redistribution of power, oceans and resources, world food problems, trade, and the environment. I don't know whether the commission itself smoothed relationships between countries, but it certainly extended and enhanced membership in the international Old Boys' Club. My dubious contribution was to keep urging David Rockefeller, a shy, self-effacing man, to be more open to the press, because I thought some of the position papers merited more publicity. Like many moneyed people, though, he was suspicious about press coverage, which probably contributed to the myth that this cabal of international heavyweights was plotting to take over the world.

During this time, my main priority certainly was not more power for men but a little more for women. In the early 1970s, that looked a lot more possible. In 1971 I remember getting a call from Marion Younger, a well-known Saskatchewan activist, who said she was going after money from the provincial government to hold a women's conference, and would I be their keynote speaker. I agreed, but privately thought they had little hope of getting the money. They didn't that year but did the next. By then, the women from the more traditional organizations had been joined by a new group of feisty youngsters—and sisterhood was flourishing. Not that all opposition had vanished. When Betty Friedan gave a lecture at the old Eaton College Street auditorium, several women stomped out and one had to be evicted to stop her from haranguing the speaker.

Just before every election, Ontario's Conservative government had been in the habit of staging one-day conferences for women around the province. At each, there would be a speaker or two, and the usual lunch of sandwiches and salad. Afterwards, it was presumed that the grateful women would go home and vote Conservative.

In the early 1970s, they made the mistake of inviting me to speak at the Toronto meeting. When I arrived at the Royal York Hotel, a small group of women were picketing the conference as a waste of tax dollars and a brazen political exercise. Stanley Randall, the minister of Consumer Affairs, constantly referred to women as "consumers" in his opening remarks and was booed. I followed with a feminist speech, and received a standing ovation. Randall and the woman who had been running these cosy get-togethers for years looked quite ill.

With so much happening so fast, we activists had little time to meet one another. In 1974 Johanna Stuckey, a forceful professor at York University, and Maryon Kantaroff, the fiery feminist sculptor, held an all-woman wine-and-cheese party in Maryon's studio. It was such a success that Moira Armour, a long-time feminist, and I staged another party six months later. These gatherings went on for another six months until they outgrew any suitable space.

Feminism was becoming acceptable and even being acknowledged. In the spring of 1973, the University of Alberta bestowed an honorary degree on me—the first of several I was to be given over the next twenty years. In April of 1975, I flew to Ottawa to receive the Order of Canada along with the actress Kate Reid and the great Quebec feminist Thérèse Casgrain, then well over seventy, who curtsied almost to the floor when she was presented to Governor General Jules Léger. One of the greatest pleasures of that evening for me was the sight of my handsome fourteen-year-old son, Stephen, who usually slouched around in dirty jeans and a T-shirt, magnificently attired in evening clothes.

All through those last years at *Chatelaine* and my first years as a single parent, I drank far too much, stayed up too late, and worked too hard. Frustrated, bored, and unhappy, I realized I had stayed too long and I would soon have to leave the magazine. Even the staff was beginning to sense that I was losing interest, and I knew it would only be a matter of time before the readers began to feel it too.

None of the people I thought would have made fine editors—Michele Landsberg, Jean Wright, Christina McCall—wanted the job. They knew, as I did, that management would want someone far more malleable than I. Having watched other long-time editors of U.S. women's magazines leave, usually followed by a period of upheaval, I wanted to depart with as little disruption to the magazine and staff as possible.

A few years before, while lunching with the novelist Margaret Laurence, I had confided that I was working on a novel and was very apprehensive about it. She sent me the following note, "Don't feel you're alone in feeling protective and apologetic and desperately uncertain about your writing. All fiction writers do (poets too). It's because we're never certain whether we've given birth to a branch of the tree of life, or a small anonymous monster under a damp stone."

Taking courage from her advice, I started getting up at six and writing every morning before work, until after two years I finished my first book, *Two Women*. Jack McClelland, the former president of McClelland & Stewart, had once said, "I'll publish any book you write, sight unseen. If it's a success, it will do us both a lot of good. If it's a failure, it will do me some good and you a lot of harm." I didn't find this very reassuring. As a professional writer, but a neophyte at writing novels, I knew I needed a good editor, and I wound up with Doug Gibson at Macmillan Canada.

By the spring of 1977, I was deeply unhappy at Maclean Hunter. Management seemed far more interested in stock splits and making money than in publishing. Bruce Drane, *Chatelaine*'s publisher, an ambitious young man at least ten years my junior, had made some useful changes when he first took over. He had shaken up the advertising department, canned some of the worse promotions, and raised my salary to $38,000.

On the negative side, Bruce was highly erratic and would burst into my office several times a day with badly thought out ideas. For example, he took a notion to expand our crafts department, which brought in a modest profit. Then, realizing it would never be a big moneymaker, he wanted to kill it entirely. One day he wanted to fire our art director, who was on maternity leave, and hire a man from New York. I of course refused. Even if one ignored the fact that we already had a fine art director, what would a New York male know about Canadian women? He disliked Canadian personalities on our covers, preferring very young models—a blonde of the month, issue after issue, would have pleased him—making us indistinguishable from our U.S. rivals.

Bruce kept pushing for far more service articles and fewer general stories. When he couldn't get anywhere with me on dubious advertising tie-ins, he began going directly to the editors, which was against company policy. By June of 1977, I had documented several of these cases and handed them, along with my resignation, to Don Campbell. Campbell's response was that it was a great mistake for me to leave just when the company was going to begin contributing fairly heavily to my pension plan. Bruce, believing I had been offered another job, stormed down to my office, demanding to know where I was going. Because I had been provoked into resigning by his behaviour, I had no trouble getting the company to agree to a year's severance pay, which I felt I had more than earned over the years.

The company gave me a fine farewell at the Harbour Castle Hotel. The best party, however, was the staff party at Winston's, where my colleagues parodied *Chatelaine* and told in-house jokes. Judy La Marsh also gave me a party, which was attended by many old friends—Keith Davey, Royce Frith, Sheila Kieran, Gerry Grafstein, Julian Porter, and Jack McClelland. While we chatted, Judy sat in the corner stroking her poodle and wondering aloud whether she should take a job teaching at the University of Western Ontario.

Floyd Chalmers took me out to lunch at the exclusive York Club. Almost deaf by then, and with a hearing aid that never seemed to be working, he talked at the top of his voice about the company and the people in it. Thankfully, only Signy Eaton and one of her sons was present to hear his complaints.

With no immediate plans and about six months before *Two Women* was to be published, I needed time to get away and think, and there was a lot to think about. Up to the 1970s my generation had enjoyed twenty-five wonderful post-war years, and we believed we were within reach of solving almost all of our social problems. It was impossible to live through the much celebrated sixties and not be affected. When discos arrived with their blaring music and flashing lights, we tried them. When our children wanted long hair like the Beatles, we went along with it and we danced in the aisles of the Royal Alexander Theatre after the opening of the musical *Hair*.

But I failed miserably in other attempts to "get with it." My hairdresser, an angelic-looking young man, told me in his soft Scottish accent that he regularly dropped LSD with his partner every weekend. Shortly after this, while seated at a dinner party beside Martin Goodman, then managing editor of the *Toronto Star*, I confessed I wanted to try pot but had no idea where to buy it.

"I'll get you some," he said.

The next day a bulky brown envelope arrived at *Chatelaine*, with enough hash to make two cigarettes. That night, after the children were in bed, David and I solemnly rolled two cigarettes and smoked them, but because I had never been able to inhale even when I smoked, I didn't get much of a buzz, and neither did he. We went back to liquor.

In many ways the sixties repelled my Depression-weathered soul. It was an age of excess—a bit like the 80s—and the true beginning of consumerism. We were told there would be no end to prosperity, if only people bought more—a conventional piece of mythology still being promoted today. We were urged to toss out perfectly good objects that were slightly out of date. All kinds of ridiculous, energy-wasting gadgets briefly became consumer goals for millions of people: electric carving knives, pencil sharpeners, and bigger, more complex washing machines, driers, and television sets.

Clothes were instantly disposable. Instead of carefully made garments you might wear for several seasons, fashions changed with dizzying rapidity. Cheap knock-off copies of U.S. styles were flung on the market, only to be labelled passé a few months later. I hated throwing away good articles for no good reason, except that a newer design was now available. I hated raising our children to waste and overconsume. The excess packaging and mountains of garbage we began to throw out sickened me.

I was fifty-five. I had been working flat out ever since I had graduated from high school, with the exception of university and that one year in Europe. Although my pragmatic side told me I should be lining up another job, nothing appealed to me. I wanted to relax for the next little while, clean out my cupboards, make chili sauce—and think about my future. Having long considered politics a natural extension of the kind of changes I had been trying to bring about as *Chatelaine*'s editor, and having penned dozens of editorials on the need for more women in Parliament, I was now seriously considering taking my own advice.

My plan was to take a four-month holiday in Europe with my two youngest sons—by this time, Peter, my eldest, was in his last year of high school and living with his father. We were to have no schedule, no itinerary, and no worries. I would come back just before my novel was published. In early October 1977, my brother Jim and his wife, Lorna, who were now living in Toronto, saw us off on an overnight flight. As the lights of Toronto disappeared, and the darkness settled in around the plane, I felt all the burdens of those last few years fall away.

My choice for our Grand Tour *en famille* would have been to travel by train and stay at moderately priced hotels. But at sixteen and fourteen, the boys had gargantuan appetites, making travelling by camper the only possibility financially. To make sure they didn't miss out on their school year, each took two correspondence courses. They usually put in a couple of hours every night while I read. Stephen chose English and European art, while Mitchell chose math. Because I had always liked math, I decided to teach myself "new math" so that I could help him. I was out of my depth in two weeks.

We covered the Netherlands, Belgium, southern Germany, France, Spain, and Portugal from September until the end of November. Occasionally, we checked into a hotel to get away from one another for a short time and enjoy the luxury of a real bed, a soak in a tub, and a general repacking and reorganizing. Most of the time, however, the accoutrements of civilization simply went by the boards. Accustomed to a mother who dressed for the office every day, my sons complained, "You keep wearing that same black outfit!"

"Well, get used to it," I replied, revelling in my new uniform of jeans, T-shirt, and a pullover.

Because I did all the driving, the boys took over all the navigating, soon becoming expert enough to guide us, with the aid of Michelin maps, through every major city in Europe. It was also their responsibility to calculate exchange rates, and check shopping, banking, and postal hours as well as useful information about the customs of each country. Every three or four days one of them would do the washing at a public launderette while I went with the other one to shop for groceries. We took turns cooking and cleaning up.

There were trade-offs, of course—the only way to make communal living bearable. I learned a lot more about motorbikes, cars, farm machinery, geology, and insects than, strictly speaking, I ever expect to use. I could stand only so many teenage jokes, imitations of animals, and recaps of old movies and TV shows. In return for a limit to this form of entertainment, Stephen and Mitchell put a quota on the number of times I was allowed to exclaim about the scenery.

The footloose feeling of being able to linger whenever we felt like it and pick up and go at random made up for hard mattresses, cramped quarters, and a "top of the line" camper that kept breaking down. The entire trip cost about $15,000. We rented the camper for $4,500 and gas averaged $20 a day. Campsites ranged from $2 to $8 nightly. The big saving was on food: in France we dined on fresh mussels, artichokes, superb cheeses, crisp vegetables, and unusual breads. The wine of the region was often as little as $1 a bottle. In Italy and Spain, restaurants were inexpensive and we gave up cooking altogether.

There was a minor crisis almost every day. We would get lost, in spite of my sons' navigational skills, or we would, out of ignorance, find ourselves in a jam—driving down the verboten-to-cars streetcar tracks in Heidelberg, or having to back up on a one-way street in a small French town. These misadventures we could laugh about later over dinner, but we found little to laugh about on two other occasions.

One afternoon in November, we were driving along Spain's scenic north coast. The road was wide but slippery with grease from the many trucks that used the highway. There were no guardrails and a long drop to the ocean beneath. It began to rain and on a particularly sharp curve the camper swerved out of control, turned around twice, then skidded and overturned, stopping with a sickening lurch on a ledge above the sea.

We scrambled out. Luckily, none of us was hurt, but the van's side window was broken, and the sliding door dented. Standing in the pouring rain, I longed for a North American towtruck. Instead, hordes of helpful Spaniards stopped, offering me water, cigarettes, beer, and brandy while an officious policeman directed traffic. Finally, after half an hour two short swarthy men in a tiny white van pulled up. They produced a rope, and while we looked on dubiously, pulled the camper upright, and changed a flat tire. They then motioned for me to get in and drive off.

I would have mounted a guillotine more happily, but there was nothing else for it. All our possessions were strewn around inside, the window was open to the rain, and it was getting dark. I climbed up, paid the men, thanked everyone, and drove off to loud cheers from the crowd.

We headed for the nearest campsite on the map. As the road got narrower and narrower, I grew increasingly apprehensive. When it became two ruts, Mitchell, who was navigating, said, "Mom, you're not going to like this, but there's a sheer cliff on this side."

My heart stopped. I immediately got out and went around to look. Sure enough the cliff dropped right off to the black ocean below—again with no guardrail. I decided to stay where we were until dawn. Just then a truck came hurtling along the road behind us with an impatient Spaniard at the wheel. He waved us on, indicating that we were blocking his way. I inched fearfully ahead, and about twenty minutes later, we found the camp.

The next morning, as I lay in bed reliving the previous day's events, Mitchell's feet appeared above me, as they did every morning, then Stephen's whiskery youthful face peered at me. I began to cry—as I did frequently for the next few days every time I looked at my sons and considered how close we had come to death.

After the camper was repaired in Madrid, a white car cut in front of the van and we collided. A man and his wife got out of the car and started screaming at me. In retrospect, I think they went on the defensive so that I wouldn't try to get the camper's dented fender fixed on their insurance. Suddenly I snapped and started yelling back at them. Words I didn't know I had in my vocabulary came tumbling out. Not knowing English, they couldn't understand me, and finally returned to their car and drove off. My sons were flabbergasted at this violent and uncharacteristic display of temper on their mother's part.

Our next disaster—and the absolute low point in the trip—also occurred in Spain. We had spent two restful weeks just outside Malaga, visiting my old friend Eva-Lis Wuorio, followed by a week in Lisbon. On our way back across Spain en route to Barcelona, I stopped at the American Express office in Madrid to collect mail and, while I stood in line, my wallet was stolen. I lost only the equivalent of $20, but the thief also got my credit cards. Although I immediately cancelled them, I was told they couldn't be reissued until we arrived in Rome, which meant we had to live on $600 in traveller's cheques for the next two weeks.

Worse was to come. While I reported this disaster to the police, the camper disappeared. Thoroughly shaken, we checked into a modest hotel, then went out and had a good meal. That night I decided if we had indeed lost everything, I would stay in Europe but send the boys home. The next morning the police told me I had parked in a legal parking zone but it had changed to a no-parking zone in rush hour and the camper had been towed away. I paid the $50 fine, depleting our money even further.

We skipped Barcelona and set out for Italy and Florence, where I had instructed my bank to forward about $3,000. By late November, even the Riviera was cold, but we stayed in campsites anyway to save money. As we crossed the border on the pass into Italy, it began to snow and the winds were so strong that the camper swayed like a bread box. In Florence the bank where the money was supposed to be was no longer in business. I phoned my bank again and was directed to another bank, where, at first, they couldn't find the draft. It took another hour of arguing to persuade them to give it to me in American traveller's cheques and not in Italian lire!

When we reached Rome in the middle of December, we left the camper at a campsite and checked into a hotel with adjoining rooms and bath, where we stayed until after Christmas. On Christmas Eve, we toasted one another with champagne—as we had always done at home—and the next morning exchanged gifts. We then left to attend the Christmas service at St. Peter's—one of the most impressive experiences of the trip.

The day quickly turned from the sublime to the ridiculous. That evening I booked dinner at a restaurant that promised to serve turkey. The only other customers were thirty Japanese businessmen, watching the band and its lead singer, a curvaceous blonde. At one point she came down, sat on Stephen's lap, and trilled "Chéri Beri Bien," while he died of embarrassment.

In Austria, the boys had a fine week of superb skiing before we headed back to Amsterdam, where we dropped the camper, then flew to London and home. Later that spring, I wrote an article for *City Woman* about the trip. When I told Stephen what I was doing, he said sardonically, "Are you telling the truth, or are you making it sound like fun?"

As the years go by, the trip becomes more and more memorable. It was a landmark in my life and theirs. I had time to think about my future and what I wanted to do with the rest of my life. My sons grew to like each other better and we all became closer, having to cope with the many challenges we encountered along the way.

Nothing could have prepared us for the shock of getting back to North America. After the confines of a camper, the house seemed far too large for three people. None of us could get over all the things we owned—and had forgotten—in those eleven rooms. Although we possessed no more than most other middle-class people, it seemed excessive after the poverty we had seen, as well as the stripped-down life we had been leading.

After I returned from the trip my inclination was to lead a much quieter life—I had cut back on drinking, once out of the publishing business. Quiet domesticity was not to be. I immediately plunged into a coast-to-coast book tour, after which I was drawn back into the old social and political life, with its rounds of meetings and parties. George Gilmour, president of Macmillan Canada, offered me a job negotiating foreign rights for the publishing firm. Judy La Marsh took me out for a fine dinner accompanied by martinis and wine. She proposed that we go into business together, although I was never quite clear what we would do and had always been wary about her free-spending ways—over dinner she confessed she was $150,000 in debt.

I joined the Ontario Press Council, which had been set up to help people with complaints about the media. Made up of editors, publishers, and members of the public and headed by the indefatigable long-time newsman Fraser MacDougall, it provided another enjoyable, voluntary job for the next five years.

I resumed my habit of parties around our backyard pool. Often guests would stay on far into the night talking about politics, media gossip, inappropriate and illogical love affairs, unhappy marriages, and whether they should quit their jobs. One of the most common questions asked of me in our work-ordered society was "What are you going to *do*?" My lack of a nine-to-five job seemed to make everyone but me extremely nervous.

CHAPTER THIRTEEN

A Short Political Polka

Soon after I returned to Canada, I had lunch in Ottawa with Keith Davey, the Liberals' national campaign co-chairman, and Senator Royce Frith. I had decided to run in the next federal election if I were offered a seat that could be won. Rosedale appealed to me, but John Evans, former president of the University of Toronto, had decided to run there. Over a generous buffet in the parliamentary dining room, I was offered Mississauga South—a long-time Conservative seat, or Don Valley West—another Conservative stronghold. Over the years I had watched too many women dispatched to hopeless ridings, so naturally I must have seemed somewhat underwhelmed. Keith didn't bother to hide his annoyance when I didn't jump at the chance to run in either of those loser ridings.

I was still serious about running, though. Long before I took over *Chatelaine*, I thought electing more women at all levels of government should be a top priority. One of my first editorials pointed this out. Soon after it appeared, I persuaded Charlotte Whitton, the mayor of Ottawa, to write an article called "Canadian Women Belong in Politics." Later I had returned to the subject regularly in the magazine.

David's involvement in the Liberal Party meant I sometimes attended nomination meetings, if he thought his favoured candidate might be short a few votes. The first time he asked me to go to one, I pointed out that I was not a member of that particular riding organization—nor was he. He assured me he had registered both of us, just in case. I began to wonder how democratic the nomination process was if people who didn't live in the riding could be on the voters' list.

I also began to question why all the meetings taking place in our living room were entirely male, when I knew many women were working in the party. Gradually, I realized that women were acceptable as secretaries, convenors of coffee parties, or telephone canvassers in elections. If they decided to run for president of the riding association or ventured to suggest they be delegates to a leadership convention, they suddenly became "difficult" and "shrill."

On one occasion in the sixties, I was invited to speak to the women's auxiliary of a riding association in North Toronto. Once there, I realized that my fiery speech, urging women to get out from behind the coffee urns and into the back rooms where policy was being made probably wasn't going to go over too well. Most of the auxiliary's members and guests present that Saturday afternoon were older women, who seemed content to be making sandwiches, pouring tea, and doing other routine campaign work. I went ahead with my speech anyway. The riding's campaign manager and its member of Parliament, who deigned to arrive for the last part of my address, were horrified. The MP took me aside afterwards and upbraided me for trying to rouse his docile female workers to rebellion. I don't think the speech was much of a success with the audience either, and the word must have spread—I was never invited to give another speech at a similar gathering.

Occasionally the best-laid plans of the male members of the party went astray. One evening in 1962, David told me he was on his way to Northumberland riding in eastern Ontario for a nomination meeting. "There's a young professor from Carleton University running," he said. "She's a great candidate, but she'll never win in a riding full of farmers. We're backing a local man who'll have a much better chance." I remember arguing with him about the heavyweights in the party ganging up on a woman. That night the professor, Pauline Jewett, won. She won because she had spent her entire sabbatical canvassing the riding, and it paid off. Later she and I became great friends.

In 1968, when Trudeaumania swept the country and my living room was once again filled with Liberals—all males—I ventured to point out that in the rush to climb on the Trudeau bandwagon, men were strong-arming women out of the way in nominations all across the country. The party was likely to end up with only one Liberal woman running in all of Canada—and she already held a seat in New Brunswick, or she too probably would have been pushed aside! After my little speech, there was a deadly pause, then everyone began talking—as though to cover up a social gaffe. The Liberals did win a resounding victory, in which every woman candidate but the NDP's Grace MacInnis was defeated. All through the next session, the House of Commons would empty when she occasionally brought up some matter related to women.

By 1971, tired of listening to Keith Davey say he was eager to run women candidates but there was no one suitable and willing to run, I phoned Barbara Frum and asked her to come into the office. Her assignment: to find possible women candidates whose pictures and CVs I planned to publish in *Chatelaine*. Without any trouble at all, she found 104 women—every one of them an outstanding potential candidate. Along with our roster of women, we ran a how-to piece on the facts of political involvement. We told women to pack nomination meetings the way men did and warned them about the "dirty" politics they would encounter—for example, riding executives shifting the date of nomination meetings without informing the candidates they didn't support.

The article caused a sensation. Later, all parties claimed they had approached the women and been turned down. I checked on those claims and, as I suspected, found that while some of the women had been approached, they were offered seats that were impossible to win. Although this was disappointing, the article paid off in other ways. Years after it appeared, I was still receiving letters from women telling me the Frum piece had spurred them to think seriously about politics. Some had won seats in provincial legislatures. Some were mayors. Others were members of city councils, or of local school boards. A few did indeed wind up in the House of Commons.

Chatelaine followed the Frum article with another by Erna Paris, who interviewed the cabinet, the shadow cabinets of the opposition parties, as well as the party leaders, on women's issues. We also sent a questionnaire on women's issues in a registered letter to every member of Parliament. From the replies, we discovered that about two-thirds of the members, including many men in the cabinet and opposition parties, were not only almost totally unaware of the concerns of women, but they considered the whole subject a joke. We decided to grade them as "Excellent," "Good," "Fair," right down to the lowest grade, "Male Chauvinist Pig."

One of the men interviewed was David Lewis, then leader of the NDP. He was graded on our report card as an "MCP." Given that he was Michele Landsberg's father-in-law, and she was on our staff, I thought I had better warn her. "That's right," she said cheerfully. "He's a nice man, but on women he's a dinosaur."

Many members hadn't bothered to reply to our questionnaire, though the letters had been registered, and we had warned them we were going to publish the names of those who didn't respond. To give them every chance, we then phoned those who had not returned the forms. The real shocker was the number of flippant and derogatory replies we received—all of them unsigned. One member suggested that poor women take up prostitution and homeless mothers solve their problem by moving into whorehouses.

When we published the results of our survey, women from coast to coast were infuriated by the ignorance and lack of seriousness displayed not only by their own MPs but also by the men running the country. They were particularly enraged that any paid member of the highest legislature in the land could be crass and vulgar about half of the electorate.

In 1973 I wrote an editorial about a women's organization in Sweden, which had worked to elect more women to government with great success. I urged Canadian women to do the same. This led to the formation of Women for Political Action, an organization that for several years held workshops for women on how to speak in public, deal with the press, write press releases, and win nominations.

That same year, a National Conference on Women in Politics was held in Toronto. Many present and future activists attended: Kay Macpherson, Margaret Campbell, Anne Johnson, Lorna Marsden, Fiona Nelson, and Yvette Rousseau. Rosemary Brown gave the keynote speech and Rita MacNeil sang. I chaired a noisy, explosive panel with lots of interruptions from the floor. It was clear that sisterhood and politics would never be a love-in.

Later in the 1970s, a Feminist Party was formed, ran three candidates, but had no success at the polls. We learned, as women in other countries had before us, that a party counting on half the population as its possible base is doomed to failure.

Under pressure to increase the number of women in Parliament, Trudeau himself—though no great supporter of women—persuaded three women to run in safe Quebec seats in 1972. Monique Bégin later became minister of Health and Welfare, and Jeanne Sauvé, after serving in the cabinet, became Canada's first woman Speaker of the House and then our first woman governor general. Slowly the pressure for more women in Parliament was building.

By the fall of 1978, the Liberal Party was in a dilemma: it had been in power since 1974, and there were fifteen vacant seats—all requiring by-elections. With both unemployment and inflation running high, and the party's popularity at almost an all-time low, their strategists knew the party faced certain defeat in an election. In a delaying tactic, they decided to hold by-elections on October 16.

Immediately after the by-election call, a problem arose in the Eglinton riding. Mitchell Sharp, who had held the seat since the early 1960s, had retired from politics in 1978. Several ambitious young men had jockeyed for this highly desirable Liberal stronghold. However, at the nomination meeting, an outsider, the Reverend Roland de Corneille, an Anglican minister, had arrived on the scene with large numbers of supporters—and won.

The by-election presented the riding with a problem. October 16, it turned out, was a Jewish holiday. De Corneille, who was active in B'nai B'rith, objected vociferously to Ottawa's lack of sensitivity in choosing a date that would offend the one-third of his riding that was Jewish. Wrapping himself in a cloak of righteous indignation, the reverend refused to run at all.

I soon received a call from Jim Coutts, Trudeau's principal secretary. Would I run in Eglinton in the reverend's place? He didn't pretend that the odds weren't daunting: the Progressive Conservative candidate, the former CBC announcer Rob Parker, had been working the riding for at least six months. The by-election was only five weeks away, and by-elections are almost never won by the party in power. The public couldn't wait to get to the polls to teach the Liberals a lesson.

On the other hand, Eglinton was an excellent riding, the best by far that I had ever been offered. In the spring its boundaries were going to be enlarged. If I made any kind of decent showing, I believed—and the Liberals gave me every reason to understand—that they were so furious with de Corneille that I would get a chance at the seat in the federal election in the spring.

I jumped in, a gamble that plunged me into five hectic weeks of pressured, non-stop crises, which, with my adventurous nature, I thoroughly enjoyed.

The riding organization was in a shambles, split between de Corneille's hostile forces and Sharp's demoralized old executive. The first call I

222 ⌐ *Rebel Daughter*

received, aside from those from the press, was from my old friend Sheila Kieran. A veteran in many a campaign, she plunged in to organize mailers, pamphlets, door cards—all handsomely designed, almost overnight, by Leslie Smart, a prominent Toronto graphic designer. The next call was from Robert Stikeman, a young man from the Liberal organizing committee. We had a gloomy lunch going over the difficulties I faced, but he helped me find an empty storefront on Bathurst Street, set up telephones, got furniture donated, and tried to find a campaign manager. The party organization had swung into action.

And that's the way things went. Regular election workers who were perfect strangers to me appeared at the riding office. Some were devoted Liberals and political pros like Sharon Van Stone, Mollie Caccia, Freda Levine, Al Brown, Donnie Wright, and Edith Land, who worked long hours almost every day. Others were people who simply loved the excitement of elections—the office camaraderie, phoning voters, checking lists, all on a diet of fast food, doughnuts, and the vilest coffee I have ever tasted.

After several people were approached about taking on the onerous job of campaign manager, Phyllis Smith, who lived in the riding and was moving to Ottawa to work after the election, volunteered.

Friends and acquaintances of every political persuasion offered to help—Adrienne Clarkson, Sylvia Fraser, Bruce McLeod, Alan Campaigne, Moira Armour, David Greenspan, Lois Harrison, Alyce Powe, Carole Buffett, Mary Jane Heintzmann, to mention only a few. Dalton Robertson of the *Financial Post* raised money. Joan Chalmers chauffeured me and my canvassers in her bottle-green Jaguar, which we had to hide on side streets—it was too tony for a candidate.

My sons also got involved, and have been politically active ever since. My ever-resourceful sister-in-law, Lorna McCubbin, worked as many hours every day as I did and bought a van to help with the sign crew. Some acquaintances, such as Izzy Switzer, sent me cheques. His was accompanied by a note saying he wanted to help a former Calgarian, but was going to vote Progressive Conservative. On the other hand, the anti-choice crowd immediately began working to make sure I didn't get elected.

Our biggest challenge was to try to persuade disaffected Jewish voters, who generally supported the Liberals, to come out on election day. All over the riding, however, there was the sense that many voters could hardly wait to whack the government over its knuckles—hard. While canvassing one day, I knocked on the door of a luxury building's penthouse apartment. A woman clothed in Italian originals, her hands laden with rings, answered. When I handed her my pamphlet, she glanced at the Liberal logo, then clutched her throat in horror.

"Trudeau!" she exclaimed. "We have suffered enough!" And slammed the door in my face.

At bus stops, some people pushed me aside as if I were handing them pornographic pictures, and several outraged citizens threw my literature on the ground or tore it up in my face. One man followed me down the hallway of a large apartment building screaming at me as if I were responsible for all the problems of his world.

I did enjoy some advantages: as I was a high-profile woman who had been advocating more women in politics for years, my own first try attracted more than the usual amount of curiosity and media. As for myself, I enjoyed the whole experience enormously. I found I liked meeting total strangers in door-to-door and bus-stop encounters. I was well enough known to make the reception generally favourable, even when people admitted they weren't going to vote for me.

The central-office Liberal machine clanked into operation. I was deluged with pounds and pounds of almost totally useless literature. Halfway through the campaign, a limousine full of bright young men, earphones permanently glued to their ears, descended on me, looked over my rinky-dink operation, and solemnly advised me to do the impossible—ditch my Citroën because it might offend voters. Nor was I to drive myself anywhere, in case there was an accident that would hurt the campaign. Their advice was idiotic. I had no other car, and no other way to get back and forth from my home, a journey of about half an hour. Most of my workers had no means to get home late at night unless I drove them.

To cheer on our little Charge of the Light Brigade, squadrons of high-profile Liberals from Ottawa kept turning up. Although they stayed only for an hour or two, we had to rejig our whole canvassing plan for the day to give them lots of profile. Monique Bégin, Jeanne Sauvé, Judd Buchanan, Royce Frith, Iona Campagnolo, John Roberts, Bud Cullen, Roy MacLaren, Barney Danson, Herb Gray, and Donald Macdonald were just some who came. Jeanne Sauvé was actually bemused by how hard we had to work: "In

Quebec, all we have to do is appear and walk around a few times on the main street before the election. We don't do any of this door-to-door stuff!"

As if they hadn't caused sufficient harm by calling the election on a Jewish holiday, the central office decided to bring Trudeau into the riding, and to compound the insult to the Jewish voters, they picked Friday, the start of the Jewish Sabbath! I immediately registered my dismay and told them that if the date couldn't be changed, not to bring him in at all. Friday turned out to be the only possible day, so instead of parading him around with lots of press, we smuggled him in for a small dinner with half a dozen workers in a back room at the Noshery, a trendy restaurant in the riding. Trudeau was friendly and sympathetic but seemed quite removed from the battle we were waging.

Jerry Grafstein, a lawyer and loyal Liberal worker who later became a senator, tried to placate the Jewish voters by arranging a weekday meeting between Trudeau and a delegation of Lubavitcher rabbis who were holding a conference in Toronto. Trudeau would endorse a statement about the importance of ethical and moral values, which had been written by the chief rabbi of New York. I was to tag along in the hope that the meeting would help my cause, but I was sternly warned not to try to shake hands or even speak to the rabbis, who are allowed to converse only with their wives.

Around noon, I dutifully appeared at the Holiday Inn behind City Hall. Trudeau and I were ushered into an anteroom, where he read the statement and said, "This is fine, but what good is this going to do Doris in Eglinton?"

Jerry replied that just the sight of Trudeau meeting these holy men would help diffuse the animosity over the election date. We were ushered into the meeting room under a blaze of TV lights, and Trudeau endorsed the statement. The chief rabbi began a long, rambling speech as the TV camera operators and press gradually slipped away.

Perhaps it did help—I don't know. A story in the *Canadian Jewish News* identified me as the woman whose back was visible in the accompanying photo. The daily press ignored the event.

When you work as hard as we had—and I think this is true of every political campaign—by election night, you half expect a miracle. I was no different. But it was all over in twenty minutes. Election night was a slaughter for the Liberals, with only two wins out of fifteen by-elections—both in Quebec. After attending the wake with my supporters, I went over to Parker's campaign office to congratulate him.

A few weeks after the election, I had breakfast with Jim Coutts at the Park Plaza. He told me that it was now up to me to start working to challenge de Corneille for the nomination. In other words, no matter how angry the party was with de Corneille, I was on my own. Faced with such an overwhelmingly negative vote, I knew the next election was going to be a tough slugfest for any Liberal. By not running in the by-election, de Corneille had consolidated his Jewish supporters, and under the circumstances, challenging him for the nomination would be madness.

Many of my workers were keen to try again in another riding. I kept my options open by remaining politically active, filling speaking engagements to Liberal groups, and attending meetings and conventions. In January 1979, I met with Keith Davey, who suggested the Beaches as a possibility; however, by February, Coutts had taken a poll and the east-end riding looked hopeless. He suggested I run against David Crombie, Toronto's popular former mayor, in Rosedale—a kamikaze mission if there ever was one.

By early spring, I had become ambivalent about politics. That short campaign had taught me something about myself. As a journalist, I had had some trouble being a good "machine" politician. Most successful backbenchers behaved like football players in a scrum—never any dissent or criticism. The concept that the party was right under all circumstances was difficult for me to swallow. If I won a seat, I knew I would chafe under that kind of strict party discipline.

As well, I had a nagging feeling of déjà vu. The Liberal Party seemed to have run out of ideas and resembled the tired organization I had encountered when I'd first met David nearly twenty years earlier. With a party seemingly headed for sure defeat in the next election, it appeared to be a poor time to be running, particularly in the dubious seats I was being offered.

I believed as much as ever that more women were needed in politics— they still made up only 5 per cent of the House of Commons—and I knew there were at least as many good women as men to choose from in the country at large. I still hoped to be one of them, but this didn't seem to be the right time.

CHAPTER FOURTEEN

The Fight for 28

In late March 1979, the Liberals began to sound me out on another matter—a job, as a possible chair for the Canadian Advisory Council on the Status of Women.

By Ottawa standards, the CACSW was, at best, a shoestring operation. There was plenty for it to do—the bureaucracy itself discriminated blatantly against women. The CACSW's mandate—to advise the government, make recommendations on legislation, hold several bilingual meetings across the country a year, carry out and distribute research—was ridiculous on a budget of $740,000.

In 1973, when the CACSW was first established, I had been asked to join its board. I would have relished being part of that first, non-partisan, feisty council along with such women as Laura Sabia and Grace Hartman, the staunch NDP head of the Canadian Union of Public Employees. I turned it down, because we planned to cover the CACSW in *Chatelaine*. Under its first chair, Katie Cooke, a seasoned bureaucrat and a committed feminist, valuable research was undertaken. Since then, the council had become much more politicized—a reward for women workers in the Liberal Party.

When I left *Chatelaine*, I was asked to join the board again, and this time I did. I could see that the CACSW wasn't working well. Not much research was being done, and there had been several staff resignations. The twenty-eight board members, who met four times a year in different cities, seemed to spend a lot of time bickering over details that had little to do with changing conditions for Canadian women.

The CACSW had one big advantage. It was independent of government and not part of the bureaucracy, which meant it could go directly to the press. If, as the Royal Commission on the Status of Women had recommended, it had been allowed to report directly to Parliament, it could have commanded the same attention for women's issues as the auditor-general's report does for taxation issues. Wisely, from its own perspective, the government chose to have the CACSW report to a cabinet minister. As the minister seemed to change frequently, the CACSW was moved about like an orphan and had a lower priority than that of a junior ministry. Because it had a very low profile, most Canadian women had never heard of it.

Always tempted by a challenge, I realized that running an appointed council would require far more diplomacy than being editor of *Chatelaine*. I was excited at the idea of turning the CACSW into a more effective tool for women. The three-year appointment would also give me a box seat from which to observe how government worked. Afterwards I could decide whether I really wanted to run again for Parliament.

Yvette Rousseau, the incumbent chair, had been a champion for Quebec's working women while raising eight children by herself. With little administrative experience, almost no English, and a distrust of the press, she had had a difficult time at the CACSW. With an election looming, the Liberals hoped my appointment would stop the criticism from women's groups and the media that the CACSW was a moribund body doing nothing for women.

When Marc Lalonde, minister of Health and Welfare, announced my appointment in April, the press criticized it as yet another political appointment—which it was. Although there were already two vice-presidents, one in Ottawa and one in Winnipeg, another was appointed for Montreal—a strikingly handsome nurse, Lucie Pepin. She had been national co-ordinator of the Canadian Committee for Fertility Research, and was one of Lalonde's protégées.

The staff of fifteen people was scattered over two floors in the dilapidated Hope Building on Sparks Street. A small research unit was headed by the very capable Julyan Reid. Several of the staff, however, were incompetent—hired by Rousseau because she felt sorry for them, or they needed a job. A sulky little translator did almost nothing, while an older woman who sent out documents was being paid far too much for such a junior job. When the receptionist couldn't understand what was being said by a caller, she would just hang up. My own secretary, having lived all her life in Paris, was totally ignorant about Ottawa and typed at a shockingly slow speed.

I immediately took over the budget. Although most research was contracted out, which made sense to me, the largest part of the budget was spent on administration and meetings rather than research. I decided to cut the staff to eleven from fifteen, which would allow me to give more money to the research unit, as well as improve our efficiency. I then caused a minor sensation by ordering a typewriter for myself so that I could type my own memos—unheard of in Ottawa. I hired a receptionist who could answer the phone in both languages and decreed that memos be replied to promptly.

Getting rid of civil servants, I found, requires months and much documentation. Even hiring a secretary, which would have been accomplished in days in Toronto, took weeks of interviewing. Most bilingual applicants knew nothing about women's issues or Ottawa and its workings (a major necessity), or their English was poor.

Translation was a problem from the first day I arrived until long after I left. In theory, everything was translated by government translators—usually badly. Council members from Quebec always complained, with justification, and I finally decided the only solution was to have everything translated in Montreal—an added expense. Although many people in Ottawa claimed to be bilingual, in all the time I lived there I found very few who could write even competently in both French and English. To reach the press in both languages, I hired two half-time media people, one for English and one for French.

I soon realized that too much success could bankrupt us. The CACSW had published some good reports, but the more publicity we received, the more money it cost us to print and distribute them free of charge. I decided only summaries of the reports and fact sheets would be free. One full report would go to all major women's groups, but we would charge for extra copies at cost. By the time I left, CACSW reports were retailing so well through the Queen's Printer that, as best sellers, they had separate sales booths at book fairs.

In my search for more money for research, I realized the Winnipeg office had a full-time employee, originally hired to work on a report on family law in Manitoba, who now seemed only to be writing speeches for our western vice-president, Win Gardner. As I gave many more speeches than all the vice-presidents put together, and wrote them myself, I reasoned that that person could be let go. I discussed this with Win, and she agreed but cautioned me not to make any changes until after the upcoming election.

On May 22, as expected, the Liberals went down to defeat.

When the new cabinet was sworn in, David MacDonald, who had been the Tories' opposition critic on women's issues, was made minister responsible for the status of women. He quickly pushed to have our budget almost doubled to $1.4 million, and also agreed to give us some input on new appointments to the council. That meant women with a background in women's concerns might join us rather than the political faithful who had licked a lot of envelopes in some campaign.

He next proposed to cancel an expensive commission set up by Jeanne Sauvé on sex stereotyping in the media. I had no trouble agreeing—more than thirty studies on this subject had already appeared—and $250,000 would be saved. Going along with my new minister did not go down well with the Liberals. I soon heard from an indignant Sauvé. How dared I agree to the cancellation of her commission?

Not long afterwards, Lloyd Axworthy, the only Liberal to have survived the PC sweep west of the Great Lakes, appeared in my office. He demanded that the speechwriter in Winnipeg, who had been fired after the election, be reinstated. I had discovered that while she was on CACSW's payroll, she had spent most of her time during the election working for the Liberals, Axworthy included. I informed him that the deed was done—approved and passed by council. He turned on his heel and stomped out. Unlike most politicians, who are friendly and polite—their job is to win votes, after all—the young Winnipeg rookie seemed rude, bullying, and overly impressed with himself.

All during this period, while I was working long hours at the office, I commuted every weekend to Toronto. I had hoped to sell my house, but the market was soft, so I rented it instead. In Ottawa I had been subletting the apartment of my friends Beverley Rockett and John Roberts. By September, when Mitchell and the dog would be moving to Ottawa with me, I had to find a bigger place. Stephen was in his last year of high school and was staying in Toronto with Peter and David, who had remarried by this time.

I was having no luck at all finding anything in the New Edinburgh or Sandy Hill area where I wanted to live. Over lunch one day with Jean Pigott, the appointments secretary for the Conservatives, I received a quick lesson in the way Ottawa works. "What real estate agent are you using?" she asked. When I told her she replied, "Sampson and McNaught are the only firm to use if you want a house in those areas, and they rarely advertise." I phoned them, was immediately shown three houses, and two days later signed a lease for a town house behind Rideau Hall. Although screening people was unlawful, it apparently was the way things worked.

Once settled, I found I enjoyed living in the nation's capital. It was smaller than Toronto and easier to get around in. The winters were less gun-metal grey, and people didn't try to ignore them as they do in Toronto. Instead, they bundled up in thick coats, heavy boots, mitts, and toques. That first year, I bought cross-country skis and a bike.

I even liked the incestuous gossip and the endless politicking. I was generously entertained. Like everyone else in Ottawa, I was rated—at the level of a deputy minister—which meant those were the people I tended to meet at party after party.

Meanwhile, I was being introduced to the byzantine world of Ottawa's bureaucracy—a place where empire building has become a fine art. People talked constantly about "person-years," meaning more staff and budgets, and endlessly polished their CVs. I was given a large, heavy briefcase (a "doc" bag), which, even empty, I could barely lift and never used.

Within days of settling in my office, I received a call from a bureaucrat concerned about my modest assets. Apparently I had to declare everything and put it in a blind trust, in case I used my position to line my pocket. I had no trouble listing my few possessions, but he spent weeks grilling me about them. (In the end, I placed my few stocks with a trust company, instructing them not to trade anything. Instead, they sold some of my remaining MH stock at a low price and bought Imperial Oil, which promptly plummeted. At the same time, Maclean Hunter split, and I lost about $20,000!)

As the weeks went by, it seemed to me that the government was like a roving beam of light: if it hit you, you could be its prisoner forever. Soon after I arrived, two accountants camped in the office for three weeks and went over every cent of our budget. I suppose Conservatives were looking for Liberal scandals. Maclean Hunter would never have allowed such high-priced help to take that long on one minuscule budget. To make matters worse, I never saw their report.

I spent hours and hours filling out forms with seven and eight copies—five year plans, two-year projections, and the like—all quite fanciful, since we had no idea what budgets we might have in the future. I often joked that I wrote more fiction while working for the CACSW than I did while writing three novels! In fact, despairing of getting anything else done, I finally hired a former civil servant familiar with the mysterious ways of government to come in a couple of half days a week and take the blizzard of paper off my hands.

Julyan Reid set up meetings with the new Conservative cabinet minis-ters and other government departments to brief them on what we did and suggest ways we could work together. We also set up a talent bank, which contained the names of suitable women for appointments to government boards and commissions.

In February 1980, less than nine months after it was elected, Joe Clark's minority government fell, and the Liberals were back in power. Although it would have been heresy to say so, I was sorry. My brief engagement with the Liberals during the by-election had convinced me that the party needed much more time out of power to renew itself. It returned as jaded and arrogant as before it had been defeated, and out of touch with many parts of Canada, including the disaffected West.

What was even more dismaying, my new minister was none other than Lloyd Axworthy. Realizing I had some fence mending to do, I dropped everything and went over to congratulate him. I think we both tried to put our disastrous first meeting behind us. I was impressed by the fact that he seemed bright, actually knew quite a bit about women's issues, and wanted to begin affirmative-action programs in key government departments.

In the Speech from the Throne, read rather haltingly by Governor General Ed Schreyer that April, affirmative action and employment strate-gies aimed at women were actually mentioned. Later that week, I happened to be at a gathering with Trudeau and congratulated him on those initia-tives. He looked at me with a stony blankness that often left me, and other people, gasping. Apparently Axworthy hadn't told his boss he meant busi-ness—either that, or the Speech from the Throne was just window-dressing.

I was even more depressed when a young man from the Prime Minister's Office dropped in to talk about appointments to the council. Jean Pigott had encouraged input from us. That ended under the Liberals. All appoint-ments would be made, the young man informed me, by cabinet ministers from each region. In other words, the party faithful would again be rewarded by being appointed to the council—forget about expertise.

That spring we added Peggy Mason, a young bilingual lawyer, to the staff, as well as a bilingual executive assistant, Wendy Lawrence. Wendy proved to be extremely efficient, with a fine mind and the ability to anticipate possible problems. I felt the staff was stronger than it had ever been.

Sue Findlay, my Ottawa vice-president, had left. As she had been appointed partly to help the former president, Yvette Rousseau, I decided we no longer needed an English-speaking vice-president in Ottawa. I wanted to use the money for research, but I had no say in the matter—or the appointment. Hellie Wilson, who had been correspondence secretary in the Prime Minister's Office, was made vice-president. Several people warned me she might be difficult and cause trouble. However, as a political appointee myself, I was expected to accommodate the government in whatever it decided to do.

Hellie would have liked to be my right-hand woman—a position from which she could wield power as if she were speaking for me. Knowing her love of gossip, and her sudden temper, I couldn't have that. To my dismay, she spent most of her time talking on the telephone to her friends in the bureaucracy. I soon felt as though I were under surveillance. (I was told later that she did indeed read all my mail and riffle through my papers when I wasn't there, under the pretext of looking for something.) I decided not to leave anything of a confidential nature around the office at all. I then tried to get Hellie interested in setting up conferences across the country, but that held little attraction for her. Finally, I hired Rachel Gauvin, a francophone from New Brunswick, to act as her secretary and work on conferences.

Lucie Pepin detested reading the research documents and found long discussions about policy tiresome. She had been urging me to hire a francophone in research, mainly to summarize everything for her in simple terms. This we did, but the delay in finding Nicole Morgan, an excellent researcher, had annoyed Lucie.

We were making good inroads into the various government departments. Bureaucrats were calling us frequently for consultation before legislation was drafted—which was what we were there for. We persuaded Statistics Canada to revise a school booklet that showed boys engaged in vigorous sports while girls passively stood about.

We were breaking new ground in our reports. We brought out the first study on battered women in Canada, by Linda MacLeod. People were shocked to read that one in ten women living in a partnership was being battered; later studies proved that the numbers were in fact much higher. We published a study on reproductive health hazards at work, showing that men's reproductive capacities were affected as well as women's. Each year we produced a report on the continuing low promotion rate of women in the public service. Studies on women in prison, handicapped women, and skilled trades for women also appeared. We had plans in the works for fourteen more papers, including ones on microtechnology and women, family property laws, pornography, and women in the arts and in sport.

In the twenty-one months I had been in the job, I felt I had made real progress. With a dedicated and highly efficient staff and better communications with our public, we were now a much more visible, credible, and effective tool for helping Canadian women. In my remaining time as chair, a little more than a year, I wanted to get on with our conferences, our expanding work with the government and the bureaucracy, and our research.

After the 1980 Quebec referendum, Pierre Trudeau's almost single-minded objective was to settle the Quebec question once and for all. To do it, he planned to patriate the British North America Act from Westminster, with an amending formula and an entrenched Charter of Rights and Freedoms.

At the CACSW, we realized few women cared a fig about the Constitution, regarding it as yawn producing, but it was clear a Charter would profoundly affect women. Its wording had to be strong, or we would be saddled with a bad and useless document for generations to come.

Reluctantly, we took on the job of informing Canadian women about what was at stake for them in these constitutional changes. We planned a conference to take place just before the premiers and the prime minister met in the fall of 1980, a move Axworthy enthusiastically supported. Julyan Reid, astute and capable as always, assigned eleven papers on the Constitution to experts across the country, including Mary Eberts, Beverley Baines, and Audrey Doerr. However, in August, when we held a press conference announcing the conference, my fears about its success seemed well founded. The press scarcely mentioned it. No one seemed interested in a constitutional conference for women.

Just before the conference, the federal translators, most of whom were women, went on strike. It was a move planned to embarrass the government, which it failed to do. The government's conference with the premiers went ahead, using managers as translators. In our case, the strike was a disaster. Because the translators were striking for more benefits, including maternity leave with pay, we supported their demands and honoured their picket lines.

I couldn't believe union women would scuttle the conference of one of the few groups supporting them, and I wanted to talk directly to the union's negotiators. Hellie Wilson, claiming her long tenure in the nation's capital made her the expert on anything to do with the government, convinced our executive that with the government in negotiation, it would be highly improper for me to do this. Instead, I had to communicate through a vice-president of the National Action Committee, an extremely unsatisfactory substitute for direct discussions.

All through that torturous weekend of phoning back and forth, I tried to find some workable compromise. My gut instinct was to go ahead with the conference, with or without translation. To Lucie Pepin and Florence Ievers, a young lawyer from Quebec, this was unthinkable. The executive voted to cancel the conference.

Ironically, the next day, no sooner had we sent out releases announcing the cancellation than the strikers agreed to provide translation. It was too late. The staff was demoralized. At the time, I believed she simply revelled in all the excitement. The NAC vice-president added to our distress by telling the media she felt the conference had been cancelled because of political pressure. That, as far as I was concerned, was completely untrue: the government considered our conference of no real importance at all.

To help women understand the issues, we released the conference papers for general discussion, and the minute the strike was settled in November, we rescheduled the conference for February. Axworthy agreed to take part in it, as before.

Concern for what a Charter might do to the rights of women was dramatically illustrated at the first ministers' conference the following week. The federal government proposed that divorce be shifted to the provinces. The attorneys general of the provinces—all men—were enthusiastically in favour of the move. It meant more power for them. The federal government foresaw some problems for women in this plan, but divorce was an easy giveaway in the negotiations.

My phone started ringing. Family-law experts were concerned, as were high placed women in the Justice and Finance departments of the federal government. A different set of divorce laws in every province would be devastating for women. Tracking down errant husbands for child support, for example, would have become even more of a nightmare than it was already. We immediately sent out a press release and started a campaign to stop the transfer. It was stopped, and we learned a powerful lesson on how badly women might suffer from future Charter decisions if we weren't alert and involved.

In October, the government released the proposed Charter, and confirmed our worst fears. The language in Section 15, which dealt with discrimination in race, religion, sex, and ethnic origin, was exactly the same wording as in the 1960 Canadian Bill of Rights. That bill had been tested ten times in the courts between 1970 and 1980, and had been found to be useless as a legal tool to help women.

Among the eleven papers the council prepared on the Charter, one dealt solely with the wording needed in any proposed Charter of Rights. It was clear, although we had sent Axworthy a full set of the papers, that neither he nor any of his staff had read them. The council prepared a statement pointing out our concerns about the wording and issued a press release. I also sent a letter to the prime minister and to Axworthy, telling them about our concerns and our intention to criticize the proposed Charter.

The prime minister was not pleased, but because he was also receiving criticism from several other quarters, I don't think our stand particularly irritated him. Axworthy, on the other hand, was furious. By misadventure, he hadn't received his letter until after the prime minister and seemed to hold me personally responsible for the sloppiness in his own office. He summoned the executive to meet with him immediately, treating us like delinquent schoolgirls up before the master to have our knuckles rapped. Faced with his bad temper, the executive collapsed, entreating him to tell them what they could do to reestablish themselves in his good graces. He contemptuously replied that we should support the government's wording as it stood and without question. I found his attitude astounding, given that the CACSW had been set up as an independent body precisely to question legislation on behalf of women. Furthermore, he threatened to cut our budget and go directly to women themselves if we didn't co-operate.

It was a bold but empty threat. Shortly afterwards, at a meeting on the Constitution in Toronto's City Hall, Axworthy asked several hundred women "to trust us." He was deservedly booed. All that fall he continued to argue that entrenching the Bill of Rights wording in the Charter would give it more clout. Few constitutional lawyers supported his stand.

The executive blamed me for getting them in trouble with the minister. Win Gardner worried that Axworthy would be so angry that she would lose her job. Lucie Pepin panicked when Marc Lalonde phoned her to register his disapproval. I don't suppose it helped when I reminded them rather sharply that our mandate was to help the women of Canada, not toady to the Liberal Party. By then my fate was sealed with the executive. I had annoyed the minister and therefore I was dangerous. That the minister had no right to threaten us and treat us like children was not questioned by these women who seemed to value their feeble attachment to the government in power far more than their commitment to women.

The crisis in which I found myself was not helped by the fact that the National Action Committee, the largest volunteer lobby group in the country, was in disarray. Racked by an internal fight between two rival factions, it was having trouble making up its mind whether we needed a Charter at all. I believed arguing about whether we needed a Charter was like discussing how many angels could dance on the head of a pin. The Liberals had a majority in Parliament and could push through any legislation they wanted. We were obviously going to end up with a Charter, and I believed our job was to make sure it was a good one and of some use to women.

I met with Edythe MacDonald, a neighbour and a brilliant lawyer who worked in the Department of Justice, and eventually re-drafted large parts of the Charter. She suggested the wording "before the law and under the law" would strengthen Section 15 ensuring that women and other groups would not be discriminated against under the Charter as they had been in the Bill of Rights.

We began to push for this change in the wording and prepared a fact sheet on the Charter and distributed it widely. We asked women to send letters and coupons demanding changes to Section 15, and thousands responded. I spoke at public meetings across Canada to explain what was at stake.

And where was the minister responsible for the status of women through all this? Miffed by the fact that a letter addressed to him had gone astray, he sulked, then went around the country saying that the CACSW was "badly informed." Finally, he hired his own lawyer to try to prove all the experts were wrong.

In the middle of all this controversy, I visited Judy La Marsh, who was dying of pancreatic cancer. We had never been close friends, but I deeply admired her principles, her fine mind, and her devotion to the cause of women. On that visit—the last time I saw her—she told me one of her deepest regrets was that she would not be around to fight for a stronger Charter.

Reluctantly realizing it was not going to be able to ram through a Charter without some input from the public, the government set up a Special Joint Committee of the Senate and the House of Commons to hear briefs on possible changes. It hoped to end the hearings well before Christmas, but with 1,208 submissions and 104 witnesses to hear, the committee hearings went on for three months.

The full council met in November, and the members were cantankerous. I could understand why: Lucie Pepin and Florence Ievers had insisted that without translators we cancel not only the September conference but our regular quarterly council meeting in September as well. The members felt left out of the decision-making process, even though they had been informed by mail and phone at every step. As president, I bore the brunt of their dissatisfaction.

On the last day of our three-day meeting, Senator Florence Bird strongly urged us to hire the best lawyer we could find to present our case before the joint committee. She seemed to think a male lawyer would be necessary. Instead, we got Mary Eberts, a former law professor at Osgoode, now in private practice, to write the brief in consultation with Beverley Baines of Queen's University and Nicole Duple from Laval.

Two days before our presentation to the Joint Committee, Lucie Pepin threw a tantrum and declared she would not appear, saying there hadn't been enough input from Duple. Mary Eberts rushed to Ottawa and spent the next day going over the brief again with Duple, and together they made minor changes. Even then, Pepin declared that if she herself blundered before the committee, "I will see that Julyan Reid is fired!"—as though any incompetence on her part would be the fault of the staff. I was shocked. Julyan and her small research staff had carried the entire burden of finding women to write our papers on the Charter, as well as researching wording at every step of the way. Instead of castigating them, we should have been applauding their work.

With its red-and-gold walls and crystal chandeliers, Room 200 of the West Block looked more like a ballroom than the birthing room of a constitution. Mary Eberts did a brilliant job at the hearings—in fact, our brief was praised as one of the best presentations made before the committee. Basking in the widespread praise in the press and particularly in Elizabeth Gray's report on the CBC's "Sunday Morning," the members seemed mollified. The ever-unpredictable Lucie Pepin even wanted to buy a bottle of champagne for Julyan!

I felt the worst of the crisis was over. The Charter was not perfect, but the main section concerning women had been changed. Other changes would probably be proposed at our rescheduled February conference. Everything was now in place for it. All original panellists, with one exception, could attend. Hotel rooms were booked. Press releases were to be dispatched at the beginning of January.

I knew the job in the coming year would be to massage the bruised egos of the executive and the council, and I was more determined than ever to solve the translation problem. Lucie and Florence Ievers had constantly carped about the translations. We had good people on staff who could do quick translations, but longer documents translated in Montreal under Lucie's direction still contained errors. To placate them, I counted on the fact that we had been commended in a report from the office of the Commission of Official Languages for our complement of staff francophones. And in spite of an eight-month delay, while my request languished in Axworthy's office, I'd managed to get our by-laws tidied up and the council's per diem fees raised in line with other boards.

At an executive meeting just before Christmas, however, I found the vice-presidents almost intolerable. They demanded that no staff be present at council meetings in future, even though the staff was constantly needed for information. Lucie Pepin objected to the amount of research we were doing, saying she didn't have time to assimilate it. I insisted, in turn, that any criticism of the staff go through me and not be directed personally at individual staff members, as Lucie had done with Julyan.

When I got back to the office on the Tuesday after the Christmas holidays, a memo from Hellie Wilson awaited me: "Heard from Nancy Connelly [Axworthy's assistant] and the minister wants regional conferences instead of a national conference."

I was flabbergasted. "How can he tell us to cancel a conference that we were accused of cancelling in the fall because of political interference? Does he want to destroy the credibility of council completely?" I raved at Hellie. She then told me she had taken it upon herself to withdraw the press release that had been scheduled to go out.

I phoned Win Gardner in Winnipeg. "He can't do that," she said. "Even Lalonde wouldn't do that!" This reassured me. Next I talked to Nancy Connelly, who reported that Axworthy seemed to be "in a funk" after his holidays. I set up a date to meet with him that Friday. After I discussed it with the executive, they insisted on attending the meeting with me.

During the week I talked extensively to all the executive by phone, and they seemed to agree that Axworthy's proposal would be damaging to the council. On the Thursday evening before the meeting, we got together for dinner. It didn't take me long to realize that the executive were not as united as they had seemed on the phone. Lucie Pepin, who always seemed to have trouble keeping a consistent line of thought, argued that cancelling the conference was not really important at all. I finally got them to agree that we would listen to Axworthy's reasons for wanting the conference cancelled but wait until we met afterwards to make a decision on what we would do.

When we arrived at Axworthy's office the next day, we were kept waiting for more than half an hour before he rushed in, looking irritated. "I'm having a bad day," he said. "And I don't want to mince words." He went on to say that the idea of a conference at that time would be potentially embarrassing for the government. Criticisms of the Charter could be used by Joe Clark, who was "fighting for his political life."

Even before he had finished speaking, Hellie was nodding in agreement. Lucie replied immediately, "I think we should cancel." Then she added, "And please Mr. Minister, could we have some more money?"—like a child who expects to be rewarded for doing what she was told. The rest of the members almost elbowed one another out of the way in their eagerness to cancel. Needless to say, I was stunned. I explained that I thought cancelling the conference for the second time would be disastrous for the

CACSW's credibility. But in my concern for the council and women, I seemed to be a minority of one in that room.

Axworthy stood up, and we were shown the door. Angry and sick at heart at what I considered a total betrayal of the CACSW and myself, I left quickly. As I looked back, I saw the other executive members crowding around Axworthy as though they expected to be patted on the head. Instead of graciously thanking them for being so accommodating, he had turned his back on them, as if, having disposed of this minor irritation, he was ready to get on with more important business.

I went for a long walk to try to calm myself before I had to face the executive again that afternoon in the board room. I had already decided to resign but wanted to hear them say to my face what possible reason they could give for their performance in Axworthy's office.

That afternoon Win argued that we had been rude to Axworthy in the fall. Now, she believed, we had to "give in." "Our credibility with our colleagues is at stake." Puzzled, I asked her, "What colleagues?" She replied, "My political colleagues." In other words, the Liberal Party—certainly not the women of Canada, whose welfare she had been appointed to protect.

Hellie's reason was that holding the conference would provoke the government's anger. Lucie dismissed the women of Canada as "not knowing what was going on," adding that we needed to "learn to play the same way they are playing with us." When I pointed out how damaging it would be for the council to cancel a conference for the second time, she shrugged. "We took shit before and we can take it again."

I argued in vain that governments moved when they realized votes were at stake, especially votes that might be lost if they didn't act. In my experience, submissively doing what governments wanted had not resulted in any major changes for women.

After we spent an afternoon arguing back and forth, a vote was held and I lost, five to one. They insisted on phoning Axworthy's office at once with the good news. In the press release announcing the conference's cancellation, I couldn't even get them to include a line saying that the conference would be rescheduled at a later date. Hellie was yawning elaborately as though profoundly bored by the whole discussion.

It was clear by now that they had been plotting behind my back all fall, and now had backed me in a corner. As president of the CACSW, I was going to be discredited along with them—or be forced to resign. The fact that I had already decided to quit probably played right into their plans.

Sick at heart, I went back to the office where Julyan Reid and Wendy Lawrence were waiting. I told them I had completely failed and planned to resign. I expected the papers would make hay over it for a day, and then it would be forgotten. As we talked, though, we decided there was one more card I could play: I could take the fight to the full council for a vote on whether to hold the conference or not.

That weekend, I drafted a press release registering my shock over Axworthy's interference and the executive's response. I ended by stating that the conference would go ahead as planned unless the full council cancelled it at their meeting on January 20.

On Monday, I phoned Axworthy and told him what I had done. For the next ten days, I spent hours on the phone trying to convince the twenty-two individual members of the council that the conference had to be held or the credibility of the CACSW would be ruined. While I was on the phone, Axworthy was being battered daily in the House of Commons by Flora MacDonald, who demanded he be censured for his interference. Pauline Jewett of the NDP accused the CACSW of harbouring a "mole" (Hellie Wilson). The press loved it, of course—a confrontation between a cabinet minister and a woman—and the affair was rarely off the front pages or television screens.

Axworthy's defence, which sounds flimsy even today, was the same one the executive used: in view of the changes the government had made to Section 15, the council had come to him on that Friday for advice about whether to hold the conference. He had merely told us he thought the timing was wrong, and claimed he had not "interfered directly" with the council. However, he certainly had interfered through his assistant, Nancy Connelly, via Hellie Wilson. In the press, he kept referring to me and other members of the council who disagreed with him as "Cadillac" feminists.

Hellie Wilson and the executive tried to strengthen their case by claiming that the research papers weren't ready. This was nonsense, of course— the research papers had been ready and fully translated since September when the first conference had been cancelled!

Finally, Trudeau had to come to the aid of his floundering minister. In the House of Commons, he read off a long list of things the Liberal Party had done for women, a performance that was truly hilarious. His puzzled expression and his stumbling over such terms as "affirmative action" and "sexual harassment" made it clear they were as foreign to him as Bantu.

At the full council meeting on the 20th, I knew the members had been heavily lobbied by the executive and probably by the party, but I was counting on the airing in the press to shame them into standing up for the CACSW. I also counted on the package of documents—a chronological sequence of events, documentation of plans for the conference, the crucial memos to cancel it, and, above all, the damning minutes of the final executive meeting—to convince the members that there had been political interference. Sadly, many took the package without even glancing at it.

As soon as the meeting started, I knew I was in for a rocky afternoon. The executive immediately brought in an affidavit declaring the secretary's minutes had been "falsified." Although she was waiting outside to testify under oath as to the accuracy of her minutes, they wouldn't hear her. The lobbyists had done their work well.

I tried to keep the discussion on the issue: the autonomy of the CACSW and the harm that would come to it if another conference were cancelled. Most of the Conservative appointees to the council supported me, of course. A few Liberals argued that they were going to vote against the conference because of "the process within the council." Others gave speeches on how proud they were to be Liberals.

After almost five hours of discussion, we took the vote. It was seventeen to ten in favour of cancelling, and split almost entirely along partisan lines. I had lost.

As I started to pack up to leave, the members began to panic. Suddenly they were leaderless. They argued about who would have to face the press, and even asked my advice about whether a reception that had been planned should still go ahead! I told them I assumed the reception would be held, but I would not be present. As for dealing with the press, it was up to them to decide how to explain why they had voted as they had. What absolutely astonished me, though, was that some of the women, who had just behaved like political ciphers, had the effrontery to try to shake my hand, tell me they admired me and hoped we could still be friends!

Outside I was met by a barrage of microphones and TV cameras. I admitted that I had lost, but that the fight had been a worthwhile one. Then I went off to dinner with some of the staff. Although bone tired, I began to put behind me the emotional turmoil of the past few days and the anguish of realizing I had been betrayed by women—some of whom I had considered friends.

Wendy Lawrence and Julie Woodsworth, who handled the CACSW's publishing and press, resigned the next day, and in the next few days five members of the council quit. In the weeks that followed, seven more staff members left—five of them with no other jobs to go to. Over the next several weeks we kept our spirits up by meeting in one another's homes for pot-luck dinners, which always ended with a singalong and a rendition of "Song of the Soul" by the feminist musician Chris Williams.

In the week following the meeting, I was interviewed by Michele Landsberg for the *Toronto Star*. I appeared on "Front Page Challenge," where Pierre Berton recognized me immediately, and on the "Fifth Estate" with Adrienne Clarkson. I flew to Vancouver to give a speech and then to Halifax to give another.

In Parliament, Axworthy continued to be pummelled by the Opposition. Flora MacDonald had obtained a copy of the be "nice to the government" minutes, which she used to question Axworthy in the House. Both Axworthy and the executive continued to take refuge behind their affidavit that the minutes had been "falsified." When asked to explain in what way, they claimed they couldn't talk because everything was "confidential." The secretary sued them for $1.3 million for besmirching her reputation. The Department of Justice paid for the defence of the executive, but the secretary had to pay her own legal costs. After her case dragged on for several months, she dropped it.

I expected the incident would disappear from the front pages in a matter of days and I could get back to some kind of normal life. But even I hadn't realized how angry women across the country were, nor how loyal Canadian women were to me.

A small group, mostly from NAC and Women for Political Action, met in Toronto and started making plans. After lining up an impressive list of speakers, they asked Flora MacDonald to book a room in the West Block. When she told them they would need at least 100 women to mount a conference, they said they thought they could bring out at least 250.

In Ottawa, women started phoning around for billets, child care, meals, and ways to get other women to Ottawa. None of them had money or any government support. What they did have was a good cause. And they were angry. They had even found a heroine—almost an anomaly in the women's movement!

Dawn Macdonald, who had worked on *Chatelaine*, was now editor of *City Woman*, and she launched a "Butterfly Campaign," to symbolize women's breaking out of their cocoons. Women all over the country wore butterfly pins, sent money, and pledged to phone ten more women to raise money to send women to the conference.

On February 14, 1981, 1,300 women from all across the country arrived in Ottawa to hold what came to be known as the Ad Hoc Conference. (If the original conference had gone ahead, we probably would have managed to attract about 500.) Many had paid their own way, while some women in the bureaucracy conveniently arranged "consultative groups" to come to Ottawa at that time. The translators' union supplied free translation, and hundreds of Ottawa women opened up their homes to billet people from out of town.

The conference was held in the very same room where the Joint Committee hearings had been staged. Instead of august members of Parliament, senators, and their attendants, it was filled with angry women.

Saturday morning started with an inspired speech from Pauline Jewett to a standing-room-only crowd. It soon became clear that even an Ad Hoc Conference of women could be politicized. Conservative women were there in force, hoping to fan the anger into such a blaze that the whole Charter would be rejected outright.

Aware of the way the debate was going, I managed to get the resolution condemning the way the Charter was being railroaded through Parliament shifted to the bottom of the agenda. Towards the end of the afternoon, Maureen McTeer, a Conservative lawyer and the wife of Joe Clark, berated the audience for not condemning the Charter out of hand. Pauline Jewett countered by pointing out that it could be an important tool for women, and since the government was hell-bent on getting it through Parliament, it was probably going to be passed. McTeer lost her temper—and the vote. A reception for Saturday night was cancelled, and everyone worked on recommendations until 11:00 p.m., including the volunteer translators.

The next morning, the list of their demands was read: Women wanted equal rights for men and women to be guaranteed without limitation in the Charter. They wanted "person" rather than such vague, problematic terms such as "individual," "anyone," or "everybody" to be used throughout the Charter. They wanted the right to reproductive freedom. They wanted Section 15 on discrimination to include marital status, sexual orientation, and political beliefs. And they wanted the three-year moratorium on Section 15 lifted so that it applied immediately.

That afternoon at the City Hall a meeting with a panel discussion on the CACSW was held. The panellists were Jill McCalla Vickers of Carleton University; Kay Macpherson, a former president of the National Action Committee; Madeleine Leblanc, president of New Brunswick's council; and myself. Out of that meeting came the following resolutions: 1. that Axworthy and the executive resign; 2. that an independent review of the CACSW be held; 3. that the CACSW report to Parliament, not to a minister; 4. that appointees to the council be people with a commitment to women.

Unfortunately, in contrast to the all the news space and air time produced during my confrontation with Axworthy, the Ad Hoc Conference received almost no press at all.

At *Chatelaine*, I had often remarked in both editorials and speeches that women frequently make the most progress when men make colossal mistakes. One of the most colossal in the history of the women's movement in Canada was Lloyd Axworthy's attempt to stop the conference on the Constitution. To this day, I believe that if the original conference had gone ahead, it would have been a bit awkward for the government. Probably the same resolutions would have come out of it, inviting some response from the government, but without the publicity, they would have been easier to ignore.

In the end, the women of Canada gained one incredible advantage they probably would never have achieved without Axworthy's blundering interference. A new section was added to the Charter—Section 28. It states simply that men and women are equal under the law.

This simple, and surely not controversial, statement is nonetheless important. In fact, it's so important that American women have been trying since 1923 to enshrine similar wording in their Constitution. They have failed every time—most recently in 1983 when the Equal Rights Amendment (ERA) was defeated. Catherine McKinnon, the renowned U.S. jurist, who taught at York University in the 1980s, was astounded at what Canadian women had achieved.

Section 28 was added to the Charter because of the furore created by the Ad Hoc Conference and the fact that a small group of about twenty-three women, headed by Linda Ryan Nye and Marilou McPhedran, stayed in Ottawa afterwards and lobbied both the government and the Opposition parties. As he had all fall, the minister responsible for the status of women continued to oppose all changes. Axworthy called the Ad Hoc group "tiresome" and—resorting to that typical stratagem of a politician cornered on women's issues—claimed we were "unrepresentative of Canadian women." He dismissed the changes we were pressing for as "not worthwhile." I was widely quoted when I remarked, "Every time Lloyd Axworthy opens his mouth, one hundred more women become feminists."

After I resigned, Win Gardner was made acting head of the CACSW. By March, Lucie Pepin had taken over as president, and Axworthy appointed six new members to the council without any consultation. Although he had agreed to an external review, the executive cancelled it in favour of an internal review to be carried out by nine members of the council, including those whose conduct was in question. The findings, of course, were never made public.

When Lucie demanded the staff take an oath of loyalty to her, four more staff members quit—by this time half the staff had departed. The CACSW's conference on the Constitution was finally held in May—long after the main debate over the Constitution had ended. Several women's groups, including NAC, boycotted it.

Today, when I look back on those days, I am still amazed at my stamina. No matter how tired I was or how much pressure I was under, I managed to cope. I think it was having the support of so many friends as well as my sons—particularly Mitchell, who was living with me. Even at sixteen, he was intelligent, sympathetic, and even wise.

To support myself, I turned back to freelancing. I wrote a column for the *Financial Post*, worked on a small Ottawa magazine, gave many speeches—some of which were paid for—and finished another book, *Rough Layout*.

In the fall, on the day I left on my cross-country book tour, Edythe MacDonald of the Justice department phoned me to say that in the final negotiations, the government and the premiers had clamped a restraining clause on both Section 28 and Section 15 in the Charter. This meant they could keep any discriminatory law they pleased on the books indefinitely, just by renewing it every five years.

I immediately phoned women in Ottawa to start lobbying both the federal and provincial governments. Once the word was out, enraged women from coast to coast took to the phones. Soon after I arrived back in Ottawa, the restraint had been lifted from Section 28 but not from Section 15. I kept wondering, Why do women have to fight like tigers again and again just to keep what we think we've already won?

In retrospect, I realize that I made some serious mistakes at the CACSW. Like many people who come from the private sector to government, I was a novice in the byzantine world of politics. Moreover, I had assumed that if I did the best job I knew how, the members and the executive would support me.

I was certainly unused to dealing with an appointed council. Although I genuinely liked and admired the work the best of them did and the knowledge they brought from their own backgrounds, too many had proved to be prima donnas who considered me just another Liberal appointee—one who had received a bigger plum from the political pie. They were uninterested in women's issues and didn't bother to read the research but expected a lot of personal service from the central office. When they didn't receive it, they found fault with both me and the staff. During the Mulroney years, some Conservative council members actually tried to change research papers to fit their current political agenda more closely! Although the CACSW improved during the presidency of Sylvia Gold and Glenna Simms, when it was dissolved under the Liberals in 1995 hardly a word of protest was raised.

I could have wooed the council members, cosied up to them, phoned them more often, but that had never been my style, and I am still not good at it. I much preferred to spend my time, as I had at *Chatelaine*, dealing with bright and dedicated staff members I had helped select.

As for me, I had been through the worst—and the best—year of my life. The experience had left me feeling somewhat bruised. Because of my new notoriety, I did not receive a single real job offer for the next two years. Nor was I asked to go on any boards that had anything to do with business: I had become something of a pariah among the business community. Politics was also out of the question, unless I changed parties and joined the NDP, as my friend Pauline Jewett was urging me to do.

The cancellation of the conference and everything that had followed afterwards had resulted in a great triumph for women—but not really for me. In fact, my life was never to be the same again. Many people, including those I admired and counted as friends, thought I had thrown away a reputation built up over twenty years at *Chatelaine.*

I had always been a revolutionary and a feminist, but something of a closet one, working under the decorous cover of *Chatelaine.* Now I had been forced to cross that invisible line between being a respected, and even powerful, woman of the establishment and being perceived as a true rebel.

CHAPTER FIFTEEN

The Real World of Women

For a short time after my resignation from the Canadian Advisory Council on the Status of Women I was a celebrity—but an inept one. I never knew what to say when a perfect stranger came up to me while I walked the dog or dashed out to buy a carton of milk wearing any old thing I happened to have thrown on. As a born observer and reporter, instead of being assured and gracious in the limelight, I was awkward and embarrassed. Thankfully, outside the women's movement, my fame subsided within a year.

One incident stands out particularly from that brief time. Pat Hacker, one of the organizers of the Ad Hoc Conference, had invited a group of us over to her house, which she was trying to sell. We were sitting in her living room, when suddenly the feminist philanthropist Nancy Jackman (now Nancy Ruth), a woman with a notoriously short attention span when bored, threw off her top. Flinging herself full length across the middle of the floor, she demanded to be massaged.

To my surprise, and as casually as though Nancy had requested a glass of water, a well-known bureaucrat dropped to her knees and began what looked to be a quite professional performance. The rest of us continued talking as though the spectacle of a very large, half-naked woman being massaged by a very thin one was an ordinary cocktail-hour occurrence.

Just then the door opened and a family of four, accompanied by a real estate agent, entered and stood in the hallway staring at the tableau. They recognized me instantly before, with great dispatch, the agent shepherded everyone upstairs. By the time they came back down, we had regrouped ourselves a little more conventionally!

For a year after my resignation from the CACSW, a lot of people, including me, were concerned about my future and whether I would ever be offered a job again. Finally, I received a proposal for a full-time job, albeit an unpaid one. The ten-year-old National Action Committee on the Status of Women (NAC) wanted me to run for president.

On the surface, it wasn't a tempting prospect from any point of view. NAC, the largest women's organization in Canada, is a loose association of member groups, who meet annually at a painfully democratic general meeting. Every year its voluntary executive is chastised for all its errors and omissions—but rarely praised—and sent back with another challenging load of even more difficult resolutions for the following year.

Among its many ups and downs, NAC had just gone through a very deep down in 1982. My assessment of the situation—which certainly would not be that of most of the principal players—was that there were two warring factions in a movement that is ludicrously presumed to exist in a constant state of euphoric co-operation and sisterhood. For the purposes of discussion, let's call one side the "old guard" and the other, the "reform group." The old guard was represented by the Toronto women who had started NAC. They had put long hours into the organization, believed they partly owned it, and wanted to keep it basically the way it was. The reform group, headed by NAC's recent president Lynn McDonald, was hell-bent on radical change. They were pushing to make the organization a truly national body with an executive drawn from across the country. They wanted NAC, as a lobby group focused on the federal government, to become independent of government handouts, and to have its head office in Ottawa.

The official conflict was whether homemakers should be allowed to join the Canada Pension Plan. The unofficial conflict was not about policy but process, and how NAC was to be run in the future. No one even on the fringes of the women's movement could be unaware of the fracas. A non-confidence vote had been brought against Lynn McDonald and a campaign mounted to remove her from office. Minutes of meetings, far from being dry recordings of motions passed, were extremely detailed and personal. (Later these highly absorbing minutes disappeared completely—a source of regret for countless Ph.D. students studying the organization.)

Because NAC's was one controversy that I had not been involved in, both sides jumped to the conclusion that I would naturally see the justice of their position and be an acceptable president. The old guard regarded me as a corporate type, unenlightened in the ways of the volunteer sector, and therefore malleable. The reform group was convinced after my fight with Axworthy that I was a true radical.

Everyone I talked to cautioned me against taking the job. They said I was a neophyte and unfamiliar with the pitfalls of running a volunteer women's group. I was warned about the Trots, the Marxist-Leninists, and the Communists. The union women, with their sharply honed skills in political manoeuvring and debate, would make mincemeat of me. Because I had no control over who was elected to the executive, I was told I would be saddled with some extremely tiresome and trying people—not to mention that I would be torn apart between the two factions.

There was some truth in all these dire predictions, but I needed to put my energies to work. Free-lance writing was keeping me busy and solvent, but I felt unchallenged. Taking on NAC would make use of my fleeting "celebrity" status to publicize a good cause. However, the most convincing argument against taking the job—and one that made it almost irresistible to me—was that this was another worthwhile women's organization in a shambles. I thought I might be able to help fix it. Never one to duck a near-hopeless mission, I accepted.

Nancy Jackman and Kay Macpherson, a past president herself, invited me for lunch and, over quiche and salad, Kay filled the novice in on the facts of life as a volunteer president. "You have to constantly hop into the breach and pick up after the slackers who don't do what they were supposed to do," she told me sternly. "You have to act a bit like a mother hen, constantly smoothing everyone's feathers and patting everyone on the head for the good job they've done—even if they haven't. You have to give everyone else credit and take none of it for yourself. In fact, you have to take all the blame for whatever goes wrong. And when you're finished," she added grumpily, "you'll end up with very little thanks for all you've done. It's certainly no picnic. I don't know why we do it."

To make sure I understood my position clearly, she added, with her typical candour, "It's just that no one else will take the job right now. You're actually the bottom of the barrel."

In the past I had attended the pressured circus of a NAC annual general meeting as an observer and thought I was fairly familiar with its roller-coaster dynamics. But the March 1982 meeting was enough to make me consider booking passage on a slow boat to Borneo.

The first evening always begins deceptively well. In spite of a Spartan reception with a cash bar, stale sandwiches, and cookies, old friends are reunited. There is nothing quite like the infectious élan of being together again for a good cause among other like-minded, dedicated women. It's truly exhilarating. A massive turn-on. A giant love-in. By the next morning, when we realize all that has to be done in one short weekend—with so many different groups from all over the country and a thousand pressing agendas—some of the euphoria evaporates and gritty reality takes over.

That year, the sessions were chaired by members of the incumbent executive, which provided a fine opportunity for rival factions to bombard them with challenges on parliamentary procedure and points of order from the floor. Halfway through the morning session, the constitutional quibbles brought the proceedings to a complete impasse. It was harrowing, as incoming president, to behold the fractious floor of that meeting. A delegate asked me as I stood at the back of the auditorium, "Do you really want to take this over? You must be a masochist!"

Somehow order and common sense were restored by tabling motions and pushing others off to be settled in committee. That night a modest banquet, accompanied by songs and humorous skits, damped down some of the rancour.

On Sunday, with a mounting backlog of business still to get through and enough policy recommendations from member groups to choke a provincial legislature for years, the infighting resumed with amendments, withdrawal of motions, and more challenges from the floor. It was a relief on Monday when we marched from the hotel to Parliament Hill for the annual lobbying of members of the three major political parties.

Every government and even the opposition parties would prefer to avoid this yearly event. The government always tries to scuttle the lobby with enticing promises of private meetings with cabinet ministers—a blatantly self-serving ploy. NAC meets with cabinet ministers privately all the time with few results. Under our system of government, there is almost no way to exert pressure on a party in power between elections except through lobbying and the media.

The media are always present and in full force at the NAC lobby. It provides a rare opportunity to question cabinet ministers and even opposition parties about weak or nonexistent positions on issues of concern to women. The media gleefully pick up flubs—and there are usually quite a few. Trudeau, who was notoriously uninterested in women's concerns, and several members of his cabinet regularly absented themselves from the lobby—which the press always duly reported. That year only twelve Liberals appeared—a deliberate snub to me.

Back in Toronto at our first executive meeting, I realized nothing had been resolved by the election of a new executive. The same warring factions were present, and almost evenly balanced. Fifteen minutes into the meeting, a blow-up on pensions for homemakers occurred again. My solution was to insist the issue be taken up in a committee, with the chief contenders on both sides charged with coming back to the table with a resolution, which would then be put to a vote. After several months of meetings, they returned with a recommendation that homemakers be included in the CPP. Once they no longer had an arena for a public fight, the desire for confrontation seemed to disappear.

Settling in as president, I realized my two-year term would be no tea party, but I already knew that it was going to be much more satisfying than my recent experience on the CACSW. Instead of an appointed board, some of whose members had little knowledge or interest in women's issues, NAC's board was elected from over two hundred organizations representing three and a half million women. NAC embraced a variety of women's organizations, from rape crisis and battered women's shelters to more traditional groups such as the IODE.

Board members ran for office because they burned with a white flame about some issues—day care, more liberal abortion laws, less violence towards women, more tolerance for minorities. Skilled and knowledgeable, they worked hard on committees as well as in their regions. Differences on the board were about ideology, priorities, and method, rarely about objectives. Being on the NAC executive was gruelling. The high demands of jobs, families—and NAC—often meant that women served only one term.

Officially nonpartisan, NAC certainly leaned more to the left than the right, and it lacked, until recently, adequate representation of women of colour, native, ethnic, and disabled women's groups. Unlike the National Organization for Women (NOW) in the U.S., NAC had never been through a destructive split over the issue of lesbianism. However, although lesbian women have always been active in the organization, the first resolution on sexual orientation was passed only in 1985.

Having spent most of my life in the business world, I had many painful lessons to learn. I could cut through a lot of office routine with great dispatch, and did so, but I found the process of talking everything out endlessly in an effort to reach a consensus both boring and frustrating. I had to learn to be patient, bite my tongue, and go along with decisions I was almost sure were wrong. Some members of the board were so suspicious of me— a woman from the corporate (male) world—that my wisest move was never to let them know where I stood, otherwise my position would automatically be opposed by them!

My strategy as incoming president was to use my high profile to get around Canada as much as possible, building support, membership, and media attention. My sympathies were with the reformers rather than the old guard, but I knew I would have to move cautiously, working with progressives from both groups.

I particularly hoped to revamp *Status*, a small NAC publication on feminism, which came out four times yearly. By 1982 there were several similar magazines. I believed its $20,000 budget would be better spent on a news bulletin to alert member groups about current priorities, whom to lobby, what letters to write, and where to send them.

I did get around the country, and the membership grew to three hundred groups almost automatically. As for *Status*, I was not even asked to its planning meetings, let alone allowed to make it over. As a former editor of the biggest magazine in Canada, I assumed, naively, that I might be useful to the little group that put it out. Occasionally they would say, "You must come to our next meeting," then never tell me the date. In any event, I was embroiled in so many other crises that I didn't need to manufacture another one. In all my time as president, I was lucky to see a copy of *Status* before it came out.

Having surveyed national women's groups in twelve industrial countries, I am convinced that NAC works better and is more democratic and representative of Canada's women than any other similar organization in either Europe or the U.S. But in 1982 it had some major weaknesses.

One of them was its dependence on the federal government's yearly hand-out—75 per cent of its $200,000 budget. The remainder was raised from modest fees from member groups and the sales of T-shirts, medallions, and so on. Soon after I took over as president, we became even more impoverished when, for no apparent reason, Gerald Regan, then secretary of state, cut our subsidy by $25,000.

Although the Toronto office used up half the budget, it was pathetically inadequate for all that was expected of it. The two full-time, overworked employees, Pearl Blazer and Janet Port, and one part-timer, Maxine Hermant, had through the years become overwhelmed by the demands made on them. Their solution was for everyone to try to do everything, with little organization. Any effort to make changes was fiercely opposed not so much by the staff but by the Old Guard, who regularly dropped in, almost as though it were a club. Wisely deciding not to meet this potentially dangerous situation head-on, I did a lot of the work a president might expect her staff to do—opening my own mail, answering many of my letters, and even typing some official letters and documents. (It was faster for me to correct a letter to a cabinet minister on my electric typewriter than to expect the overburdened office staff to do it on their antiquated equipment.)

In my first six months, we prepared six briefs and presented them to various parliamentary committees in Ottawa. Preparing briefs is time-consuming but the women on the executive knew far more about the Criminal Code, rape laws, and federal housing than most of the politicians and bureaucrats before whom we appeared.

One of the first things every new member of NAC's executive wanted was to go immediately to Ottawa. Each was convinced that if only she could buttonhole the right cabinet minister and explain the facts of life about pay equity or disabled women or whatever, everything would magically change. What they didn't seem to realize was that ministers see half a dozen lobbyists a day, an increasing number of whom are well-paid professionals from the wealthy business sector.

It was fairly easy to set up a meeting with a cabinet minister. The trick was to convince them that there would be a political advantage in changing legislation. As president of NAC, I took part in one or two of these presentations every month. In 1982 Louise Delude, our expert on pensions, and I went to see Monique Bégin, minister of Health and Welfare, a warm, expansive woman deeply concerned about social issues. Unlike most of her male colleagues, she gave us a full two hours to talk about including homemakers in the Canada Pension Plan.

Louise presented a brilliant argument: two out of three older women were living in poverty without pensions because they had stayed home looking after children—a role society endorses as the proper thing to do. Backed up by thousands of letters supporting the inclusion of homemakers in the CPP, Louise proposed that middle- and upper-class husbands pay the premiums for their wives but poor women be subsidized by the state. She had even worked out a scheme whereby the survivor benefits for wealthy women could be taxed away to be used for pensions for poor women, saving the government money. Unfortunately, I could see from Bégin's expression that as a political strategy, it was dead in the water.

I spoke to groups at least a dozen times a month in churches or community centres, basements and hockey arenas. Sometimes there were challenges from the floor and always complaints about what NAC was doing, or, more often, not doing. Right-to-lifers regularly turned up to try to turn the session into a free-for-all about choice. In Calgary I was heckled by a Marxist-Leninist who insisted that Albania was the only true democracy. At another meeting a man interrupted my speech, delivered a mini-speech himself in the question period, and harassed me all the way out to my car. The organizers apologized profusely, but I wondered how long I—or any other woman—would have lasted using such tactics at an all-male conference!

In February 1982, I debated Barbara Amiel on the subject of feminism before a standing-room-only audience at the University of Lethbridge. She opened by claiming to be a friend of mine—which she certainly was not—and then called me a "swine." She went on to state that feminism encroached on society's freedoms. Affirmative action and nonsexist language were just "exchanging one injustice for another."

I argued that far from being unfair to men, most of the legislation to date, including equal pay and affirmative action, had been quite ineffective. I pointed out that Amiel's brand of neo-conservatism, far from being new, contained the same arguments used by Phyllis Shaffly to defeat the Equal Rights Amendment in the U.S. I suggested she stop claiming she had "made it on her own" and either acknowledge her debt to the women's movement or stop taking advantage of all the hard-earned gains other women had won for her.

It was a brisk exchange that got a lot of press in the western papers, but I doubt that we changed many minds either way.

At a Board of Trade dinner in Montreal, the atmosphere was so hostile that only the president, his wife, and the woman who had invited me would sit beside me at dinner. However, after my purposely low-key speech, the members were so relieved that I wasn't a man-eating dragon that they would hardly let me go.

Sometimes I would be put up in a hotel on some freebie arrangement, but more often I was billeted in a home—usually in a child's room with a Donald Duck or Bo-Beep motif. The rightful occupant, naturally curious about the large lump in his or her bed, would wake me with a poke. Mother would be preparing breakfast in the kitchen and coping with the other children, while a grumpy husband flipped pancakes as if he did it every morning—to prove what a liberated household I was visiting!

Soon after I took over the presidency of NAC and while I was still living in Ottawa, Pat Carney, at that time a Conservative MP, invited me to dinner along with Pauline Jewett and Flora MacDonald. A niece of Byrne Hope Sanders, my predecessor at *Chatelaine*, Carney not only looked like her famous aunt but also had a lot of her flair. On the day of the dinner, she phoned to say she had put her back out but gamely offered to carry on with the dinner anyway. I, of course, offered to host it instead. Carney arrived wearing a dramatic cape and carrying a walking stick. She and Pauline spent the evening making hilarious suggestions about what I should do with NAC—move it out to Calgary, or to Tobago, for example. Flora MacDonald who, even in that relaxed atmosphere, was guarded and partisan, sat on the couch looking uncomfortable amid all the merriment.

As president of NAC, I was the recipient of all kinds of requests. Women asked for advice about jobs, legal information, marriage counselling, violent husbands, spouses intent on kidnapping children. My practice was to reply not with advice but with information about where to get help. I was amazed at the well-to-do women who abhorred feminism and NAC—until their marriages broke up or they ran into discrimination at work. Turning overnight into feminists, they would appear in our office demanding help, and be infuriated when we didn't drop everything to attend to them.

The worst—and most hopeless—part of my job by far was the same problem I had had at the Advisory Council. I spent hours and hours trying to master the jargon and the byzantine bureaucratic process as I wrote submissions to the secretary of state in order to get our yearly grant. No matter how many times I redid the submission, it was never right. The torment by paper continued every fall, right up to the point where we were going to have to close the office and send the staff home because we couldn't pay them. And then, miraculously, we would receive a dribble of money.

I soon lost any feeling of guilt about taking government money. Having experienced how much money was wasted in Ottawa, how few women there were in the House of Commons, and how little most MPs and bureaucrats knew about women's issues, I thought the government was getting excellent value for the paltry sums they doled out to women's groups. We greatly improved legislation in bill after bill, thanks to down-to-earth input from women actually working with rape victims, child-care groups, single mothers, teenage runaways, and minority groups. One of the bills we lobbied for and substantially altered for the better was Jean Chrétien's 1982 changes to the Criminal Code sections on sexual assault.

In 1981 an organization called REAL (Realistic, Equal, Active, for Life) Women had been formed. It professed to represent the "real" women of Canada, but its main purpose was opposition to abortion under any circumstances. Its members were also against day care, the equality clauses in the Charter of Rights, equal pay for women, affirmative action, and family law reform. They were for much tougher divorce laws that would make it harder for both men and women to end a marriage. Claiming to be pro male—but only in the sense that they wanted men to take care of them— they labelled all other women's groups "radical."

At its zenith, REAL Women claimed no more than fifty thousand members—many fewer than dozens of member organizations of NAC. Yet they demanded half the funding for women's groups from the secretary of state Women's Program. Turned down because they were not working for equality, they then lobbied to wipe out the entire program, which helped support more than six hundred women's organizations.

The media, always on the lookout for stories with two protagonists to pit against each other, frequently gave REAL Women equal time with NAC simply because they presented "another point of view." Enhancing their image as "real" women, they would arrive at the House of Commons with freshly baked muffins and cookies and receive the red-carpet treatment from many Conservative MPs in return. They were like a bad case of static all during my presidency.

In August 1982, I made the move back to Toronto, with a great farewell party at one end and a big welcome-back party at the other. With my sons either at university or on their own, I had planned to sell my major asset, my Toronto house, and buy a more modest home, using any extra cash to generate some income. But housing prices had plummeted by the time my tenant's lease was up, and after three years of being rented, the house looked shabby. The only thing to do was move back into it, fix it up myself, and hope for an upturn in the market.

I set about fixing eavestroughs and broken windowpanes and repainting the house on the inside, doing as much as possible myself to save money. In the spring, the market improved and I sold the house for about half of what it would have brought two years before. I then bought a much smaller place in Cabbagetown, which was still big enough to accommodate my sons when they came home. I have never regretted selling the old house when I did. It had been a gloomy, sad time living there by myself in a house creaking and echoing with memories of happier times. I wanted to get on with my life.

I found Toronto quite changed. It was a less safe and comfortable place to live in. Once I had felt confident sending my children off on the subway to hockey and music lessons, but that was changing for younger parents. Two young women had recently been brutally raped and murdered. In response, Metro had set up a commission headed by the very capable Jane Pepino to see what could be done to make the city safer.

I became a member, heading up a subcommittee on pornography. It recommended some control over violent pornography, most of which was imported from the U.S. That immediately brought me into conflict with some friends in the media and even some feminists.

I can't help comparing violent pornography to cigarettes. In the early 1960s, reports identifying cigarette smoking as a main cause of lung cancer started to appear. Rejected by the powerful tobacco industry, those reports were generally ignored until statistics proved conclusively that smoking killed more than forty thousand Canadians a year. Many studies have linked violent pornography to a growing callousness towards victims, more than 90 per cent of whom are women. But none has been considered "conclusive," despite the fact that when a movie shows a man torching a subway-ticket office, or a gangster ambushing a policeman, an immediate connection is made to similar crimes in society.

In the Scandinavian countries, where pornography was once freely available, its sale is now strictly controlled. Because we control many things such as hate literature in our society, I see no reason to refuse to exercise control over where and to whom pornography is sold, as well as banning violent and child pornography entirely. The main argument for some restriction, in my opinion, is that we have to clearly inform the public that violent, degrading pornography is unacceptable in the same way that laws in the past educated and stopped people from abusing minorities, throwing garbage out the window, or spitting in public.

My first annual general meeting as NAC's president was fast approaching. We had completely overhauled the constitution and tightened up the nomination process. Previously, almost anyone could go into the Toronto office, look at the in-coming nominations from across the country, and then phone around to try to line up more agreeable people.

The biggest conflict, I realized, would be over my plan to move the office to Ottawa. The Toronto "club" was opposed to the move, but a year as president had convinced me that it was necessary. We were a lobby group, after all, with the federal government our chief target. We were also supposed to be a national, bilingual organization. I firmly believed that national organizations supposedly representing all of Canada, including Quebec, could not be unilingual with a Toronto head office. I also hoped the move would cut office expenses: NAC would be able to share space and equipment with several other national women's organizations already located in Ottawa.

I did manage to solve one problem that had plagued the last annual meeting. I eliminated a lot of the politicking from the floor by appointing neutral chairs instead of members of the executive. The three women who took on this thankless task and did it as long as I was active on the board were Jill Vickers, from Carleton University, and Susan Mann and Caroline Andrews, from Ottawa University. They not only chaired the meetings with magisterial calm and logic, but they also weathered at least one rebellion every year. Some women, unused to parliamentary procedure, would demand that Bourinot's rules be tossed out of the window and "the meeting adopt its own women-made rules."

"You can do anything you like," Jill Vickers would tell them calmly, "but everyone has to agree to the same rules, or the meeting can't go forward." The idea of stopping the meeting to get agreement on a whole new set of "women's" rules dampened the rebels, and the meeting would once again stagger forward.

That year committee reports whistled through on Friday night with scarcely a mutter of dissent. Even the constitutional changes the next morning passed in record time, for such a potentially explosive issue.

On Monday morning, our lobby, led by Michelle Swenarchuk and Laurel Ritchie, bristled with penetrating questions for all three parties, and the media coverage was excellent. When the hem of my dress fell just as we were about to march in to face the MPs in a blaze of television lights, I hastily tacked it up with the Scotch tape that some enterprising feminist had in her purse and carried on.

It was a triumph of renewed sisterhood for NAC, compared with the vicious infighting that had afflicted the organization over the previous three years.

Moving the office was another matter. The Toronto old guard out-flanked us right from the start. With plenty of time on their hands in the weeks before the meeting, they had canvassed member groups all across the country. They argued that a move to Ottawa would put NAC in dire danger of being "co-opted" by the government and the bureaucracy (even though other women's organizations had not met with this grievous fate.) They suggested that because we didn't have strong representation from Quebec, there was no reason for the move to Ottawa, as if the move were not to strengthen our Quebec ties. They even had a Quebec woman speak to that argument!

After two hours of debate, a vote was taken—an open show of hands. This was a mistake, I realize now. The result was an exact tie. We had lost.

In the aftermath of the vote, to try to mend matters, my old friend Kay Macpherson, leader of the stay-put faction, moved that we set up an office in Ottawa and make the Toronto office bilingual! Of course, there was no money to accomplish either objective properly. I had not only lost the vote but I now also had a daunting task to try to carry out.

We advertised, and after almost six months of interviewing, managed to hire a young, bilingual woman for Ottawa, Mary Lou Murray. She was excellent, but her job was almost impossible. She had to try to stay on top of all legislation going through Parliament, answer all kinds of questions from across the country, and do it with no support staff and almost no budget.

Meanwhile, attempts to make the Toronto office more efficient and introduce bilingualism were equally difficult. We couldn't add a bilingual person without letting someone else go. By summer, as a compromise, we hired a bilingual student whose salary was covered under a student loan program. Although I managed to get the budget increased, the changes left us $5,000 in debt.

The following fall, I took a trip to New York to meet with some of the members of NOW to find out why they were so much more successful in raising money than we were. It was no mystery. NOW is structured differently from NAC. It has branches all over the U.S., as if it were a service club. Unlike NAC, it is also much more middle class and less representative of U.S. women. Over forty people work in the head office just raising money.

Many of our member groups were not middle class and could pay only modest fees. Although many middle- and upper-income Canadian women supported NAC, unlike U.S. women, they are unaccustomed to writing large cheques. In trying to tap this group more effectively, we launched an aggressive direct-mail campaign in my last year as president.

In the spring of 1983, I and Jennifer Keck, a member of the executive, appeared before the Royal Commission on the Economic Union and Development Prospects for Canada, chaired by the former cabinet minister Donald Macdonald. Its purpose was to explore the proposed free trade agreement with the U.S. Canadian women had a small, minimal social safety net with paid maternity leave for eighteen weeks, a minimum-wage scale, and some laws protecting them from unhealthy working conditions. Many states south of us had no such protection. We were concerned by the business-oriented focus of the hearings and the large numbers of women working in electrical and textile industries who would lose their jobs under a free trade agreement. What kind of retraining was being planned for them—or, for that matter, for men who would also be displaced by free trade?

I had no sooner begun to speak than one of the women on the commission interrupted me to say the commission was concerned about "people," not women. I replied that NAC would happily begin to talk about "people" when Canada's poor were not disproportionately women, when half—not 2 per cent—of top executives in major corporations were women, when the average salary of women was equal to, not 68 per cent of, men's salaries. And when at least half, not 5 per cent, of the members of the House of Commons were women.

In the fall of 1983, we returned for another session with the commission, which was by now acknowledging that free trade might throw thousands of low-paid workers out of work. They wanted us to do an in-depth analysis of the problem for women, which was ludicrous. We had no budget for that kind of work—they did. The cost of running the commission for less than a week, and from the same pot of taxpayers' money, was more than our total annual budget!

With another election coming up, five women's organizations decided it was time to tackle the government about better funding for women's programs and to demand we get it with fewer hassles. The Canadian Congress for Learning Opportunities for Women, the Canadian Research Institute for the Advancement of Women, the National Association of Women and the LAW, Relais-Femmes from Quebec, and NAC got together. After researching what was being spent on other groups, we discovered that multiculturalism received $8.3 million, natives' programs $26.7 million, official languages $19.8 million. Women's programs, in contrast, totalled $3.2 million, which worked out to 10 cents a woman a year—and we had to grovel for that!

In June, armed with a strong press release detailing these figures, we met with Judy Erola, who had replaced the truculent Lloyd Axworthy as minister responsible for women. She was sympathetic but pessimistic about the possibility of getting more money or improving the method. Somewhat subdued, we went off for our next meeting with the secretary of state, Serge Joyal.

I have always believed, in our Canadian first-past-the-post political system, that the only real pressure we can put on government is just before an election. After that meeting, I was sure of it. We had hardly begun our presentation when Joyal capitulated with hardly a murmur. He not only increased the budget to $13 million but early in the following year the funding process was streamlined and greatly improved.

At my last annual general meeting in 1984, with an election in the offing, all three party leaders—John Turner, Brian Mulroney, and Ed Broadbent—turned up for the NAC lobby. They were all committed to changing the 1876 Indian Act so that native women married to non-natives would no longer lose their treaty rights. NAC had supported the cause of native women since 1973, when Janet Lavell first challenged the act before the Supreme Court of Canada—and lost. The Liberals promised as well that they would make divorce easier and set up a national registry to help enforce child support.

Again that year we tried to get the office moved to Ottawa. This time both sides were well organized but again we were outmanoeuvred. The opposition's ace in the hole was a small organization from Quebec claiming to be the "Voice of Quebec" in NAC (I had never heard of them). They pleaded that their funding might be cut if the office were moved—a patently ridiculous idea, since we hoped the move would attract many more Quebec groups to join. We lost the vote 175 to 160.

When Chaviva Hosek took over as NAC's president in 1984, although she had been part of the faction in favour of keeping the office in Toronto, she realized it badly needed reorganizing. A consultant was hired, and after a lot of anguish, a threatened lawsuit, and $30,000 that was paid out in compensation, staff changes were made. All this took two years. In retrospect, I continue to think that moving the office would have been not only the logical thing to do but also might have avoided a great deal of distress for everyone.

For the next two years, NAC, which now represented more than five hundred women's groups, was much better off. It had more money from both government and its new source, direct mail. Under its new executive director, Judy Campbell, and a staff of six, the Toronto office became a model of efficiency. A pension plan was brought in and a union. However, the problem of the Ottawa office, where one lone woman was doing all the political work, was never adequately solved.

Chaviva Hosek's big coup as NAC's president was to arrange a two-hour nationally televised leaders' debate on women's issues before the 1984 election. After the broadcast, the media reported that it had been "flat and tedious." Appearing on "Canada AM," I said it had been "music to my ears" to hear women's issues taken seriously for a change. On the same program, Flora MacDonald declared that she had been so bored that she had turned it off. As I reported in the *Toronto Star*, I thought the leaders came off pretty much as they were. Mulroney looked like the boy who would offer you anything to get you into the back seat of his father's car. Turner, even on camera still persistently patting the backside of his party's president, Iona

Campagnolo, came off as the high-school jock. Ed Broadbent was the brain you went to the April hop with—if no one else asked you.

In trying to pin down the three parties more explicitly about their stand on women's issues, a group of us staged Luncheons with Leaders. Brian Mulroney, the first leader to attend and be grilled on what he planned to do for women, provided the most astonishing answers. He promised to do everything we asked him—a telling example of what was to become his political style—promise anything during the campaign and do whatever you want afterwards.

The magazine, *Status*, also changed after I stepped down as president in 1984. For a short time under a new communications chair, it tried to compete on the newsstand and make money through circulation, a plan that flew in the face of the experience of every small magazine in this country. The idea failed and *Status* was replaced by Action bulletins—exactly what I had wanted from the beginning.

When Judy Rebick became president, the number of executive meetings was cut in half to save money. Judy, a natural media personality, did a fine job of attracting press as well as establishing stronger links with labour and other groups. Women's program cuts under the Tories resulted in even greater efforts to raise money. Today only one-third of NAC funding still comes from government.

To make it possible for women who can't afford to take two years off without pay to run NAC, the presidency became a paid position. The small number of visible-minority women—which had been a nagging criticism of the organization even before my time—was corrected and many more groups were brought in. Before Sunera Thobani stepped down as president, she and half the executive were visible-minority women. Women's groups in Quebec still have a very tentative relationship with NAC.

In the 1990s, with many more government cuts, the NAC office has had to move many times—but always in Toronto. And after keeping two offices for several years, NAC closed the Ottawa office in 1995 for budgetary reasons.

I remained on the NAC board as past president for two years and continued for another two years in that office when Chaviva Hosek became ineligible, as a member of the Ontario legislature. In the summer of 1985, I attended the UN Conference in Nairobi as NAC's representative on the official delegation.

At the opening ceremonies, Daniel T. arap Moi, president of Kenya, laughed and joked with his henchmen all through the secretary-general's speech. After his own speech, he and his entire entourage walked out before Margaret Kenyatta, daughter of Kenya's first president, spoke. No one was surprised when Moi's government censored all but a few of the films from the National Film Board's women's unit, Studio D.

The Film Board was making a documentary on Nairobi and asked me and other Canadian delegates to be in it. I was to be filmed talking to Betty Friedan. Friedan had already established herself in Nairobi as a guru of the women's movement. Every day she stationed herself under a tree, where she held forth to anyone who cared to listen.

When we met on the morning of the film shoot, she pretended she didn't know me and actually refused to have me in the shot at all, saying she wanted to be surrounded by African women. That was fine, except that this was a Canadian film crew, which meant at least a token Canadian had to be in it. I finally had to explain to her, "If I am not in this shot, then neither are you."

Realizing her faux pas, she suddenly became quite friendly, "Why, Doris!" she exclaimed. "I didn't recognize you!"

In the film, we were supposed to be talking together, but as far as I was concerned there was no dialogue. She talked nonstop, as she usually does. Afterwards, the crew interviewed me separately. In the final cut I ended up at Friedan's feet, which really did not please me.

In one humorous incident, Walter McLean, our minister responsible for women, addressed the assembly. After a paragraph or two in English, he switched into mangled French. The assembly was astonished. Why was this poor man murdering the French language when the assembly provided excellent translation in twelve different languages? We Canadians were, of course, surprised at all the fuss. If a Canadian government minister hadn't spoken in both official languages, there would have been hell to pay, both in Nairobi and Canada!

Back home, and in the middle of cooking the family Thanksgiving dinner, I received a phone call from a young woman who wanted me to take part in a conference called Post Nairobi the following Sunday. Having just returned from three weeks out of town, I suggested several other people for the panel she was organizing. She insisted she had to have me, giving me the impression she was a desperate, overworked volunteer who had been trying to organize the conference over her coffee breaks.

To help her out, I agreed, but asked her to send me some background material. By Thursday, when no material had arrived, I phoned for more details and learned that the conference had been planned for months. International guests were being brought from Africa and Latin America on the $35,000 budget. Far from being an overworked volunteer, the "desperate" young woman was a well-paid employee.

The purpose of the conference was to discuss the problems of minority women—women of colour, disabled women, and lesbian women. They all felt, with some justification, that they had been shut out of the mainstream of Canadian life and out of the women's movement.

On the Sunday panel, as past president of NAC, I became the target of a lot of anger that had been building all weekend. NAC as an organization and I personally were accused of being racist. I was challenged for daring to talk about Third World women at all. I was lectured that I could never understand what it was like to be a minority women, which was obviously quite true. In the process, I endured everything short of being spat upon, tarred, and feathered.

After the panel was over, I left the platform with as much dignity as possible under the circumstances. A few women—not many—came over to console me for the battering I had taken. It was an exercise many of us were to go through over the next few years. (Although she was never deeply involved in the women's movement, it would even touch June Callwood years later, as a result of her attitude—misconstrued as racist—in dealing with women of colour on the board of a hostel she had founded.)

One June day I received a call from my great friend, Norma Scarborough, long-time president of the Canadian Abortion Rights Action League, and an executive member of NAC. "I've got a problem," she said. "I've got a letter with all the names of our honorary board members, and opposite each name is the date when that person is to be killed. What do you think I should do?"

"Phone the police," I suggested.

"I've done that."

"Then phone the first person on the list," I said helpfully.

"You're the first person on the list," she informed me.

I was obviously not bumped off by an anti-choice maniac in the next few weeks, but I understood a little better what kind of tension Norma and her family had put up with over the years.

In 1986 I finally left the executive of NAC, although I am still active in fund raising for the organization. I especially enjoyed the last years as past president. With little power, I was treated as if I were everyone's favourite aunt. "It was almost worth all the agony of being president to become past president," I remarked in my farewell speech.

My association with NAC was one of the most challenging, rewarding—and humbling—experiences of my life. I met exceptional, dedicated, visionary women who are still among my closest friends. I learned a great deal about the dynamics of women's organizations, which are far more democratic, inclusive, and caring of people, the environment, and society than most hierarchical, competitive male structures. I am more firmly convinced than ever that unless there is more input from women in our society at every level, the world is doomed.

CHAPTER SIXTEEN

And the Next Millennium?

With two sons in university, I needed more financial stability than free-lancing provided, and in 1982 I became a columnist for the *Toronto Star*, a job I thoroughly enjoyed for the next ten years. Used to a three-month lag between finishing an article and its appearance in print, I loved the imme-diacy of a daily paper, as well as the scope I was given to write about any-thing from politics to pop art.

Any spare time I had was taken up with travelling, writing books, and serv-ing on voluntary boards. In 1984 I was appointed to the Judicial Council of Ontario, the body to whom the public takes its complaints about the courts. Jean Augustine, who later became an MP, and I were the only two lay members. We were outnumbered three to one by the chief justices and the treasurer of the Law Society, who tended to be protective of their profession. Usually any high-handed, sexist, or racist behaviour on the part of a judge resulted in a reprimand and a fine covering the cost of conducting the hearing.

The council also approved appointments to the bench. Few women or non–Anglo Saxons appeared before us until Ian Scott, as attorney-general, broke up the Old Boys' Club by setting up an independent advisory council to make recommendations from among a broader selection of lawyers. Although the new system works well, the Harris government is threatening to go back to the Old Boys' route again.

In 1991, I became chancellor of the University of Prince Edward Island, a position I greatly enjoyed. At the same time I joined the board of Harbourfront Centre, a unique complex where theatre, art, dance, festivals for children, and the largest reading series in the world takes place on the Toronto waterfront.

In the fall of 1986, I spent a month in China along with nine other Canadian women. As guests of China's All-Women's Federation, we were able to visit day nurseries, retirement homes, hospitals, a reform school, and several factories. I liked the way women were portrayed in the media, not as sex kittens but as serious, capable people.

While sampling green tea and sweet cakes, we compared notes with our Chinese hostesses. Because we are able to marry for love, they wanted to know why our divorce rate is so high compared with China's 4 per cent. With arranged marriages in decline, they were confident Chinese weddings would soon be forever. We were extremely dubious. They also couldn't understand why, with all our freedom and access to education, we hadn't yet achieved equality. It puzzled us too.

On our side, the Maoist slogan Women Hold Up Half the Sky seemed quaint. Although many more fathers and grandfathers look after children than in Canada, Chinese women, like women all over the world, seemed to be shouldering far more than half the work and receiving far less than their fair share of credit and rewards.

My fourth book, *The Unfinished Revolution*, published in 1991, was a true labour of love. In my search to discover what had been accomplished after twenty years of the women's movement, I travelled all over Europe and North America interviewing more than three hundred leading feminists.

The next year, while Mitchell, my youngest son, was in India on an Aga Khan fellowship, we spent a month touring that fascinating country together. The following year on my own, I visited Thailand, Singapore, Indonesia, and New Zealand. In the spring of 1994, I was one of thousands of international observers sent to South Africa during its first democratic election. That fall, determined to see for myself how Americans actually live, I took a bus trip with Virginia Rock, an academic and seasoned traveller, all through the U.S. Midwest. I wanted to see more of the world while I was still healthy and vigorous. Travel is still a high priority.

Both my older brothers are now dead, but I see my younger brothers, who are retired, every year. Two of my sons are in Vancouver, the other in Kingston, Ontario. One is a dedicated environmentalist, the second works for the prestigious *Queen's Quarterly*, and the third is between jobs.

Over the past ten years, I've experienced several personal losses. David, my former husband, and I had remained friendly. In 1985 he told me he had cancer. The following June, after three operations and a gallant fight, he lost the battle against that dreaded disease.

In 1988 my great friend Pauline Jewett retired from politics and, after her appointment as chancellor of Carleton University, moved from Vancouver to Ottawa. She looked forward to more travel and a lot more time at her beloved cottage near Eganville, Ontario, where I had been a guest every summer. In 1990 she was told she had lung cancer, and after two operations was given only three months to live. All through the spring of 1992, her friends—Margaret Mitchell, Marian Dewar, her niece Pauline Coupar, myself, and others—took turns staying with her. She died while I was with her, early in July. In her will, she set up an ongoing fund to help needy high-school students stay in class with the hope that they would continue on to university.

I will be seventy-five this fall, and feel about fifty-five. Although it's hard to be cheerful about aging in our youth-obsessed culture, I've found that growing old has many advantages. Long ago I gave up high heels, downhill skiing, trying to make passable pie crust, and worrying about balancing my bank account to the cent. Finally, I am able to smile at a man with no fear that he may interpret it as a pick-up!

Faced with a finite number of years, I read only books that either enchant me or challenge me with new ideas. I spend as much time as possible with people I enjoy and love, and indulge myself more than ever, in whatever I really feel moved to do at the moment.

With so many people close to me gone, I find it impossible not to contemplate death. It seems a terrible travesty to spend millions keeping people alive, often in distress and pain, for a few more months in the last years of their lives, while during their most impressionable early years we skimp on care for little children. Over ten years ago, I signed a living will instructing my doctor and family not to resuscitate me when my faculties fail. However, I want much more control than that: I want to be able to legally leave this world when I choose. And if I am no longer mentally capable of making the decision myself, I want my loved ones to carry out my written wishes and suffer no legal consequences.

As I look back on my life, I realize that growing up in the Great Depression, followed by a world war, had one great advantage: since childhood, my life and those of most of my generation has steadily improved.

When I was young, racism was not only common but acceptable among supposedly decent people. Sexism was the norm and women rarely dared to step out of their place. Disabled people were scorned and ignored, while gay people lived in terror.

Protestant prayers in school were compulsory, regardless of the religious beliefs of students. Generally, only rich people attended university, enjoyed regular holidays, frequented restaurants and theatres, and regularly visited doctors and dentists. By old age, after a lifetime of work, most people were dependent on the generosity of their children.

Every one of these circumstances has either been improved or eliminated in my lifetime.

Until fairly recently, many of us believed life would go on improving for everyone. A world free of poverty, famine, injustice, and inequality seemed within our grasp. Instead, although we have avoided a world war, conflicts between ethnic and religious groups have rarely been more vicious, and everywhere social unrest, violence, and threats to the environment increase year by year.

Clearly, two changes are responsible for much of the present instability—technology and our rapidly shrinking world through international trade and communication.

Knowing technology would free us from all robot-like assembly line jobs, we naively expected to work fewer days a week. With our freed-up time, we thought we would be able to lead much richer lives and look after everyone much better: superb child care, pleasant homes for the aged, and help for all disadvantaged people. (Interestingly, even though some people were in institutional warehouses back in those unenlightened times, there were hardly any beggars or homeless people on the streets.) With everyone working at more rewarding jobs, we were confident violence and crime would almost vanish. Another priority was protecting and leaving the environment in much better condition for our grandchildren. We planned state-of-the-art cities filled with inviting parks, fast, efficient public transportation, and few cars.

We reasoned that everyone had contributed through work and taxes to the world's progress up to this point in our evolution and we all naturally would share in its benefits.

Were we deluded in our expectations?

No. The delusion is the agenda now being imposed on us.

The last one hundred years—a mere blip in billions of years of the earth's progress—have been both its most progressive and destructive era. Age-old forests that have functioned as the planet's lungs are now being wantonly ravaged. Many cities are now so polluted they are almost unin-habitable. Even our oceans are endangered, their fish stocks depleted. We disregard ecologists who say we have seriously damaged the ozone layer, and we gobble up scarce resources at a ruinous rate. All our recycling and new technological breakthroughs can never replace what we are so impru-dently squandering in the latter part of the twentieth century.

Two of our biggest growth industries are disposing of all the garbage we spew out, and bigger police forces and prisons to control and house our rapidly increasing criminal population. And the sole panacea for these deplorable problems: more taxes on ordinary people, and more slashes to social programs such as health, education, and welfare. The rationale: we must control the deficit.

No one could be more supportive about being fiscally responsible than I am. However, even a casual glance at the revenues brought in through taxes during the past forty years will reveal that our problem is not welfare mothers living lavishly on the public purse or our other social and medical costs but a huge shift in taxation from corporations to ordinary citizens. This switch means every country has far less money than it did thirty years ago to carry out its social commitments.

At the same time, technology has eliminated millions of jobs. The employed population now falls into two segments: a small group of tech-nicians and professionals who work longer hours than ever just to maintain their present status, and an ever-increasing number of people who will, under the present system, never again enjoy the kind of well-paying, secure jobs with benefits they used to assume as their right. If this present trend continues, most young people will never achieve anything like the same standard of living their parents enjoyed. At most, they will subsist on part-time work, intermittent welfare—and, for some, petty crime.

The costs to the state of such a way of life for large numbers of formerly middle-class people will be far more expensive than any money saved through slashed social-welfare programs. If we don't make it possible for average citizens to support themselves adequately, we will face a real break-down in society. Our excellent health care and universal education systems as well as our tolerant Canadian way of life—recently the envy of the world—is already seriously threatened. But instead of seeking solutions, the victims themselves are being castigated in these hard scrabble times.

Big business and neo-conservatism now completely dominate the agenda of almost every western nation. Business also bankrolls almost all major political parties. But business, with its single-minded push for profits, has never been particularly competent at running anything but business itself—and sometimes, in my own experience, not even that. Adam Smith, the father of modern economics, believed raw capitalism would always have to be tempered by enlightened government intervention.

But today one priority of neo-conservatism is as little government as possible. Government's role is now not to create jobs, and even taxation is considered a "distortion" of the market. There must be no benefit programs for the public. A large number of unemployed is desirable to keep down labour costs and inflation and to weaken unions.

The motto, repeated like a mantra, is "Let market forces prevail and everything else, such as jobs and prosperity, will follow." After twenty years of neo-conservatism in the United States, it's clear that such ideology has created only a mirage.

Even the logic is grossly flawed. How can a market economy function while we put more and more potential customers out of work? Nor will the Third World provide new buyers with millions of people working for subsistence wages. Reducing taxes in the hope that jobs and buying power will increase is laughable in face of the large numbers of unemployed and the economic realities of today. Few businesses are interested in preserving resources or cleaning up the environment. With mind-boggling shortsightedness, they gobble up dwindling oil and minerals like rampaging dinosaurs.

With the Soviet Union no longer a target, many right-wing ideologues seem intent on attacking democracy itself as if it were the Evil Empire. Paradoxically, although they demand a free hand to make money, they insist on using the state to impose their own narrow moral constraints on everyone else. They want religion back in the schools. Only traditional families are to be tolerated. And they absolutely oppose any kind of freedom in sexual orientation and choice in abortion.

In contrast to the tight moral code expected of the rest of the population, business ethics have never been more blatantly self-serving and unprincipled. People are rewarded for being dishonest—as long as they don't get caught. Employing battalions of lawyers, they "win" by bending the rules as far as they legally can. Society not only condones such behaviour but also glorifies its successful white-collar crooks. "Greed is good" and "He wins who dies with the most toys" are today's accepted mottos.

Nor is business occupied today in producing goods and jobs. Its most profitable ploy over the past twenty years has been to run up the value of a company until it is ripe for a take-over, and then sell off its assets. All executives and stock holders handsomely profit. The workers lose their jobs and often their pensions.

Politicians are also rewarded not for being wise, humane, and balancing the needs of various members of the electorate against one another but for behaving like cold-blooded CEOs. Aping the tycoons who fill their election coffers, they compete with one another in slashing public-service jobs, cutting social programs, and privatizing everything in sight.

What is not rewarded in society today are all the virtues we used to revere: honesty, compassion, a sense of community, and a belief that those of us who have been more fortunate have an obligation to help those who have not.

Far from taking a leading role in guiding us out of our present debacle, the U.S. is itself a striking case study of what will happen to the rest of us if we continue on our present course. Its vast gaps between rich and poor, its fixation on the accumulation of individual wealth, and its decaying inner cities with its apartheid-like walled and guarded suburbs are stark examples of our possible future. Top executives are being paid obscenely large salaries including handsome severance packets—even if they fail—while the standard of living for ordinary people has steadily decreased. Many now labour in sweat shops for below minimum wages, and when they are fired they are left with no money and no prospects.

Celebrated as the world's greatest democracy, less than half of its citizens bother to vote. Although it floods the world with its movies, TV, books, and magazines, its own people are among the most badly informed of any western nation. Instead of news and thoughtful comment, its media is filled with salacious diversions such as the O. J. Simpson trial.

Its crime rate is ten times that of most other western countries, with more than fifty offenses now carrying the death penalty. In many states, after three felonies people face permanent imprisonment. In care of its people, particularly children, it rates far below any comparable European country, and even some Third World nations.

It seems to me that we stand at a fork in the road: one fork leads to a world divided into haves and have-nots, accompanied by environmental devastation. The other is a different, more women-centred world.

Like many feminists, I never dreamed—or wished—to be rich. We wanted far more than that: we wanted to change the world. The greatest accomplishment of the women's movement has been to give women a sense of their own worth, and men the courage to explore other aspects of their psyches besides the constraining macho option. Realizing we share far more traits than differences, men and women rob each other of potential growth when they allow themselves to be shoehorned into narrow traditional roles.

If I had had a daughter, I always knew what I would tell her. First of all, I would try to counter all the outdated stereotypical claptrap that girls are commonly told about their sex—that women are valued far more for their sexual characteristics than their character and brains—and encourage her to be a truly independent person. Only in knowing who she is herself will she be able to find her own life's work and make good decisions in choosing a partner and having children.

Love has been defined as the absence of fear, but how can one partner not be fearful when the other controls most of the money and is allowed by tradition to dominate? True intimacy without fear or game-playing can only be achieved between equals with respect for each other.

I would also tell her—as I have told my sons—that it isn't good enough to pass through this world concerned only with your own well-being. If everyone—and we are all capable—tried to leave the world a little better place than he or she found it, most of our troubles would be over.

When men dream of changing the world, they tend to return to a nostalgic past and talk of "traditional" values, which means mostly restrictions on women and children. Women are far more daring. They want to wipe out poverty not only on this continent but all over the world. Pioneers in both the nuclear ban and environmental movements, they want far less violence both internationally and domestically, and much more concern for people and the planet. Above all, they want an end to sexual and racial exploitation, and the winners-take-all game of settling conflicts.

Some of the questions women want answered are:

1. How is it that the world has never been more awash with money, yet

there is so little, apparently, for solving the obvious problems of people?

Many banks and corporations have more funds at their disposal than half the small countries of the world. One trillion dollars is traded every single day on the international money markets. But only about $1 in every $6 traded—or gambled, to be more accurate—results in any goods being produced or jobs created. Most of the transactions are speculation—a huge, ongoing international crap game involving currencies and future commodities.

James Tobin, the U.S. economist and Nobel Prize winner, has suggested that a tax of as little as .05 per cent would completely wipe out all poverty in the world, adequately support the United Nations, equip it with its own peace-keeping force, and completely clean up the environment. He suggests an international organization be set up to manage such a tax and distribute the revenues.

2. Why do we not follow the European rather than the American model?

Europe has preserved its inner cities, avoiding both the malignant downtown areas and the suburban sprawl so characteristic of this continent. Most European countries provide a far more stable social safety net than we do in North America, as well as more generous support for the arts. If half a dozen European countries and Canada banded together to come up with a proposal such as the Tobin plan, we would have more than enough money. Why are none of our political parties or leaders even talking about such a possibility?

3. Since governments seem incapable of dealing with our problems, why isn't there a movement to reform the system, which has always happened before when democracies encountered disrupting change? The upheaval of the Industrial Revolution brought in universal suffrage (for men), education, better laws for working people, and health-protection measures.

Why not eliminate the dependency of governments on business for money to run political campaigns? (In the U.S., every member of Congress must raise at least $3,000 a day solely to finance the next election campaign!)

Some European countries have banned contributions from all pressure groups—business, unions, and special-interest organizations. Money from the public purse is used to run much shorter, modest campaigns with ample TV time for debates among the political parties, and limits on contributions from individual citizens.

4. Why does Canada cling to its antiquated electoral political system—now only used by the U.S. and the U.K.? In our first-past-the-post election process, a party can win an overwhelming majority with less than 40 per cent of the vote, and between elections do whatever it chooses, and there is no way to get rid of it. With such high stakes, all parties tend to crowd into the middle so that there is little to differentiate among them.

Proportional representation, used by most western democracies, is much fairer, more representative, and accommodates itself to a much wider diversity of political opinion. Each party gets the same proportion of members in parliament as they garner in votes. (For example, in the 1993 election under P.R., the Progressive Conservative Party would still be the opposition, making for a far better balanced House of Commons today.)

5. Why can't we settle the Quebec question as fairly as possible and stop the destructive debate that has been tearing us apart and absorbing most of our energies for the past thirty years? Most women have no problem recognizing Quebec as different and distinct. During the run-up to the Charlottetown accord, women were much more concerned about the devolution of so much power to the provinces, weakening the federal government. Although this plan was enthusiastically supported by several premiers, women were afraid Canada would no longer be a viable country.

Why can't Quebeckers be given a clear choice: either stay in Canada with generous control over only those powers needed to protect its own culture, or vote for sovereignty association, while understanding thoroughly what that would entail: Quebec would send no more members to the House of Commons; it would lose its present dominance in Canadian life. (Over the past forty-eight years, for example, we have had a prime minister from Quebec for thirty-five of them. Today with less than 30 per cent of the population, the leader of the opposition, the chief justice of the Supreme Court, the leader of the Senate, the Clerk of the Privy Council, the Speaker of the House of Commons are all from Quebec.)

Quebec would have to assume its share of federal debt—about 25 per cent, and give up all future transfer payments. Minorities within Quebec—including its native population—would have to be protected.

As for using Canadian money and passports, why not? If it is a possible option for the European Union to use a common currency and passport system, it certainly should be possible for two peoples who have lived together in peace for more than two hundred years. Another level of government would have to be set up to deal with the mutual concerns we still might share such as defence, transportation, and trade. It's a settlement that has worked well for Belgium—divided as it is between the Walloons and the Flemish.

6. Why can't we put first things first? For women, the bottom line is how well we look after our greatest investment, our children. Every child must be given as fair a start in life as possible. Schools must be co-ed and encourage academic excellence and participation among girls as much as boys. Sex education, co-operation, and sharing must start for both boys and girls in nursery school. Any two-tiered system of schools or medical care is feudal, socially destructive, and wasteful of our most precious resource—the talents and abilities of all our future citizens.

7. It took us from 10,000 B.C. to the beginning of this century to reach a world population of 1.6 billion. Yet in the past one hundred years we have almost quadrupled that number. When women have control over their own fertility, they invariably choose to have fewer children and take care of them a lot better. Isn't it time to leave these matters to women, including all decisions about whether to carry a pregnancy to term?

Finally, if women had more say in how the world was run, we wouldn't be worrying about the next quarter's profit picture, or whether Moody's is going to award us an A++ rating. Our priorities would be more focused and practical than that: we would be thinking of nothing less than the future of the planet and its inhabitants for the next millennium.

Isn't it time women stopped holding up half the sky and began making at least half the decisions right down here on earth?

Index